THE ANARCHIST COOKBOOK

Keith McHenry

with

Chaz Bufe

See Sharp Press ◆ Tucson, Arizona

For information contact:

    See Sharp Press LLC
    P.O. Box 1731
    Tucson, AZ 85702

    www.seesharppress.com

The Anarchist cookbook / by Keith McHenry with Chaz Bufe –
Tucson, Ariz.: See Sharp Press, 2015.

154 p. : ill. ; 28 cm.
Includes bibliographical references and index.

ISBN 978-1-937276-76-8

Contents:

1. Anarchism. 2. Cooking, American -- Recipes. 3. United States --
Economic conditions -- 21st century. 4. Food -- Political aspects.
5. Food relief. I. McHenry, Keith. II. Bufe, Charles.

             320.57

Portions of this book previously appeared in somewhat different form in *Hungry for Peace*, by Keith McHenry, *Provocations*, by Chaz Bufe, *The Complete Manual of Pirate Radio*, by Zeke Teflon, and *You Can't Blow Up a Social Relationship*, by our favorite author, Anonymous.

Contents

This book is dedicated to

INTRODUCTION

Julien Benda in his 1927 classic "The Treason of Intellectuals"—*La Trahison des Clercs*—argued that we are faced with two options in life. We can serve the goals of privilege and power or the virtues of justice and truth. But, Benda warned, the more we make concessions to privilege and power the more we diminish the capacity for justice and truth. This is a truth any anarchist understands.

"As long as social injustice lasts we shall remain in a state of permanent revolution," the French anarchist Elisée Reclus said in the same vein.

This, to me, is what it means to be an anarchist. Peter Kropotkin made this point when he said that anarchists do not seek power for themselves but understand "the close dependency on everyone's happiness upon the happiness of all; and of the sense of justice, or equity, which brings the individual to consider the right of every other individual as equal to his [or her] own." Anarchists understand that power is always the problem. It does not matter who wields it. And to remain steadfast to the virtues of justice and truth we must be eternally alienated from and antagonistic to all forms of power.

Kropotkin also grasped that the indiscriminate violence and terrorism practiced by some in the anarchist movement was a grotesque caricature of anarchism. Violence, he warned, demoralized and ultimately corrupted any revolutionary cadre. It justified the harsh counter violence of the state and discredited anarchism in the eyes of the public. Those who employ violence against the enemy, he knew, soon employ violence against internal rivals, as the Bolsheviks amply demonstrated. Revolutions are nonviolent. They succeed by appealing to the consciences of people within the structures of power who will no longer defend a discredited elite. No revolution succeeds until a significant segment of the organs of internal security and the state bureaucracy defect or refuse to use coercion to defend

the *ancien régime*. This was as true in revolutionary France as it was in revolutionary Russia.

It is only, Benda wrote, when we are *not* in pursuit of practical aims or material advantages that we can serve as a conscience and a corrective. All those whose primary allegiance is to the practical aims of power and material advantage—even if they defend this allegiance as one that will lead to justice and truth—are corrupted intellectually and morally. Anarchists, like the intellectuals Benda lauds, must be indifferent to popular passions. They must "set an example of attachment to the purely disinterested activity of the mind and create a belief in the supreme value of this form of existence." They must look "as moralists upon the conflict of human egotisms." They must preach "in the name of humanity or justice, the adoption of an abstract principle superior to and directly opposed to these passions." Benda conceded that those who hold fast to these principles are often unable to prevent the powerful from "filling all history with the noise of their hatred and their slaughters." But they did, at least, "prevent the laymen from setting up their actions as a religion, they did prevent them from thinking themselves great men as they carried out these activities." In short, Benda asserted, "humanity did evil for two thousand years, but honored good. This contradiction was an honor to the human species, and formed the rift whereby civilization slipped into the world." But once the intellectuals began to "play the game of political passions," those who had "acted as a check on the realism of the people began to act as its stimulators."

All forms of centralized power, from Vladimir Lenin and the Bolsheviks to the corporate state, seek to crush this spirit, which is the spirit of anarchism. The Russian revolutionary Victor Serge understood this when he wrote "every revolutionary government is by its very nature conservative and therefore retrograde. Power exercises upon those who hold it a baleful influence which is often expressed in deplorable occupational perversions." Power seeks, even when in the opposition, to make cadre loyal to its doctrine and its hierarchy. It seeks, in short, to capture the individual conscience and make it serve the ends of power. This is done through the promise of lofty ideals and goals. But all who surrender to the dictates of any power structure became captives to the basest instincts of human existence.

Mikhail Bakunin, who foresaw the counterrevolution that would be imposed by the Bolsheviks, also made this point. A genuine revolution he said "does not foist upon the people any new regulations, orders, styles of life, but merely unleashes their will and gives wide scope to their self-determination and their economic and social organization, which must be created by themselves from below and not from above." It must "make impossible after the popular victory the establishment of any state power over the people—even the most revolutionary, even your power—because any power, whatever it calls itself, would inevitably subject the people to old slavery in new form."

Anarchists are the guardians of liberty. Their role, holding fast to justice and truth, is to thwart the lust by centralized power for absolute control. This means, unlike the protestations of black bloc self-styled anarchists, engaging in strategies and tactics that keep the powerful fearful of a public that refuses to be chained and that will revolt if they are manacled. And this makes anarchism the most important creed of our era, for it places its faith in perpetual resistance rather than the accumulation of power. The most successful examples of anarchist power took place in Russia after the 1917 revolution with the rise of the Soviets and during the civil war in Spain. These anarchist achievements, before being crushed by force, made visible the egalitarian and decentralized structures that are led by the people as opposed to a new class of bureaucratic mandarins. These structures must be our model as we enter an age of diminishing resources and corporate totalitarianism.

We have undergone a corporate coup d'état. It is over. They have won. A handful of corporate global oligarchs have seized everything—wealth, power and privilege—and the rest of us struggle as part of a vast underclass, increasingly impoverished and ruthlessly repressed. These oligarchs have cemented into place the most sophisticated and terrifying security and surveillance apparatus in human his-

tory. They have militarized police and given them license to kill with impunity. They have stripped us of our most basic civil liberties, including the right to privacy, can hold us in indefinite detention without access to the courts or due process, and have authorized the government to order the assassination of fellow citizens. At the same time, the corporate state through its corrupted elected officials and courts have established another set of laws and regulations for the power elite, ones that legalize criminality and perpetuate what is little more than a global mafia. Electoral politics is a charade. Money has replaced the vote. The consent of the governed is a cruel joke. And, handing us our death sentence, corporations have unleashed fossil fuel industries to ravage the planet, threatening the viability of the human species, along with all other species.

There is nothing in 5,000 years of economic history to justify the absurd doctrine that human societies should structure their behavior around the demands of the marketplace. The false promises of the market economy have, by now, been exposed as lies. The ability of corporations to migrate overseas has decimated our manufacturing base. Wages have been driven downward, impoverishing our working class and ravaging our middle class. Huge segments of the population—including those burdened by student loans—suffer from crippling debt peonage. And the elites stash an estimated $18 trillion in overseas tax havens while corporations such as General Electric pay no income tax. Corporations employ virtual slave labor in Bangladesh and China, making obscene profits. As corporations suck the last resources from communities and the natural world, they leave behind vast sacrifice zones, horrific human suffering and dead landscapes. The greater the destruction, the more the corporate apparatus is used to crush dissent and exact tribute in the name of "austerity." This is the terrible algebra of corporate domination.

Anarchism is about steadfast defiance. Anarchism is about resisting forces of oppression as Mumia Abu Jamal, Edward Snowden, Jeremy Hammond, Chelsea Manning, and Julian Assange have resisted. Anarchism means refusing to succumb to fear. It means refusing to surrender, even if you find yourself, like Manning, Hammond, and Abu Jamal, caged like an animal. It means saying no. To remain safe, to remain "innocent" in the eyes of the law in this moment in history is to be complicit in a monstrous evil. Anarchism is about, as Benda and Kropotkin, knew, living morally. Rebellion is not defined for an anarchist by what he or she achieves, but by what he or she becomes. And all the great rebels including Christ, Buddha, Sitting Bull, Harriet Tubman, Emma Goldman, and Malcolm X preached this truth. All the great rebels also knew that they could not let fear—the primary instrument those in power use to maintain control—cripple resistance.

"Repression," Serge wrote, "can really only live off fear."

"But is fear enough to remove need, thirst for justice, intelligence, reason, idealism—all those revolutionary forces that express the formidable, profound impulse of the economic factors of a revolution?" Serge asks. "Relying on intimidation, the reactionaries forget that they will cause more indignation, more hatred, more thirst for martyrdom, than real fear. They only intimidate the weak; they exasperate the best forces and temper the resolution of the strongest."

The anarchist does not succumb, not because he or she is assured of victory, but because to be ruled by fear, to bow before the demands of power, means one is no longer an anarchist. Anarchism is a state of being.

In his poem of resistance, "If We Must Die," the poet Claude McKay reminded us that rebellion, like anarchism, is finally about personal dignity and independence. The act of rebellion alone defines us. If they come for us, if we are cornered, if as McKay said we must die, then let us be defined as rebels, and "let it not be like hogs/Hunted and penned in an inglorious spot/While round us bark the mad and hungry dogs."

—Chris Hedges
Princeton, New Jersey

ITS AUTHOR ON THE ORIGINAL "ANARCHIST COOKBOOK"

Forty-four years ago this month, in December 1969, I quit my job as a manager of a bookstore in New York City's Greenwich Village and began to write the *Anarchist Cookbook*. My motivation at the time was simple; I was being actively pursued by the US military, who seemed single-mindedly determined to send me to fight, and possibly die, in Vietnam.

I wanted to publish something that would express my anger. It seems that I succeeded in ways that far exceeded what I imagined possible at the time. The Cookbook is still in print 40 years after publication, and I am told it has sold in excess of 2m copies.

I have never held the copyright, and so the decision to continue publishing it has been in the hands of the publisher.

I now find myself arguing for it to be quickly and quietly taken out of print. What has changed?

Unfortunately, the source of my anger in the late 60's and early 70's—unnecessary government-sanctioned violence—is still very much a feature of our world. The debacle of the US invasion of Iraq is yet another classic example. It still makes me very angry. So my change of heart has had less to do with external events than it does with an internal change.

Over the years, I have come to understand that the basic premise behind the Cookbook is profoundly flawed. The anger that motivated the writing of the Cookbook blinded me to the illogical notion that violence can be used to prevent violence. I had fallen for the same irrational pattern of thought that led to US military involvement in both Vietnam and Iraq. The irony is not lost on me.

To paraphrase Aristotle: it is easy to be angry. But to be angry with the right person, at the right time and to the right degree, that is hard—that is the hallmark of a civilized person. Two years ago, I co-authored a book entitled *Becoming an Emotionally Intelligent Teacher*. Although written for educators,

the book serves as an implicit refutation of the emotional immaturity of the Cookbook. The premise is that all learning takes place in a social context, and that teachers with a high degree of emotional intelligence construct relationships with students that enhance learning. I continue to work hard, in an Aristotelian sense, to be more civilized.

For the last 40 years, I have served as a teacher and school leader in Africa and Asia, working in some of the poorest and least developed countries of the world. Together with my wife, I have been involved in supporting schools around the world in becoming more inclusive of children with learning challenges. We have written books on the subject and speak regularly at international conferences. In 2010 we founded, together with other colleagues from international schools, the Next Frontier: Inclusion, a nonprofit organization dedicated to helping schools be more inclusive of children who learn differently—children with developmental delays, dyslexia, ADHD, and autism.

I suspect that these children have taught me a great deal more than I have taught them.

So what is the connection between the needs of these children with learning disabilities and my wish to see the Cookbook go out of print?

For one thing, children with learning challenges are often ostracized; sometimes informally by peers, sometimes more formally by schools that deny them admission, and sometimes by teachers who fail to understand their academic, social and emotional needs. No child should have to earn the right to belong.

The Cookbook has been found in the possession of alienated and disturbed young people who have launched attacks against classmates and teachers. I suspect that the perpetrators of these attacks did not feel much of a sense of belonging, and the Cookbook may have added to their sense of isolation.

Schools need to be safe places. Students and teachers need to feel physically and psychologically safe. Learning is greatly inhibited when fear pervades the schoolhouse. Learning is also greatly inhibited when children and young adults do not feel a sense of belonging.

I do not know the influence the book may have had on the thinking of the perpetrators of these attacks, but I cannot imagine that it was positive. The continued publication of the Cookbook serves no purpose other than a commercial one for the publisher. It should quickly and quietly go out of print.

—William Powell, author of the original
Anarchist Cookbook

(This piece originally appeared in the December 19, 2013 issue of *The Guardian*. Reproduced here by permission of the author.)

ANARCHISM

ANARCHISM

WHAT IT IS AND WHAT IT ISN'T

There are many popular misconceptions about anarchism, and because of them a great many people dismiss anarchists and anarchism out of hand.

Misconceptions abound in the mass media, where the term "anarchy" is commonly used as a synonym for "chaos," and where terrorists, no matter what their political beliefs or affiliations, are often referred to as "anarchists." As well, when anarchism is mentioned, it's invariably presented as merely a particularly mindless form of youthful rebellion. These misconceptions are, of course, also widespread in the general public, which by and large allows the corporate media to do what passes for its thinking.

Worse, some who call themselves "anarchists" don't even know the meaning of the term. These people fall, in general, into two classes. The first, as the great Italian anarchist Luigi Fabbri pointed out a century ago in *Influencias burguesas sobre el anarquismo*, consists of those who are attracted to the lies in the mass media. By and large, these people are simply looking for a glamorous label for selfish, antisocial behavior. The good news is that most of them eventually mature and abandon what they consider "anarchism." The bad news is that while they're around they tend to give anarchism a very bad name. As Fabbri put it:

> [These are] persons who are not repelled by the absurd, but who, on the contrary, engage in it. They are attracted to projects and ideas precisely because they are absurd; and so anarchism comes to be known precisely for the illogical character and ridiculousness which ignorance and bourgeois calumny have attributed to anarchist doctrines.[1]

The second class consists of those who equate anarchism with some pet ideology having essentially nothing to do with anarchism. In modern times, the most prominent of these mislabeled beliefs have been primitivism and amoral egotism. Again, the identification of such beliefs with anarchism tends to give anarchism a bad name, because of, on the one hand, the absurdity of primitivism and, on the other, the obvious antisocial nature of amoral egotism. To put this another way, the identification of anarchism with chaos, mindless rebellion, absurdities (such as primitivism), and antisocial attitudes and behaviors (such as amoral egotism) has three primary undesirable effects: 1) it allows people to easily dismiss anarchism and anarchists; 2) it makes it much more difficult to explain anarchism to them, because they already think that they know what it is and have rejected it; and 3) it attracts a fair number of what Fabbri calls "empty headed and frivolous types," and occasionally outright sociopaths, whose words and actions tend to further discredit anarchism.

So, if we're ever to get anywhere, we need to make plain what anarchism is and what it isn't. First, let's deal with the misconceptions.

What Anarchism Isn't

Anarchism is not terrorism. An overwhelming majority of anarchists have always rejected terrorism, because they've been intelligent enough to realize that means determine ends, that terrorism is inherently vanguardist, and that even when "successful" it almost always leads to bad results. The anonymous authors of *You Can't Blow Up a Social Relationship: The Anarchist Case Against Terrorism* put it like this:

> You can't blow up a social relationship. The total collapse of this society would provide no guarantee about what replaced it. Unless a majority of people had the ideas and organization sufficient for the

1

creation of an alternative society, we would see the old world reassert itself because it is what people would be used to, what they believed in, what existed unchallenged in their own personalities.

Proponents of terrorism and guerrillaism are to be opposed because their actions are vanguardist and authoritarian, because their ideas, to the extent that they are substantial, are wrong or unrelated to the results of their actions (especially when they call themselves libertarians or anarchists), because their killing cannot be justified, and finally because their actions produce either repression with nothing in return, or an authoritarian regime.[2]

Decades of government and corporate slander cannot alter this reality: the overwhelming majority of anarchists reject terrorism for both practical and ethical reasons. In the late 1990s, *Time* magazine called Ted Kaczynski "the king of the anarchists"; but that doesn't make it so. *Time*'s words were just another typical, perhaps deliberately dishonest, attempt to tar all anarchists with the terrorist brush.

This is not to say that armed resistance is never appropriate. Clearly there are situations in which one has little choice, as when facing a dictatorship that suppresses civil liberties and prevents one from acting openly—which has happened repeatedly in many countries. Even then, armed resistance should be undertaken reluctantly and as a last resort, because violence is inherently undesirable due to the suffering it causes; because it provides repressive regimes excuses for further repression; because it provides them with the opportunity to commit atrocities against civilians and to blame those atrocities on

their "terrorist" opponents; and because, as history has shown, the chances of success are very low.

Even though armed resistance may sometimes be called for in repressive situations, it's a far different matter to succumb to the romance of the gun and to engage in urban guerrilla warfare in relatively open societies in which civil liberties are largely intact and in which one does not have mass popular support at the start of one's violent campaign. Violence in such situations does little but drive the public into the "protective" arms of the government; narrow political dialogue (tending to polarize the populace into pro- and anti-guerrilla factions); turn politics into a spectator sport for the vast majority of people[3]; provide the government with an excuse to suppress civil liberties; and induce the onset of repressive regimes "better" able to handle the "terrorist" problem than their more tolerant predecessors. It's also worth mentioning that the chances of success of such violent, vanguardist campaigns are microscopic. They are simply arrogant, ill-thought-out roads to disaster.[4]

Anarchism is not primitivism. In recent decades, groups of quasi-religious mystics have begun equating the primitivism they advocate (rejection of science, rationality, and technology—often lumped together under the blanket term, "technology") with anarchism.[5] In reality, the two have nothing to do with each other, as we'll see when we consider what anarchism actually is—a set of philosophical/ethical precepts and organizational principles designed to maximize human freedom. For now, suffice it to say that the elimination of technology advocated by primitivist groups would inevitably entail the deaths of literally billions of human beings in a world utterly dependent upon interlocking technologies for everything from food production/delivery to communications to medical treatment. Primitivists' fervently desired outcome, the elimination of technology, could only come about through means which are the absolute antithesis of anarchism: the use of coercion and violence on a mass scale, as it's inconceivable that a majority of human beings would voluntarily give up such things as running water, sewer systems, modern medicine, electric lights, and warm houses in the winter.[6]

Anarchism is not chaos; Anarchism is not rejection of organization. The idea that anarchism equals rejection of organization is repeated *ad nauseam* by the mass media and by anarchism's political foes, espe-

2

cially marxists, who sometimes know better. Even a brief look at the works of anarchism's leading theoreticians confirms that this belief is in error. Over and over in the writings of Proudhon, Bakunin, Kropotkin, Rocker, Ward, Bookchin, et al., one finds not a rejection of organization, but rather a preoccupation with it—a preoccupation with how society should be organized in accord with the anarchist principles of individual freedom and social justice. For over a century and a half, anarchists have been arguing that coercive, hierarchical organization (as embodied in government and corporations) is not equivalent to organization *per se* (which they regard as necessary), and that coercive organization should be replaced by decentralized, nonhierarchical organization based on voluntary cooperation and mutual aid. This is hardly a rejection of organization.

Anarchism is not amoral egotism. As does any avant garde social movement, anarchism attracts more than its share of flakes, parasites, and outright sociopaths, persons simply looking for a glamorous label to cover their often pathological selfishness, their disregard for the rights and dignity of others, and their pathetic desire to be the center of attention. These individuals tend to give anarchism a bad name, because even though they have very little in common with actual anarchists—that is, persons concerned with ethical behavior, social justice, and the rights of both themselves *and others*—they're often quite exhibitionistic, and their disreputable actions sometimes come into the public eye. To make matters worse, these exhibitionists sometimes publish their self-glorifying views and deliberately misidentify those views as "anarchist." To cite one example, several years ago the publisher of an American "anarchist" journal published a book by a fellow egotist consisting primarily of *ad hominem* attacks on actual anarchists, knowing full well that the "anarchist" author of the book is a notorious police narcotics informant who has on a number of occasions ratted out those he's had disputes with to government agencies. This police informer's actions—which, revealingly, he's attempted to hide—are completely in line with his ideology of amoral egotism ("post-left anarchism"), but they have nothing to do with actual anarchism. Amoral egotists may (mis)use the label, but they're no more anarchists than the now-defunct German Democratic Republic (East Germany) was democratic or a republic.

The full absurdity of identifying amoral egotism—essentially "I'll do what I damn well please

and fuck everybody else"—with anarchism will become apparent in short order when we'll consider what anarchism actually is.

Anarchism is not "Libertarianism." Until relatively recently, the very useful term "libertarian" was used worldwide as a synonym for "anarchist." Indeed, it was used exclusively in this sense until the 1970s when, in the United States, it was appropriated by the grossly misnamed Libertarian Party.

This party has almost nothing to do with anarchist concepts of liberty, especially the concepts of equal freedom and positive freedom—that is, access to the resources necessary to the freedom to act. (Equal freedom and positive freedom are discussed in the following section of this essay.) Instead, this "Libertarian" party concerns itself exclusively with the negative freedoms, pretending that liberty exists only in the negative sense, freedom from restraint, while it simultaneously revels in the denial of equal positive freedom to the vast majority of the world's people.

These "Libertarians" not only glorify capitalism, the mechanism that denies both equal freedom and positive freedom to the vast majority, but they also wish to retain the coercive apparatus of the state while eliminating its social welfare functions—hence widening the rift between rich and poor, and increasing the freedom of the rich by diminishing that of the poor (while keeping the boot of the state firmly on their necks). Thus, in the United States, the once exceedingly useful term "libertarian" has been hijacked by egotists who are in fact enemies of liberty in the full sense of the word, and who have very little in common with anarchists.

This is what anarchism isn't.

What Anarchism Is

In its narrowest sense, anarchism is simply the rejection of the state, the rejection of coercive government. Under this extremely narrow definition, even such apparent absurdities as "anarcho-capitalism" and religious anarchism are possible.[7]

But most anarchists use the term "anarchism" in a much broader sense, defining it as the rejection of coercion and domination in all forms. So, most anarchists reject not only coercive government, but also religion and capitalism, which they see as other forms of the twin evils, domination and coercion.

> "The anarchist . . . is not a utopian . . . He does not want to plunge mankind into a condition of life for which its nature is not fitted—a charge often repeated by kindly and well-meaning people who cannot rid themselves . . . of the belief that government must exist to restrain the selfishness of man. They forget that a man with the forces of government at his command has the power to indulge his selfishness multiplied a thousand times.
>
> The anarchist does not deplore the instinct of selfishness. He simply recognizes it and is guided accordingly. . . . The anarchist is not so foolish as to think that one set of men, because they belong to a different party, or hold different opinions in politics or economics, are any better or worse than any other set. He knows that all men are made from the same clay, and that placed in the same position they will act the same way. . . . He insists that selfishness must not be perverted by being placed in positions of authority, where it can enslave mankind, and that the way to protect ourselves from selfishness is to strip it of all power, except the power each person possesses within himself."
>
> —Jay Fox, *Mother Earth*, November 1917

They reject religion because they see it as the ultimate form of domination, in which a supposedly all-powerful god hands down "thou shalts" and "thou shalt nots" to its "flock."

Anarchists likewise reject capitalism because it's designed to produce rich and poor, and because it's designed to produce a system of domination in which some give orders and others have little choice but to take them. For similar reasons, on a personal level almost all anarchists reject sexism, racism, and homophobia—all of which produce artificial inequality, and thus domination.

To put this another way, anarchists believe in freedom in both its negative and positive senses. In this country, freedom is routinely presented only in its negative sense, that of being free from restraint. Hence most people equate freedom only with such things as freedom of speech, freedom of association, and freedom of (or from) religion. But there's also a positive aspect of freedom, an aspect which anarchists almost alone insist on.[8]

That positive aspect is what Emma Goldman called "the freedom to." And that freedom, the freedom of action, the freedom to enjoy or use, is highly dependent upon access to the world's resources. Because of this the rich are in a very real sense free to a much greater degree than the rest of us. To cite an example in the area of free speech, Donald Trump could easily buy dozens of daily newspapers or television stations to propagate his views and influence public opinion. How many working people could do the same? How many working people could afford to buy a single daily newspaper or a single television station? The answer is obvious. Working people cannot do such things; instead, we're reduced to producing 'zines with a readership of a few hundred or putting up pages on the Internet in our relatively few hours of free time.

Examples of the greater freedom of the rich abound in daily life. To put this in general terms, because they do not have to work, the rich not only have far more money (that is, access to resources) but also far more time to pursue their interests, pleasures, and desires than do the rest of us.

To cite a concrete example, the rich are free to send their children to the best colleges employing the best instructors, which the rest of us simply can't afford to do; if we can afford college at all, we make do with community and state colleges employing slave-labor "adjunct faculty" and overworked, underpaid graduate teaching assistants. Once in college, the children of the rich are entirely free to pursue their studies, while most other students must work at least part time to support themselves, which deprives them of many hours which could be devoted to study. If you think about it, you can easily find additional examples of the greater freedom of the rich in the areas of medical care, housing, nutrition, travel, etc., etc.—in fact, in virtually every area of life.

This greater freedom of action for the rich comes at the expense of everyone else, through the diminishment of everyone else's freedom of action. There is no way around this, given that freedom of action is to a great extent determined by access to finite resources. Anatole France well illustrated the differences between the restrictions placed upon the rich and the poor when he wrote, "The law, in its majestic equality, forbids the rich as well as the poor to sleep under bridges, to beg in the streets, and to steal bread."

Because the primary goal of anarchism is the greatest possible amount of freedom for all, anarchists insist on equal freedom in both its negative and positive aspects—that, in the negative sense, individuals be free to do whatever they wish as long as they do not harm or directly intrude upon others; and, in the positive sense, that all individuals have equal freedom to act, that they have equal access to the world's resources.

Anarchists recognize that absolute freedom is an impossibility, that amoral egotism ignoring the rights of others would quickly devolve into a war of all against all. What we argue for is that everyone have equal freedom from restraint (limited only by respect for the rights of others) and that everyone have as nearly as possible equal access to resources, thus ensuring equal (or near-equal) freedom to act.

This is anarchism in its theoretical sense.

In Spain, Cuba, and a few other countries there have been serious attempts to make this theory reality through the movement known as anarcho-syndicalism. The primary purpose of anarcho-syndicalism is the replacement of coercive government by voluntary cooperation in the form of worker-controlled unions coordinating the entire economy. This would not only eliminate the primary restraint on the negative freedoms (government), but would also be a huge step toward achieving positive freedom. The nearest this vision came to fruition was in the Spanish Revolution, 1936–1939, when huge areas of Spain, including its most heavily industrialized region, came under the control of the anarcho-syndicalist *Confederación Nacional del Trabajo*. George Orwell describes this achievement in *Homage to Catalonia*:

> The anarchists were still in virtual control of Catalonia and the revolution was in full swing. . . . the aspect of Barcelona was something startling and overwhelming. It was the first time that I had ever been in a town where the working class was in the saddle. Practically every building of any size had been seized by the workers and was draped with red flags or with the red and black flag of the anarchists; . . . Every shop and café had an inscription saying it had been collectivized; even the bootblacks had been collectivized and their boxes painted red and black. Waiters and shop-workers looked you

> in the face and treated you as an equal. Servile and even ceremonial forms of speech had temporarily disappeared. . . . The revolutionary posters were everywhere, flaming from the walls in clean reds and blues that made the few remaining advertisements look like daubs of mud. . . . All this was queer and moving. There was much in it that I did not understand, in some ways I did not even like it, but I recognized it immediately as a state of affairs worth fighting for.

This is anarchism. And Orwell was right—it is worth fighting for.[9]

---

1. *Bourgeois Influences on Anarchism*, by Luigi Fabbri. Tucson, AZ: See Sharp Press, 2001, p. 16.

2. *You Can't Blow Up a Social Relationship*. Tucson, AZ: See Sharp Press, 1998, p. 20.

3. It may be that now due to apathy, but in violent/repressive situations other options are cut off for almost everyone not directly involved in armed resistance.

4. For further discussion of this matter, see *You Can't Blow Up a Social Relationship: The Anarchist Case Against Terrorism* and *Bourgeois Influences on Anarchism*.

5. Ted Kaczynski is in some ways quite typical of this breed of romantic. He differs from most of them in that he acted on his beliefs (albeit in a cowardly, violent manner) and that he actually lived a relatively primitive existence in the backwoods of Montana—unlike most of his co-religionists, who live comfortably in urban areas and employ the technologies they profess to loathe.

6. For further discussion of this topic, see *Anarchism vs. Primitivism*, by Brian Oliver Sheppard. Tucson, AZ: See Sharp Press, 2003 (available online at www.libcom.org). See also the "Primitive Thought" appendix to *Listen Anarchist!*, by Chaz Bufe. Tucson, AZ: See Sharp Press, 1998.

7. Indeed, there have been a fairly large number of admirable religious anarchists, individuals such as Leo Tolstoy and Dorothy Day (and the members of her Catholic Worker groups, such as Ammon Hennacy), though to most anarchists advocating freedom on Earth while bowing to a heavenly tyrant, no matter how imaginary, seems an insupportable contradiction. To the best of my knowledge there have been no such shining examples of anarcho-capitalists, with the notable exception of Karl Hess.

8. To be fair, marxists also tend to emphasize positive freedom, but for the most part they're curiously insensitive, and often downright hostile, to "negative" freedom—the freedom from restraint (especially when they have the guns and goons to do the restraining).

9. Of course, this discussion of anarchism is necessarily schematic, given that this essay is intended as an introductory 10-minute read. For elaboration see the many books on anarchism listed in the bibliography, especially *Anarchism and Anarcho-Syndicalism*, by Rudolf Rocker; *What Is Communist Anarchism?*, by Alexander Berkman (now published by AK Press as *What Is Anarchism?*); *Fields, Factories and Workshops Tomorrow*, by Peter Kropotkin; and *Anarchy in Action*, by Colin Ward.

"And Sue said to me, 'But Richard, how can someone as sensitive as you and a practicing humanitarian take this job?' And I said, 'Sue love, I genuinely believe that by doing so I can alleviate some of the worst excesses of the system.'"

You Can't Blow Up
A Social Relationship

You Can't Blow Up a Social Relationship was originally published as a pamphlet in 1979 by several cooperating anarchist and libertarian socialist groups in Australia, who encouraged others to reproduce it. In 1981 the short-lived Anarchist Communist Federation (ACF) published a Canadian edition, and in 1985 See Sharp Press published the first U.S. edition and has kept it in print ever since. Why? You Can't Blow Up a Social Relationship is in all likelihood the best critique of urban guerrillaism and terrorism ever written, and remains as timely now as the day it first appeared.

Events in recent years have amply demonstrated the correctness of its main points: 1) That means determine ends—the use of horrifying means guarantees horrifying ends; 2) That urban guerrillaism almost always leads to repression and little else—which makes it very difficult to engage in constructive political work such as organizing and education; 3) That "successful" urban guerrillaism leads to authoritarian outcomes; 4) That these results are determined by the nature of guerrillaism.

Guerrillaism relies upon the capitalist media for much of its impact, presenting political acts as spectacles divorced from the day-to-day lives of ordinary people (reducing them to passive spectators), while providing the corporate media with a perfect opportunity to frighten the public into the "protective" arms of the state. To put it another way, guerrillas presume to act for the people—attempting to substitute individual acts for mass actions—thus perpetuating the division between leaders and followers (in this case, vanguardists and spectators).

While the authors of You Can't Blow Up a Social Relationship reject terrorism, it should be emphasized that they are not arguing for political passivity. They are not arguing against the many forms of direct action which form an essential part of any mass movement for fundamental social change. (Examples of such direct action include wildcat strikes, factory occupations, and civil disobedience.) Neither do they discount the quieter but equally essential efforts of those doing educational work. Finally, it should be noted that the authors are not pacifists; they believe that situations may arise in which armed self-defense becomes necessary.

The changes made in the text in this edition fall into two categories: 1) minor spelling and punctuation changes made solely to bring the text in line with standard American usage (substituting jail for gaol, for example); and 2) minor copy editing changes made solely for the purpose of clarification.

We've retained most of the comments added to the text in the 1981 ACF edition and have added a few of our own. These comments appear either as endnotes or in brackets within the text. The bracketed notes and comments within the text are ours. Our initials appear after the footnotes we've added; all other footnotes are from the ACF edition.

* * *

You Can't Blow Up
A Social Relationship

The Sydney Hotel bombing of March 1978 raised the issue of terrorism in Australia.[1] The deaths of three innocent people gave this incident a human as well as political significance. Statements of the press and politicians about this absurd and sinister act amounted to a catchcry for the erosion of democratic rights. Many statements by public figures and articles in newspapers also showed an ignorance of the past because, for some time now, Australia has had organized terrorist groups.

In fact, there have been numerous incidents over the last few years which only by good fortune did not result in deaths. Has the attempted assassination of Arthur Calwell in 1966 really been forgotten?[2] Australia has long been the base for overseas terrorist operations. The Croatian Ustasha[3] had been carrying out arms training and a number of bombings under what appeared to be the beneficent arm of Liberal rule at the time. Yugoslav travel agencies and consulates have been attacked and murders attempted in the Yugoslav community. In September 1972 sixteen people were injured by a bomb in a Yugoslav travel agency. Raids were mounted into Yugoslavia by commandos trained in Australia. The September 1978 raid on an arms training camp indicates that Ustasha is still militarily active. As well, Australian Nazis possessed extensive weaponry (and undoubtedly still do) and petty harassments and announcements of death lists have occurred frequently. Bricks, guns and firebombs were all used by the Nazis to damage property, and terrorism occurred when they bombed the Communist Party headquarters in Brisbane in April 1972. Another attempt was made in Perth. In the Brisbane bombing people at a CPA meeting when the bomb exploded were lucky to escape without injury. The origin of the letter bombs sent to Queensland Premiere Bjelke-Petersen and Prime Minister Fraser in 1975 was not discovered and, though it was blamed on the left and a number of left-wing households were raided on flimsy grounds, it is by no means clear that it did not more truly serve the interests of the right at the time. Certainly, no leftists were prosecuted.

There have been some incidents originating from the left as well. There were some incidents of property damage during the Vietnam War and, recently, there was the bombing of the woodchip facility in Western Australia. The only personal attack was the bailing-up [holdup] at gun point of an official by a black activist. None of these incidents has revealed the hand of an organized group of leftist terrorists.

What is noticeable then in the history of terrorist activity in Australia has been the existence of organized right-wing terrorism, though even this has been of relatively minor significance. It certainly did not provoke official or media campaigns for military involvement, massive security measures or expanded political police forces.

Fraser took advantage of the Hilton bombing for precedent-setting military histrionics which even security commentators attacked. He announced a new emphasis on security which will soon be seen to be at the expense of rights. Finally, a general attempt was made to exploit the deaths to take the heat off political police under attack after the South Australian investigations of the Special Branch. Calls were made for a strengthening of their organizations.[4]

Despite all this, in sections of the press and especially in letters to the editor and street interviews (notably at Bowral, New South Wales) evidence existed that many people were keeping things in proportion. Overseas experience has shown that the most powerful weapon in the hands of those trying to use the existence of terrorism as an excuse to weaken democratic rights has been the creation by the media, police, and politicians of an atmosphere of hysteria. Then the real impact of terrorism can no longer be sensibly gauged. But more than this will be required if people are to stand up to the pressure to acquiesce in a gradual growth of repression. For example, justifying political police activity by invoking the fear of subversion was not really questioned in the 1978 South Australian inquiry into that state's Special Branch. Subversive activities, according to Liberal-National governments, have not been those of Ustasha and other extreme right-wing groups, but those of all leftist, unionist and reform groups and even those of the ALP [Australian Labour Party]. This was spelled out by sacked South Australian Police Commissioner Salisbury, who said at a press conference that, before the Second World War, an ASIO [Australian Security Intelligence Organization, the central government secret police force] equivalent organization would have concentrated on the right wing, but that since the war [WWII] the left has definitely become the chief object of concern for intelligence services.

We have already pointed out that since the war it is the right that has dominated the few incidents of terrorism that have occurred. The current balance of forces within the Liberal Party has resulted in police attention to Croatian rightists. This has not changed the function of political police, which is to limit political debate, not to prevent violence. Subversion for today's political police is not merely questioning the status quo—it is questioning the Liberal-National status quo, which makes the connection of the ALP with the setting up of the political police all the more reprehensible. It seems that Dunstan's will remain an isolated act in Australian social democracy. Despite Attorney General Murphy's raid on ASIO headquarters during the Whitlam government's term of office,[5] the ALP's main concern regarding the political police was not to question their function but merely to make them more efficient. What really upset some people about the South Australian revelations was that judges and other upright citizens were being watched. "What a waste of time," they say, "when the police should be concentrating on those weird folk who think that capitalism should be reformed or done away with." If these people cannot be awakened to a concern for basic rights, they should at least be reminded that one thing leads to another and that it might be their rights endangered tomorrow. Subversion is in the eye of the beholder, and the beholder is the ruling class.

Furthermore, the recent past has shown that democracies will use the opportunity created by political violence to disrupt or repress the left as a whole. They will even incite or conspire in terrorism to justify their own actions. An ex-member of a German terrorist group, now living incognito, has written a book critically appraising the guerrilla experience [*How It All Began*, by Bommi Baumann]. In it he tells how their first bombs and weapons were supplied by a police agent: "Unwittingly, we were a very specific element of the bulls' [police] strategy." (p. 37) Stupidly, he does not follow the obvious implications of this: "It isn't clear to me even today what role one plays in that game." (p. 85)

The famous American Sacco and Vanzetti case of the 1920s is an archetypal case of the preparedness of the police to frame dissenters on charges of political violence. They were charged with robbery and murder. It is now generally accepted that these charges were trumped up. It is officially admitted that the anarchists did not get a fair trial. Despite massive international campaigns over a period of years for their release, they were executed in 1927. Such was the determination of the rulers of the time. Cases like this, and there are many others, should be kept firmly in mind when assessing bombings and court cases arising from them. The state, therefore, can be very ruthless in persecuting such people. However, when left-wing terrorism is being carried out in a consistent way in society, it gives the state extra leverage in using political repression against individuals and the left in general.

When by their own actions terrorists serve such ends, they are contributing to the destruction of politics and the closing of various options for the spreading of ideas before they have been fully utilized.

Of course, the state will readily use various repressive methods if it meets any substantial resistance or if it has to handle a social crisis which is creating resistance. Terrorism and guerrillaism cannot be attacked just because they produce repression. Even more important is the fact that there is nothing to have made it worthwhile. In the end the guerrillas get wiped out and there is nothing left but repression (and a law and order mentality amongst the people).

A developing mass movement will produce repression, but it will also produce numbers of people with clear aims and the organized means of reaching them. It will be able to build far more lasting means of armed defense. In a social crisis in which all sorts of positive developments begin, a separate guerrilla or terrorist group dashing about creating ultimately irrelevant confrontations concentrates political debate in too narrow a compass—"have they (government or guerrillas) gone too far?" etc. instead of—"should the workers have occupied those factories?" etc. Terrorism and guerrillaism destroy politics.

Terrorism by the State

Terrorism, of course, does not belong solely to small bands in Italy and Germany. The most brutal and ruthless agent of terror, now, as throughout human history, is the ruling class. Read history. Alternatively recall that throughout the world our humane rulers have the nuclear weaponry to kill everyone on Earth 24 times over (Ruth Legar Sivard in *Bulletin of the Atomic Scientists*, April 1975). Or think of the implications of the property-preserving, life-destroying neutron bomb. The point must be made that state terrorism is stronger, more prevalent and much more destructive than vanguardist terrorism.

It is a question of the degree to which the state feels challenged that determines its use of terror, not constitutions or democratic principles. When they are threatened by a serious organized revolutionary movement, the Western democracies will display the full range of horrific methods. The massive use of torture by France in Algeria, its use by Britain in Aden and Northern Ireland, police and army murders and conspiracies in Italy are a few examples of their readiness to apply ruthless methods in varying situations. This readiness for brutality flows from the very nature of the state as expressed by the French Anarchist, Pierre-Joseph Proudhon in 1851 [in *General Idea of the Revolution in the 19th Century*]:

9

To be governed is to be watched over, inspected, spied upon, directed, legislated at, regulated, docketed, indoctrinated, preached at, controlled, assessed, weighed, censored, ordered about, by men who have neither the tight, nor the knowledge, nor the virtue. To be governed means to be, at each operation, at each transaction, at each movement, noted, registered, controlled, taxed, stamped, measured, valued, assessed, patented, licensed, authorised, endorsed, admonished, hampered, reformed, rebuked, arrested. It is to be, on the pretext of the general interest, taxed, drilled, held to ransom, exploited, monopolised, extorted, squeezed, hoaxed, robbed,- then at the least resistance, at the first word of complaint, to be repressed, fined, abused, annoyed, followed, bullied, beaten, disarmed, garrotted, imprisoned, machine-gunned, judged, condemned, deported, flayed, sold, betrayed, and finally mocked, ridiculed, insulted, dishonoured. Such is government, such is justice, such is morality.

In South America state-sponsored undercover police death squads and the systematic use of torture have been recurrent. In the "white terror" in Guatemala literally thousands died each year (2,000 to 6,000 was the estimate for 1967–1968). The military dictatorships that have ruled Brazil since the coup in 1964 are notorious for their police-based death squads. The U.S. brought members of these squads into Uruguay to train police in torture of urban guerrillas. The U.S. is deeply involved in the development of torture in this region.[6] The police-based AAA [Argentine Anti-communist Alliance] killed 1,000 people in 1975.[7] The full mobilization of the Chilean regime into terror and killing is probably the worst anywhere since the war.[8] Of course state terrorism is not practiced by corporate-capitalist countries alone. It is also an integral part of the practice of such state-capitalist countries as the Soviet union.[9]

The Urban Guerrilla Strategy of Revolution

Around the world the word "terrorism" is used indiscriminately by politicians and police with the intention of arousing hostility to any phenomenon of resistance or preparedness for armed defense against their own terroristic acts. Terrorism is distinguished by the systematic use of violence against people for political ends. Assassination, sniping, kidnappings, hijacking and the taking of hostages from amongst the public, and assaults and bomb-ings deliberately aimed to kill, maim or affright the populace are methods used particularly in non-state terrorism. Within this category a distinction can be made between attacks on the public and those on individuals in power, without implying approval in either case. Clearly attacks on the innocent are worse than those on people guilty of some crime.

In general it is important to differentiate between terrorism and what could be called intimidation. The state is constantly involved in trying to prevent the expression of political opinions by the threat of slander, harassment or disruption. Much activity of the state falls under the term intimidation. Some elements in the Australian left have attempted various types of intimidation against other leftists. We must also be careful to differentiate between terrorism and the damaging of property. Although it is clear that intimidatory activity and property damage are not usually as serious as terrorism, leftists should recognize the ease with which a preparedness for such activities can lead to worse consequences. This is not to argue that revolutionaries should have a reverent attitude toward private property, merely that they should see that there is a vast difference between, say the destruction of a nuclear facility building site by a mass occupation and the blowing up of that site by a few individuals.

Just as the rulers prefer the word "terrorist," terrorists prefer the description "urban guerrilla" [or "armed resistance" or "militants"] as it lends them a spurious romantic air. Nevertheless, we believe that there is a distinction between terrorists and those revolutionaries who adopt the ideology and practice of "guerrillaism," which is to promote armed struggle as *the* revolutionary strategy. Especially in rural warfare these people can use nonterroristic armed action. This usually involves armed clashes with the police or army. However, because of the circumstances of urban guerrilla warfare, this method automatically leads to terrorism as will be discussed below.

In South America the increased use of urban guerrilla warfare was largely a result of the failure of the rural strategy, which had become obvious by the sixties. The rural strategy was based on tenuous theoretical conclusions drawn from an idealized view of what happened in the Cuban revolution. However, the strategy of the urban guerrilla was not in essence different from that of the rural campaigns. Both were based on the vanguardist concept of the armed group whose specifically military confrontations with the ruling regime's repressive forces would provide the small motor (the well known "foco") to start the big motor of political revolution. In this strategy, successful military operation is the propaganda.

The Uruguayan Movement for National Liberation (called the Tupamaros), most successful of the urban guerrillas, expressed this strategy thus:

> The idea that revolutionary action in itself, the very act of taking up arms, preparing for and engaging in the actions which are against the basis of bourgeois law, creates revolutionary consciousness, organization and conditions.'

What a monomania! What simplistic reasoning! The total defeat of the urban guerrillas in Venezuela in 1962–1963, who had support from the countryside and even the Communist Party, should have warned them that the strategy was flawed.

It is fractured thinking to identify the essence of revolution as illegality or as armed confrontation with the repressive instruments of the state. This totally obscures the essence of our objection to this society which is not simply a disgust with state violence—the uses of jail, brutality, torture, murder, etc.—but with hierarchical relationships among people, with competition instead of cooperation. The "very act of taking up arms" may defy the law but it says nothing about what is being fought for. The essence of revolution is not armed confrontation with the state but the nature of the movement which backs it up, and this will depend on the kinds of relationships and ideas amongst people in the groups, community councils, workers councils, etc. that emerge in the social conflict.

The job for revolutionaries is not to take up the gun but to engage in the long, hard work of publicizing an understanding of this society. We must build a movement which links the many problems and issues people face with the need for revolutionary change, which attacks all the pseudo-solutions—both individual and social—offered within this society, which seeks to demystify those solutions offered by the authoritarian left and instead to place the total emphasis on the need for self-activity and self-organization on the part of those people willing to take up issues. We need to present ideas about a socialism based on equality and freedom.

> "Kings and emperors have long arranged for themselves a system like that of a magazine-rifle: as soon as one bullet has been discharged another takes its place. The king is dead, long live the king! So what is the use of killing them?"
>
> —Leo Tolstoy, *Thou Shalt Not Kill*

Political Rackets

Both in the corporate capitalist world and the Third World, guerrilla movements have made a very poor showing in the area of ideas. That the state is repressive and that it can be fought is only a very small part of revolutionary ideas, but this constitutes almost the whole content of what guerrillas attempt to communicate to the people. It is based on the assumption that there is little to think about to make a revolution. All that is required is to convince the people that they can defeat the state. Nothing could be further from the truth. If people do not want to see repeated again and again the old pattern of the revolution placing in power a new group of oppressors, then they will have to realize that the responsibility for a new society rests with them. They will have to think about how to structure this new society so that it remains democratic.

Since it depends on them, they will have to think about their attitudes, and this includes their attitudes in their personal lives.

It is often argued that such demands are ridiculous in the context of immediate basic needs in the Third World. In fact, self-organization on cooperative lines is becoming a feature of Third World struggles. The econometric arguments about Third World struggles would seem to be linked with the idea that Western-style leaps into industrialization are the solution, when in fact decentralization is the key, and this certainly makes the type of personal change we are thinking of easier.

A few leaflets scattered about the site of an action is as much as some groups offer in the way of ideas. The communiques of the German Red Army Fraction (Baader-Meinhoff) never rose above the political level of slogans like "Expropriate Springer [a reactionary German press magnate], Fight for

11

class justice, Fight all exploiters and enemies of the people, Victory to the Viet Cong," etc.

Their pamphlet, "The Concept of the Urban Guerrilla," is a transference of the same strategy as quoted above to Western capitalism. The same goes for the American Weathermen (later Weather Underground), the British Angry Brigade, Japanese Red Army, Symbionese Liberation Army (SLA), etc. Usually these groups have shown a sycophantic third worldism which saw activity within imperialist nations as supportive of the "real revolution" in the Third World. The Weather Underground Organization (WUO) elevated this into their whole ideology and strategy. They denied the task of spreading revolutionary ideas to the majority of people in their own country. Instead the U.S. was to be made immobile while the victorious Third World revolutionaries brought revolution from outside. The WUO later became orthodox marxist-leninists.

Baumann, author of the book mentioned before, was in the June 2nd Movement. He reveals the same kind of thinking; though, unlike the marxist-leninist Red Army Fraction (RAF), they (June 2nd) called themselves "anarchists":

> It would be hard to find a "strategy" that was less anarchistic, less libertarian. The third-hand Lenin on the labor aristocracy, the vanguardism, the profoundly elitist millenarian vision of total destruction, etc., all absolutely exclude anything but a dictatorial outcome.

Baumann described how after Vietnam their line was "people would get involved in Palestine" (p. 50)—and the various German and Japanese terrorists have certainly appeared in Palestinian actions. But this only reveals all the more clearly their total removal from the real struggle in their homelands. And it does not display any substantial concept of internationalism, as they were acting totally above the heads and completely out of the control of the people they were supposedly representing. They were content to work with groups which themselves were merely acting as "terrorist pressure groups" attempting to gain concessions from various ruling classes.

For example, the creation of Black September was a result of the defeat of the Palestinians at the hands of the Jordanian forces in 1970 and of the failure of the various organizations to successfully mobilize the people—instead they turned to international publicity. Now that the PLO has successfully organized itself as a state amongst the Palestinians, terrorism is used as an instrument of state policy. It is the avenue through which the PLO can threaten to explode the situation in the Middle East. [Since this was written, the PLO/Fatah has renounced terrorism in favor of the intifada strategy; and while some Palestinians still resort to terrorism, this is now almost the exclusive province of the fundamentalist religious group Hamas.]

On the whole, struggles revolving around groups oppressed as a culture or nationality are those in which terror against the public and terrorism as a sole strategy is most often found. As a refuge for conservative, authoritarian or vanguardist ideas, nationalism masks them as "progressivism." Terrorism does not conflict with such ideas. If the aim is to place a new group in power whose only requirement from the people is that they are of the same culture or nationality, any method which works will be consistent. The more one wishes to change existing relationships by an aware, self-active populace initiating and controlling a movement, then the more counterproductive and contradictory terrorism becomes because of the elitism and manipulation inherent in it.

Nationalist ideas, as ruling classes know well, allow the presentation of a dehumanized concept of the enemy from another nationality (or religion), which justifies immoral actions against them and excludes the idea of real unity. In South America the groups typically rely on denunciations of tyrants and U.S. imperialism. It would be hard to overestimate the role of U.S. imperialism in the area, but when the enemy is phrased simply in these terms and the goal is national liberation, real liberatory ideas are excluded.

As has already been suggested, the guerrilla creed is that successful military operation is the propaganda. Born of reaction to the stultifying South American communist parties which opposed all action which could possibly get out of their control, guerrillaism is a philosophy of action, an irrational faith in action and the purity of violence which propounds few ideas and produces programmatic statements mostly dedicated to the need for more action of the same kind.

Worse, guerrillaism reproduces the old trap of a passive people who are being fought for, struggling vicariously through the guerrilla group suffering for them. While the sympathetic masses watch this drama played out, time passes and with it their own chance to develop their own response to the social crisis. By the time the drama has become tragedy and the guerrillas lie dead about the stage, the audience of masses finds itself surrounded by barbed wire, and, while it might now feel impelled to take the stage itself, it finds a line of tanks blocking it and weakly files out to remain passive again. Those individuals who continue to object and call on the audience to storm the stage are dragged out, struggling, to the concentration camps. Guerrillaism is in the tradition of vanguardist strategies for revolution. While in general it merely leads to repression, should the strategy succeed it can only produce an authoritarian leftist regime. This is because the people have not moved into the building of a democratic movement themselves.

The Chinese and Cuban successes (and the Indo-Chinese and African struggles of the time) were the great models inspiring assorted rural and urban guerrillas and terrorists. But in looking to these examples the imitators made little realistic adjustment to the general conditions in their own countries. They especially did not make an analysis of the link between the type of governments established by these struggles and the methods used. Of course, for most of these groups the authoritarian governments established in China and Cuba were entirely admirable. But for libertarians and anarchists this is not so.

Those armed groups in Spain and elsewhere who called themselves anarchist or libertarian drew much of their specific justifications from the Spanish revolution and war and the urban warfare that continued there even past the end of the Second World War. For our argument the civil war in Spain is exemplary because the slogan of "win the war first" was used against politics, to halt the revolution and then to force it back under the stalinist-dominated republican governments. In fact, the enthusiasm and determination of the people who first threw back Franco's 1936 coup was based on the fact that at the same time they were seizing the factories and coordinating them through cooperative means.

The defeat in war necessarily followed the defeat of the revolution. Furthermore, the popular army was reorganized into an ordinary military and the original egalitarianism was stamped out under typical militaristic discipline and hierarchy. The post-war libertarian guerrillas were aware of this, but they did not analyze the experience sufficiently. They did not see the absolute primacy of politics over armed struggle. They did not see the vanguardist nature of armed groups seizing the

initiative. They did not see the need for whatever armed activity is necessary to be organized from an existing democratic movement and to remain under that movement's control.

One libertarian movement in Spain, the Iberian Liberation Movement (MIL), founded itself on the theory of guerrillaism (though it was involved in political activity). It carried out a number of bank robberies and during arrests a policeman was killed. As a result an MIL member was garrotted in 1974. The reason the MIL is mentioned here is because they dissolved their organization after general defeat by the police, but also because of the realization that their strategy was wrong. "It is now useless to talk of politico-military organizations and such organizations are nothing but political rackets." (Congress of Dissolution) They decided instead to work to deepen the anarchist communist perspectives of the social movement. Surely a lesson for all.

"Nothing Radicalizes Like Pigs in the Park"

A democracy can only be produced if a majority movement is built. The guerrilla strategy depends on a collapse of will in the ruling class to produce the social crisis out of which revolution occurs, whether the majority favors it or not. Any reading of guerrilla strategists reveals that it (guerrillaism) is a philosophy of impatience. While a collapse of will in the ruling class is surely a vital element in any revolution, unless a mass movement with democratic structures for running the country exists, then an elite will take power. Always lurking in the background and sometimes boldly stated is the idea that guerrilla warfare or terrorism aims to produce a fascistic reaction which would radicalize the people. The Provisionals (IRA) quite obviously followed this strategy. But groups like the RAF and June 2nd also shuffled this idea with their third-worldism, especially as the Third World stabilized into dictatorships and state capitalism, and Western collapse appeared a receding prospect.

Of the state apparatus, Bommi Baumann says, "We knew that if it was touched anywhere, it would show its fascistic face again." As horrible as many aspects of the West German state are, it is not fascist. A clearer understanding of the situation would reveal that it is yet another example of the fact that dictatorial methods have always been and will continue to be part of the arsenal of social control in a

13

capitalist parliamentary democracy. Such methods will be used with abandon in a social crisis. More important still is the revelation that these guerrillas are completely unable to understand in a social-psychological sense that oppression is maintained by consent, and that violence is a secondary phenomenon.

In general it can be seen that these groups are un-embarrassed by any awareness of how major events have changed leftist thought on a whole range of issues (or confirmed elements of libertarian thought which had been suppressed by the dominance of marxism). For example, an interpretation of France 1968 or Hungary 1956 seems to have passed them by entirely.

In March 1972 the Tupamaros stated that they wanted to "create an undeniable state of revolutionary war in Uruguay, polarizing politics between guerrillas and the regime." There is even some suggestion that they discussed the possibility of carrying out actions designed to prompt an invasion by Brazil in the belief that this would galvanize the total population into action.

The RAF put it this way:

> We don't count on a spontaneous anti-fascist mobilization as a result of terror and fascism itself . . . And we know that our work produces even more pretexts for repression, because we're communists—and whether communists will organize and struggle, whether terror and repression will produce only fear and resignation, or whether it will produce resistance, class hatred and solidarity . . . depends on the response to repression. Whether communists are so stupid as to tolerate such treatment . . . depends on this response.

What is revealed completely in this quote is the absolute arrogance of these groups—"Sure we're hoping for a radical response to the state repression we bring down on your heads, but if that doesn't occur, well, that will go to prove you are all stupid." They ignore the actual conditions, like all guerrillas, demanding that everyone else miraculously achieve their "advanced" consciousness, when, as has already been shown, their ideas are superficial and without value and merely a rallying cry for a massacre.

The reason for the occurrence of this ugly strategy derives from the limitations of urban guerrilla warfare. Since they depend on armed action for their existence, all guerrillas can only develop their struggle by escalating their engagements. If they do

"Anarchism . . . it's not terrorism. The agent of the government—the cop who wears a gun to scare you into obeying him—is the terrorist. Governments threaten to punish any man or woman who defies state power, and therefore the state really amounts to an institution of terror."

—Fred Woodworth, *Anarchism*

not they will be forgotten. Dynamism is everything. But rural guerrillas can do this by establishing and expanding their territory of action—liberated zones. They can choose to take on army formations according to their situation. But urban guerrillas can hold no territory, for to attempt to hold a neighborhood or building is to take on the entire armed might of the city. In any engagement the size of army forces cannot be ascertained since they arrive in minutes.

Urban guerrilla warfare must become terrorism in order to develop. There is no other avenue for escalating the struggle. Furthermore, the warfare cannot stretch out indefinitely without withering away. This is the appeal of the polarization and militarization of society strategy. It is the ultimate in manipulation—an intentional attempt to create suffering among the people for the ends of the guerrillas who assume that they know best and that the people will be better off in the long run. Of course the strategy usually results only in repression.

The Tupamaros came to prominence in 1968. In 1967 the democratic government had begun responding to Uruguay's first major economic crisis since the war by attacking the working class and introducing repressive legislation. So they entered the right social situation. They had also spent all the sixties preparing. They were always efficient and planned well. They had links in the unions and other legal movements that were not only maintained but grew. They had elan, imagination and humanity. But by 1971, the year of elections, the paucity of their strategy was becoming apparent and even they were indecisive. How could they go one step further without losing support? They depended on transitory support that was impressed with their seeming invincibility and their restrained use of violence.

14

Inevitably they would prove beatable, inevitably much blood would flow. Then it would be revealed that they had no mass base. After the elections the army was let loose and soon up to 40 Tupamaros were being tried every day. They were defeated before the military junta came to power in 1973.

Just because they were so good within the limits of urban guerrilla strategy they prove the basically flawed nature of the theory. It was quite clear that the ruling class of Uruguay was going to respond to the economic crisis by gravitation to dictatorship. But if the energy expended by the Tupamaros had gone into the spreading of ideas encouraging people to organize, the resistance would have been larger and more profound and therefore had more chance of success.

Headline Hunters

Another component in the foolishness of guerrillaism is that it looks to the media as the agency of its propaganda. According to Baumann:

> RAF said the revolution wouldn't be built through political work, but through headlines, through appearances in the press, over and over again, reporting: "Here are guerrillas fighting in Germany." This overestimation of the press, that's where it completely falls apart. Not only do they have to imitate the machine completely, and fall into the trap of only getting into it politically with the police, but their only justification comes through the media. They establish themselves only by these means. Things only float at this point, they aren't rooted anymore in anything, not even in the people they still have contact with.

This is especially absurd given the role of the most popular news sources in stimulating and maintaining the most irrational elements in people's response to acts of political violence. They deliberately try to obscure political issues by omission and commission. Take the Middle East as an example—How many people remember that 106 passengers and crew were killed in a civilian plane shot down by an Israeli jet over Sinai? How many people know that Israeli bombs killed 46 children in a village in the Nile delta? How many know that 1500 were killed and 3000 napalmed in Palestinian refugee camps and villages by Israel from 1969 to 1972? In November 1977 rocket attacks by Palestinian guerrillas into Israel killed three people. In response Israeli planes bombed nine villages and three refugee camps which they claimed harbored guerrillas.

More than 100 civilians were believed to have been killed. A *Guardian* reporter (November 20, 1977) visited one village and one camp to find that they were not guerrilla outposts. The Israelis also used delayed action bombs so that people were killed during attempts to find survivors. Yet the terrorist acts of Palestinians are the ones which people abhor because they were the acts extensively reported.

Before too long the killing of civilians by the Israelis in their incursion into Lebanon will be forgotten. But you can bet that the killing of civilians by the PLO's terror squad will be remembered. In fact, the hypocrisy and cynicism of Israeli planning relies on this amnesia.

The media seek to obscure politics further by treating incidents as spectacles. This does suit the apolitical nature of guerrilla strategy in which their struggle is supposed to take on bigger and bigger proportions in the media in order to call forth a ruling class response.

The real effect amongst the people, however, is to confirm the idea that politics is a removed realm to be viewed passively—usually as dreary routine, but occasionally as a spectacle. Even if people "support" the guerrillas, this hardly has any real meaning in terms of their own involvement in politics. Instead, the usual result is to provide an organizing base of vicious attitudes for the rulers to exploit for their ends.

The hypocrisy of the media is illustrated by their tendency to play up the significance of political violence compared with their failure to raise any stir about industrial accidents and disease. Car accidents are treated, even sensationalized, but with a kind of primitive fatalism, when in fact they are a serious social and political problem. Many people die of these causes, many more are maimed. Who cares?

The existence of media manipulation should not, however, obscure its basis in reality. Leftists are inclined to dismiss people's outrage as "reactionary." But the killing of school children, placing of bombs in underground stations or machine gunning people at an airport can never be dismissed no matter what the context. People's response is, on the whole, genuine moral outrage. This is manipulated into law and order hysteria which allows legislation to be passed and the left to be crushed. But it is typical of the elitism of many passive leftists lacking in principled ideas who sycophantically devote themselves to any active cause somewhere else, carried out by someone else, to pour contempt on the reactions of people to real outrages.

15

Military Madness

There is undoubtedly much evidence of a tendency toward glorification of death and violence by terrorists and guerrillas. [Ahmad] Jebril [head of the Popular Front for the Liberation of Palestine], one of the leaders of the Palestinian rejection front, sends his troops into Israel with orders not to return (that is, to die) and was quoted as saying, "We like death as much as life and no force on Earth can prevent us from restoring Palestine . . ." putting himself in the same category as the Spanish Falangists (fascists) who shouted "Long live Death!" It must be admitted that this trend of love of death has been prominent amongst various terrorists. WUO leader [Bernardine] Dohrn made a public and positively gloating rave of support for the murders of the Charles Manson gang. There is an element here of the "counter-cultural fascism" which saw the U.S. divided between "pig amerika vs. woodstock nation." A section of the counterculture made a cult of Manson. Baumann mentions that, at the time, they did not think Manson was "so bad." In fact they thought him "quite funny."

What should be avoided, however, is a tendency to explain terrorism by the alleged insanity of the actors, because the acts arise in specific situations of oppression and provocation—the obvious example being nationalities suffering embittering oppression.

In West Germany there were specific incidents such as exceptionally brutal police behavior, leading to the death of a demonstrator, the attempted assassination of a student leader, the venality of the major Springer press (many times worse than Packer or Murdoch [right-wing Australian publishers]), the social democrat Brandt's introduction of *berufsverbot* in 1972 (an employment ban [in government] against leftists, reformists, etc. who are "not loyal to the constitution," which was later applied in some states to social democrats themselves), the attempt to smash all extra-parliamentary or nonunion movements, of which the ban is only the best known part. All of these things provided the background for political violence.

The whole Nazi experience was constantly enlivened by the fact that ex-Nazis, war criminals and Nazis who were still active in right wing politics all held positions in the judiciary, bureaucracy, business, etc. (an expedient policy of the allies who wanted reliable law and order people in the political vacuum of the post-war world). Since this was also the case in Italy it may be no accident that these two countries are the most prominent areas for terrorism in Europe.

All this is not an excuse for terrorism, but such considerations are part of an overall explanation. Concentrating on the supposed insanity of the guerrillas or terrorists is an attempt to provide a justification for murderousness towards them and for the introduction of general repression.

Many of these people become involved in terrorism merely by circumstances and associations, as Baumann's book shows. They get mixed up in an environment of self-glorification and isolation from the world. Even their relationships with supporters are one sided rather than broadening. This unreal situation produces features of madness such that an escalating series of acts is seen as justified and rational. But any attempt by the media, police and politicians to create a caricature of demonic, blood-thirsty monsters will be for the purpose of excusing their own barbarity and corruption. (See the film or read the book by Heinrich Boll, *The Lost Honor of Katarina Blum*.)

Erich Fromm has written:

> We can witness the phenomenon among the sons and daughters of the well-to-do in the United States and Germany, who see their life in their affluent home environment as boring and meaningless. But more than that, they find the world's callousness toward the poor and the drift toward nuclear war for the sake of individual egotism unbearable. Thus, they move away from their home environment, looking for a new lifestyle—and remain unsatisfied because no constructive effort seems to have a chance. Many among them were originally the most idealistic and sensitive of the young generation; but at this point, lacking in tradition, maturity, experience, and political wisdom they become desperate, narcissistically overestimate their own capacities and possibilities, and try to achieve the impossible by the use of force. They form so-called revolutionary groups and expect to save the world by acts of terror and destruction, not seeing that they are only contributing to the general tendency to violence and inhumanity. They have lost their capacity to love and have replaced it with the wish to sacrifice their lives. (Self-sacrifice is frequently the solution for individuals who ardently desire to love, but who have lost the capacity to love and see in the sacrifice of their own lives an experience of love in the highest degree.) But these self-sacrificing young people are very different from the loving martyrs,

who want to live because they love life and who accept death only when they are forced to die in order not to betray themselves. Our present-day, self-sacrificing young people are the accused, but they are also the accusers, in demonstrating that in our social system some of the very best young people become so isolated and hopeless that nothing but destruction and fanaticism are left as a way out of their despair.

Baumann shows that he has learned this lesson through harsh experience (though he still misses that there is a tradition of human values which has survived even "the machine" and that this tradition is asserted, for example, in many episodes of mass revolutionary activity such as the Spanish revolution in 1936, the Hungarian revolution in 1956, and the French revolt in 1968):

Making a decision for terrorism is something already psychologically programmed. Today, I can see that—for myself—it was only the fear of love, from which one flees into absolute violence. If I had checked out the dimension of love for myself beforehand, I wouldn't have done it . . . Until now it has been assumed that there is no simultaneity of revolutionary praxis and love. I don't see that, even today I don't. Otherwise, I might have continued. But I saw it like this: you make your decision, and you stop and throw away your gun and say: Okay—the end.

For me, the whole time it was a question of creating human values which did not exist in capitalism, in all of Europe, in all of Western culture—they'd been cleared away by the machine. That's what it's about: to discover them anew, to unfold them anew, and to create them anew. In that way, too, you carry the torch again, you become the bearer of a new society—if it is possible. And you'll be better doing that than bombing it in, creating the same rigid figures of hatred at the end. Stalin was actually a type like us: he made it, one of the few who made it. But then it got heavy. [Stalin was a gangster (bank robber, etc.) for the Bolsheviks before the revolution.]

You can see how bad it was in Schmuecker's case— they shot him down (Ulrich Schmuecker was a former member of the June 2nd Movement who was assassinated in 1974 after informing on the group). He was just a small harmless student. They forced him into one of these situations, not asking themselves if he was far enough along to handle it. He couldn't have talked that much anyway, and they did him in. That's real destruction; you just can't

see it any other way. The murder of Schmuecker reminds one strongly of Charles Manson. It really is murder, you have to see that." (pp. 105–106)

Minimize Violence by Emphasizing Politics

The very essence of libertarian revolutionary strategy is the idea that there is an inextricable link between the means used and the ends proposed. While there may be a link between the rotten authoritarian ends of nationalists and marxist-leninists and rotten terrorist means, it is unquestionably clear that libertarian ends must disallow terrorist means. In fact, the majority of marxist-leninist groups oppose terrorism, though, as Lenin says in *Leftwing Communism—An Infantile Disorder*, "It was, of course, only on grounds of expediency that we rejected individual terrorism." Leninists are the proponents of vanguardism par excellence. They also are proponents of terrorism by the state—as long as they control it.

Libertarians look at history and at the ruling classes of the world and conclude that a libertarian movement will face state violence, and armed struggle will be necessary in response. It is quite obvious that political activity could not even commence in certain conditions without taking up arms immediately. Also in certain conditions, as in peasant-based societies, it would be necessary to set up armed bases in the countryside. But the aim here would not be to carry out "exemplary" clashes with the military but to protect the political infrastructure to enable the spreading of ideas to continue. This may involve some guerrilla tactics, but it cannot mean the strategy of guerrillaism. Nor can it mean the creation of a separate, hierarchical, military organization, which is not only anti-libertarian but is also vulnerable and inefficient. The Tupamaros were, being marxist-leninists, hierarchically organized. One of the factors in their defeat was the treason of Amodio Perez, a "liaison director" in the organization, i.e., a second-level institutionalized leader who knew so much that he was able to single-handedly put police onto large sections.

In Baumann's book he makes it quite clear that the capture of members of groups was often the result of betrayal by sympathizers. This was not even a result of hierarchical structuring as this did not exist in the group he belonged to. Though the police did use virtual torture methods on some sympathizers, this was not the main factor either. It rather follows from the life of illegality:

> Three people who were illegal would sit in one apartment and two or three legal ones would take care of them . . . (p. 56)

> You only have contact with other people as objects, when you meet somebody all you can say is, listen old man, you have to get me this or that thing, rent me a place to live, here or there and in three days we'll meet here at this corner. If he has any criticism of you, you say, that doesn't interest me at all. Either you participate or you leave it easy and clear. At the end it's caught up with you—you become like the apparatus you fight against.

> Because you're illegal, you can't keep contact with the people at the base. You can no longer take part directly in any further development of the whole scene. You're not integrated with the living process that goes on. Suddenly you're a marginal figure because you can't show up anywhere. (p. 98)

It is obvious that these aspects of such a life are counter-productive for libertarians. On the whole then it would seem that such organizations could only have a survival function for certain people under threat of murder or torture by the state. At one stage the Tupamaros were able to stop systematic torture by threatening torturers, but once the state resumed the offensive, torture was resumed. To prevent executions and torture, armed activity might be justified, but its anti-political features would have to be weighed carefully.

Armed struggle means people would be killed and there is no getting away from the fact that violence threatens humanism. But libertarians would hope to preserve their humanism by ensuring that armed struggle would merely be an extension of a political movement whose main activity would be to spread ideas and build alternative organizations. The forces of repression (police, army) and the rulers themselves would not be excluded from such efforts. In fact much effort would be devoted to splitting them with politics to minimize the necessity for violence. In this situation everyone would have a choice. Libertarians are extending to people the hope that they can change. We are extending to people our confidence that a self-managed society will be more satisfying for all people. This includes our rulers, even though we recognize the limitations created by the characters people have developed in their lives, especially those adapted to the exercise of power.

Small groups operating outside the control of a mass movement and often in the absence of any mass resistance at all, who take upon themselves decisions of "class justice" in the name of groups who are unrepresented but whose interests are affected by action based on these decisions, are nothing but dangerous. The SLA killed a school superintendent after a community coalition failed to prevent the introduction of draconian disciplinary measures in schools. This failure was a reflection of the political level of the community and exactly the opposite of an invitation for the SLA to kill a mere pawn of the Board of Education. "The SLA recognizes but its own will which identifies with the will of the people in much the same manner that many psychopathic killers claim to be instructed by God. It has killed a defenseless individual whose guilt is not only not proved, but is mainly a fantasy of his executioners."

These comments of *Ramparts* magazine apply to many similar incidents. If in these cases guilt can at least be attributed as a justification, what can be said of those actions against the public at large (indiscriminate bombing, taking hostages, hijacking planes, etc.)? Usually terrorists will attempt justification in terms of the kinds of strategies described above. The expected end results from these strategies supposedly justify the means used. Enough has been said about these strategies. But it should be emphasized again that foul means, far from being justified by distant ends, merely provide a guarantee that the ends achieved will be horrible.

You can't blow up a social relationship. The total collapse of this society would provide no guarantee about what replaced it. Unless a majority of people had the ideas and organization sufficient for the creation of an alternative society, we would see the old world reassert itself because it is what people would be used to, what they believed in, what existed unchallenged in their own personalities.

Proponents of terrorism and guerrillaism are to be opposed because their actions are vanguardist and authoritarian, because their ideas, to the extent that they are substantial, are wrong or unrelated to the results of their actions (especially when they call themselves libertarians or anarchists), because their killing cannot be justified, and finally because their actions produce either repression with nothing in return or an authoritarian regime.

To those contemplating political violence, we say, first look to yourselves. Is destructiveness an expression of fear of love? There are political traditions and political possibilities you have yet to examine.

To the society which produces the conditions of poverty, passivity, selfishness, shallowness and destructiveness in which the response of political violence can grow, we say take warning. These conditions must be overthrown. As a French Socialist said in 1848: "If you have no will for human association I tell you that you are exposing civilization to the fate of dying in fearful agony."

---

1. Early in the morning of February 3, 1978, a bomb exploded in front of the 42-storey Hilton Hotel in Sydney, the location of a conference of leaders of Asian and Pacific Commonwealth countries. The bomb had been placed in a trash can and killed two garbage collectors and a bystander, but injured none of the distinguished delegates. According to press speculation, the bombing was directed at the Indian prime minister by the fanatical Buddhist sect, Anand Marg, whose members believe their leader, convicted of murdering defectors from his group, is the incarnation of God.

2. June 21, 1966, Australian Labour Party leader Arthur Calwell was slightly injured by broken glass when a bullet was fired through his car's window. His 19-year-old assailant was later sentenced to life imprisonment.

3. The Croatian Ustasha was founded in 1929 with the Italian fascist movement as a model. With Nazi support it ruled Croatia 1941–1945.

4. On January 17, 1978, the Labour Party premier of South Australia, Donald Dunstan, fired State Police Commissioner Harold Salisbury following a judicial report critical of undercover activities in the state. These activities included the surveillance of over 40,000 persons and organizations, most of them Labour Party supporters.

5. On March 16, 1973, Attorney General Lionel Murphy led an unprecedented raid on the ASIO headquarters in Melbourne. Murphy was searching for information about the Croatian Ustasha, which he believed the ASIO was shielding. The raid was precipitated by the imminent visit of the Yugoslav premier to Australia.

6. See *Inside the Company: CIA Diary*, by Philip Agee for details. — CB

7. Estimates of the total number of those murdered by the police and the military (who were primarily responsible for the killings) during the "dirty war" against leftist urban guerrillas are in the neighborhood of 9,000 to 10,000. — CB

8. Not really. Following the 1973 coup, the Chilean military murdered at least 3,000 people, with some estimates in excess of 10,000. During the decade 1975–1985 alone, the U.S.-backed regimes in Guatemala and El Salvador murdered, according to conservative estimates, 70,000 of their own citizens. Other estimates run to as high as 100,000. — CB

9. And China. In June 1989 the People's Liberation Army slaughtered 3,000 unarmed students in Tiananmen Square. Nor should Cambodia be forgotten. Estimates of the number of those killed by the Khmer Rouge (which, revealingly, the U.S. government supported as the "legitimate representative" of the Cambodian people at the UN from 1979 to 1993) run between one and three million. —CB

"The deep-rooted conservatism of the 'revolutionaries' is almost painfully apparent: the authoritarian leader and hierarchy replace the patriarch and the school bureaucracy; the discipline of the Movement replaces the discipline of bourgeois society; the authoritarian code of political obedience replaces the state; the credo of 'proletarian morality' replaces the mores of puritanism and the work ethic. The old substance of exploitative society reappears in new forms, draped in a red flag, decorated by portraits of Mao (or Castro or Che) and adorned with the little 'Red Book' and other sacred litanies."

—Murray Bookchin, *Listen Marxist!*

INTERNATIONAL PROLETARIAN
HAMMER THROWING & RHETORIC FLINGING
COMPETITION

On: MAY 1, 1984. At: (where else?)
MARX MEADOW in GOLDEN GATE PARK

CONTEST RULES

You will have two hours to compose a manifesto using the terms *struggle, heroic, vanguard, revolutionary, reified, liberated zone, workers party* (penalty for use of apostrophe), *people's army, revolutionary government, youth* (as a plural), *people of color* (**not** *colored people*), *phallocracy, womyn, wimmin, wimin, wimmen, wymyn, white skin privilege, petit bourgeois, trade union consciousness, moral imperative, revolutionary duty, infantile, objectively reactionary, objectively counterrevolutionary, islamophobic, bosses, stooge, puppet, decadent, exploitation, fight, smash, hands off, build, stop, unleash, free* (fill in the blank—Bob Avakian is a good choice), *revisionist, fascist, opportunist, deviationist,* and *running dog.* You **must** use all terms!! (Special prize for the most inventive neologism. Last year's winner: *cisgender.*)

You will then have two hours to put your manifesto into publishable form. Supply your own tools. **Preferred typesetting equipment**: old manual typewriter (extra points for worn ribbons, broken or filled-in characters, handwritten corrections).

The longest, most unreadable entry wins. The triumphant manifesto will then be copied on a 15-year-old xerox machine which hasn't been cleaned in a decade, bound with a staple in one corner, and distributed to contest participants. Losers will have the moral duty to read it. Those who refuse will be unmasked as objectively counterrevolutionary petit bourgeois anarchists and will face the revolutionary justice of the people's democratic dictatorship.

Graphic from *The Heretic's Handbook of Quotations*

REVOLUTIONARY NONVIOLENCE

The popular graffiti tag "Anarchy is love" speaks to the roots of revolutionary action, action taken by those seeking to make anarchism real. As we seek to replace coercive, hierarchical organizations with positive, life-affirming projects such as info shops, community gardens, worker-managed collectives, free schools, and other do-it-yourself efforts, we must organize against coercion, exploitation, and domination in all their forms.

Nonviolent resistance and noncooperation are probably the most effective ways to achieve long-lasting, positive social change. There is dignity in nonviolent resistance, a dignity needed to sustain change. To be effective, it is often necessary to have large numbers of supporters and to be persistent. Your intentions should be clear to both the institutions resisting change and the people you intend to attract as supporters. Honesty and truth are your most important allies. While often difficult, compassion and respect for your opponents, combined with truth and honesty, are essential to undermining the power of even the most ruthless and inhumane institutions. The longer and more violent the repression, the harder it is to remain compassionate, but by retaining your integrity in the face of extreme conditions you will often attract increased popular support and weaken the resolve of those hired to stop your efforts. Participants in nonviolent resistance will increase their feelings of empowerment and pride the longer they remain dedicated to nonviolence.

Nonviolence is not just a theory; it means responding to injustice with action. Nonviolence should not be confused with inaction. Withholding support and refusing to cooperate with institutions and policies of violence, exploitation and injustice is a principal tactic of nonviolent resistance.

"The overwhelming importance attributed to an act of violence or individual rebellion is the daughter of the overriding importance attributed by bourgeois political doctrine to a few 'great men.'"

—Luigi Fabbri, *Bourgeois Influences on Anarchism*

Just because participants are dedicated to nonviolence, you can't expect the authorities to restrain their violence. Often the state will increase its violence if it believes your campaign is succeeding, but as repression grows so will your support. What might seem like months, maybe years of failure can change suddenly.

San Francisco Food Not Bombs (FNB) persisted in sharing food every week for seven years of near daily arrests that became violent due to the police; and, in 1995, the local media, which had been very critical of FNB, finally started ridiculing city officials for wasting money and resources on stopping our meals for the homeless. Their reports reflected the perspective of their corporate owners and politicians in San Francisco who came to see it was not possible to stop Food Not Bombs. Our persistence and dedication to nonviolence attracted public support. Our volunteers would not give up, knowing that, if we did, future efforts to silence Food Not Bombs groups in other cities were more likely.

The San Francisco police officers hired to arrest and beat us withdrew their support for the campaign against Food Not Bombs and started to see themselves as allies of our volunteers against those ordering the repression. Seven years of building relationships with the officers caused the department leaders to first issue an order to "stop fraternizing" with our volunteers, and once it became clear that they could not count on their patrol men and women to continue arresting and beating us with enough enthusiasm, they called off the whole project. The officers grew to see we were honest, caring people and not anti-American criminals bent on disobeying the law out of self-interest, as they had been told by their superiors.

Corporate and government leaders ended their repressive campaign in order to protect their illusion of control; worried that if it became clear to the public that our persistence and relationships with the police had worked, more sectors of the community might have withdrawn support for their authority. Imagine if the patrol officers were perceived by the public as refusing orders. What would be next?

It is extremely important that we act in a manner which is consistent with our values. We want a future without violence and exploitation. Means determine ends. It is never in our interest to use violence against the police or others.

Campaigns of violence, even against the most unethical opponents, can be very disempowering and, even if successful will usually install new institutions that rely on violence to protect their authority. If power changes hands after a campaign of nonviolence, it is more likely that the new institutions will have popular support and maintain their power through consent of the people.

On the practical side, the dominant power usually can muster significantly more violent force than we can. The authorities strive to engage their opponents in realms where they have the advantage, notably armed conflict. But, more philosophically, we don't want to use power for domination in our efforts for social change. Imagine if San Francisco Food Not Bombs adopted a strategy of throwing rocks at the police when they came to arrest us. Instead of the public understanding our message that the government and corporations are intentionally redirecting resources toward the military while letting thousands go without food, the impression would have been that the police were justified in using violence to protect themselves and the community from criminals who have no respect for the public, let alone for the police. (The media reported extensively for years about how violent our volunteers were after several frustrated activists tossed bagels over a line of riot police to hungry people blocked from getting to the food.) We want to create a society based upon human rights and human needs, not dependent on the threat and use of violence. We do not want to dominate. We want to seek the truth and support each other as we work to resolve conflicts without violence.

University of Denver political science professor Erica Chenoweth, co-author with Maria J. Stephan of the book *Why Civil Resistance Works: The Strategic Logic of Nonviolent Conflict*, was surprised to find that "campaigns of nonviolent resistance were more than twice as effective as their violent counterparts." She, like many others, assumed that the most effective way to topple dictatorships and other repressive regimes is to use military tactics. Chenoweth's and Stephan's research showed that "uprisings were 50 percent more likely to fail if they turn to violence."

Washington Post reporter Max Fisher put it like this:

> Political scientist Erica Chenoweth used to believe, as many do, that violence is the most reliable way to get rid of a dictator. History is filled, after all, with coups, rebellions and civil wars. She didn't take public protests or other forms of peaceful resistance very seriously; how could they possibly upend a powerful, authoritarian regime?

A nonviolent uprising can evolve into long lasting change since its power comes from popular support and participation of a substantial number of people. It was once believed that it would take the participation of at least 5% of the population to force change, but Chenoweth and Stephan found that in most uprisings since 1900 it took only 3.5% of the population to bring down a dictator.

Their research also showed that when a government changed hands through the use of violence, the new government turned to violence to stay in power. Using violence to take power often reduces popular support, and so increases the "need" for more violence.

Chenoweth believes that "a violent uprising is more physically demanding and dangerous and thus scares off participants, but I'd add that violence is controversial and can engender sympathy for police and soldiers at the other end of dissidents' rifles."

She tells the *Washington Post* that "The data shows the number may be lower than that [3.5%]. No single campaign in that period failed after they'd achieved the active and sustained participation of just 3.5% of the population." She adds, "But get this: every single campaign that exceeded that 3.5% point was a nonviolent one. The nonviolent campaigns were on average four times larger than the average violent campaigns."

Public support for Occupy Oakland was at an all time high after 26-year-old Iraq war veteran Scott Olsen was nearly killed on October 25, 2011 by Oakland police who deliberately fired a tear gas canister into his head. The Oakland City Council even scheduled a special meeting to vote on a proposal to endorse the occupation.

22

Support vanished overnight after people claiming to support "diversity of tactics" vandalized Whole Foods and several local small businesses on November 2, 2011.

Rebecca Solnit's November 2011 essay, "Throwing Out the Master's Tools and Building a Better House: Thoughts on the Importance of Nonviolence in the Occupy Revolution," describes her decades of activism and her direct experience of radical anarchist successes being derailed by macho acts of violence.

Solnit participated in the "N30" protests that blockaded the World Trade Organization Ministerial Summit in Seattle in 1999. She writes, "To shut down the whole central city of Seattle and the World Trade Organization ministerial meeting on November 30, 1999, or the business district of San Francisco for three days in March of 2003, or the Port of Oakland on November 2, 2011—through people power—is one hell of a great way to stand up. It works. And it brings great joy and sense of power to those who do it." She could have also mentioned the week-long blockade of the San Francisco federal building during the first Gulf War, which she also participated in.

Anarchists in places around the world, including Zagreb and Manila, have asked me if I participated in the "heroic black bloc" assault on the windows of Starbucks and Nike during the 1999 Seattle protest. They were surprised to learn that we shut down the WTO summit *despite* those "heroic" assaults. They had never heard of the years of organization or the Direct Action Network and its pledge of nonviolent action, and the months of nonviolence preparations that went into shutting down the WTO meeting.

Anarchist and *New York Times* best-selling author Starhawk wrote an essay called "How We Really Shut Down the WTO." She writes about seeing news of the protests after having been freed from the King County jail:

The reports have pontificated endlessly about a few broken windows, and mostly ignored the Direct Action Network, the group that successfully organized the nonviolent direct action that ultimately involved thousands of people. The true story of what made the action a success is not being told.

Food Not Bombs organized the UnFree Trade Tour in 1997 visiting 60 cities in North America explaining the dangers of the WTO and advocating a mass mobilization to shut it down if it ever held a ministerial meeting in North America. A year later the WTO announced it would meet in Seattle in November 1999, and the organizing started in earnest with formation of the Direct Action Network. Organizers came to consensus to present a pledge to participants to take nonviolent action. Activists agreed to "refrain from violence, physical or verbal, not to carry weapons, not to bring or use illegal drugs or alcohol, and not to destroy property."

Starhawk notes:

We were asked to agree only for the purpose of the 11/30 action—not to sign on to any of these as a life philosophy, and the group acknowledged that there is much diversity of opinion around some of these guidelines.

She goes on to say:

In the weeks and days before the blockade, thousands of people were given nonviolence training— a three hour course that combined the history and philosophy of nonviolence with real life practice through role plays in staying calm in tense situations, using nonviolent tactics, responding to brutality, and making decisions together. Thousands also went through a second-level training in jail preparation, solidarity strategies and tactics and legal aspects. As well, there were first aid trainings, trainings in blockade tactics, street theater, meeting facilitation, and other skills.

Rebecca Solnit's response to the black bloc attack on local businesses in Oakland in 2011 comments on the literature within the anarchist community glorifying violence. She writes:

CrimethInc, whose logo is its name inside a bullet, doesn't actually cite examples of violence achieving anything in our recent history. Can you name any? The anonymous writers don't seem prepared to act, just tell others to (as do the two most high-profile advocates of violence on the left).

Solnit continues:

CrimethInc issued a screed in justification of violence that circulated widely in the Occupy movement. It's titled "Dear Occupiers: A Letter from Anarchists," though most anarchists I know would disagree with almost everything that follows. Midway through it declares, "Not everyone is resigned to legalistic pacifism; some people still remember how to stand up for themselves. Assuming that those at the front of clashes with the authorities are somehow in league with the authorities is not only illogical . . . It is typical of privileged people who have been taught to trust the authorities and fear everyone who disobeys them. . . ."

[Despite the smear quoted above that privileged people oppose them, theirs is the language of privilege. White kids can do crazy shit and get slapped on the wrist or maybe slapped around for it . . . [Those with skin of a different] color face far more dire consequences.

As do families with children and older people who are in danger when the black bloc provides the opportunity for the authorities to use violence—with the blessing of a public disturbed by images of rampaging thugs.

Anarchists dedicated to nonviolent direct action are not opposed to all forms of property damage. It can be an effective strategy if the decision to do it involves all participants, the target chosen is one that will guarantee no one who is not part of the action could be injured, and the method used does not frighten the public. If those participating also take credit and destroy property that is clearly injurious, that sends a clear message to both those who are being targeted and the public; that type of property damage can be empowering to those participating in it and can serve as an inspiration to those you want to join you.

A simple example is the Food Not Bombs actions taken the night of August 19th and at lunch time on August 20, 1981. Food Not Bombs shared vegan meals outside a weapons bazaar at Boston University the day after we spray-painted the outline of "dead" bodies on the ground, stenciled mushroom clouds with the word "Today?" and wheat-pasted "War is Murder for Profit" posters along the route that the weapons buyers and sellers would take from their hotel to the conference hall. We stood outside the conference holding poster boards with the mushroom cloud image that we had stenciled dozens of times outside the Student Union and along Commonwealth Avenue, taking credit for hundreds of dollars in graffiti damage to Boston University's property. Who did this frighten into the arms of the state? No one.

Solnit explains anarchist support of property damage this way:

I want to be clear that property damage is not necessarily violence. The firefighter breaks the door to get the people out of the building. But the husband breaks the dishes to demonstrate to his wife that he can and may also break her. It's violence displaced onto the inanimate as a threat to the animate.

Quietly eradicating experimental GMO crops or pulling up mining claim stakes is generally like the firefighter. Breaking windows during a big demonstration is more like the husband. I saw the windows of a Starbucks and a Niketown broken in downtown Seattle after nonviolent direct action had shut the central city and the World Trade Organization ministerial down. I saw scared-looking workers and knew that the CEOs and shareholders were not going to face that turbulence and they sure were not going to be the ones to clean it up. Economically it meant nothing to them.

French farmer and anti-globalization activist José Bové has taken part in several actions involving property damage during campaigns of nonviolent resistance. Bové declared, "I am an anarcho-syndicalist. I am closer to Bakunin than Marx. My references are the Jura Federation in the First International in the [19th] century and the Spanish CNT of 1936."

Bové participated an a nonviolent direct action destroying genetically engineered maize in a grain silo in Nérac in the department of Lot-et-Garonne, France. At his trial he stated, "Today, I am present in this court together with Rene Riese and Francois Roux, accused of committing a serious crime according to the law. The alleged crime is the destruction of sacks of genetically modified maize (corn). Yes, on January 8, I participated in the destruction of genetically modified maize, which was stored in Novartis' grain silos in Nerac. And the only regret I have now is that I wasn't able to destroy more of it."

On August 12, 1999 Bové participated with activists from the *Confédération Paysanne*, the second largest farmers' union in France, in the "dismantling" of a McDonald's franchise that was under construction in Millau, Aveyron, France. Bové was sentenced to three months' imprisonment for his role in the destruction. He was imprisoned for 44 days and released on August 1, 2002. The actions of the *Confédération Paysanne* helped bring global attention to the policies of the World Trade Organization and neoliberal structural adjustment/economic austerity programs. Over 40,000 people attended the trial of Bové and his co-defendants.

Anarchism is fundamentally about collective action using the nonhierarchical process of consensus in the decision-making process to include all those

ANARCHISM: The theory that all forms of government rest on violence, and are therefore wrong and harmful, as well as unnecessary.

ANARCHY: A condition of society regulated by voluntary agreement, cooperation and mutual aid instead of government.

—Emma Goldman

affected. Actions such as those taken by the black bloc cannot by design be agreed to by all those who are affected. Rather, they're *imposed* on other participants in actions.

Solnit writes:

> The euphemism for violence is "diversity of tactics," perhaps because diversity has been a liberal-progressive buzzword these past decades. But diversity does not mean that anything goes and that democratic decision making doesn't apply.

I participated in the protests against the Democratic National Convention in Denver in 2008. While staffing the Food Not Bombs table I witnessed two white vans arrive in Civic Center Park in the early evening of August 25, unloading twelve buff men in black Obama for President t-shirts, black pants, and black bandanas covering their crewcuts. Two of these men had a knapsack. The vans drove away leaving the 12 "black bloc" men. They divided into two groups, one headed to the west side of the protesters preparing to march to the convention and the other six went to the east end of the gathering. I followed those walking to the west side and was joined by a reporter from the *Denver Post*. He asked me if I thought they were policemen. I told him that I just saw them get out of two vans driven by uniformed officers.

Before long the "black bloc" on the west side was taunting the riot police. Then all of a sudden they turned and rushed into the crowd and seconds later the riot police started firing pepper spray, mace, and other crowd control weapons into the protesters. Riot police surrounded the march along a one-block stretch of 15th Street between Court and Cleveland. A total of 96 people were arrested that evening. I spoke with a woman who watched the protest on her local Fox TV station, and she felt the arrests were justified because of how violent the black bloc had been, throwing stones through windows and taunting the police. When the arrests started I returned to the Food Not Bombs table. The twelve "black bloc" men arrived soon after and stood before me talking. After about ten minutes the two white vans returned and the "black bloc" climbed in and the vans drove away from Civic Center Park. (This is not to say that the black bloc are police agents, just that their tactics

> "Laws! We know what they are and what they are worth! They are spider webs for the rich and mighty, steel chains for the poor and weak, fishing nets in the hands of the government."
>
> —Pierre Joseph Proudhon, *What Is Property?*

make it very easy for police provocateurs to impersonate them and disrupt demonstrations.)

Some people who were not police agents joined them in their provocations. The domination, exploitation, and destruction of capitalism is brutal and it is not difficult for the state to encourage sensitive people to buy into the romantic vision of "revolutionary" resistance personified by the black bloc.

CrimethInc published a personal account of the Denver protests from a young person who attempted to join the black bloc:

> Donning a black shirt and jeans, I raced down the street on my scooter, wind in my face, to catch up to my friend. It was the first day of the Democratic National Convention and we were running late for the black bloc protest in Civic Center Park. Having grown up in Denver, an overlooked bastion of liberalism in the Rockies, I never thought I would be able to get involved in a nationally publicized protest without moving to Washington D.C. or New York. This was the first major political action in which I had the chance to participate, and I wasn't about to miss it.

Solnit's essay on the Oakland assault on Whole Foods is pertinent here: "This account is by a protestor who also noted in downtown Oakland that day a couple of men with military-style haircuts and brand new clothes put bandanas over their faces and began to smash stuff." She thinks that infiltrators might have instigated the property destruction, and Copwatch's posted video seems to document police infiltrators at Occupy Oakland.

One way to make the work of provocateurs much more difficult is to be clearly committed to tactics that the state can't co-opt: nonviolent tactics. If an infiltrator wants to nonviolently blockade or march or take out the garbage, well, that's useful to us. If an infiltrator sabotages us by recruiting others to commit mayhem, that's a comment on what such tactics are good for.

Solnit quotes Oakland Occupier Sunaura Taylor: "A few people making decisions that affect everyone else is not what revolution looks like; it's what capitalism looks like."

Peter Marshall's book on the history of anarchism, *Demanding the Impossible*, points out that "The word violence comes from the Latin *violare* and etymologically means violation. Strictly speaking, to act violently means to treat others without respect ... A violent revolution is therefore unlikely to bring about any fundamental change in human relations. Given the anarchists' respect for the sovereignty of the individual, in the long run it is nonviolence and not violence which is implied by anarchist values."

26

AVOIDING FBI ENTRAPMENT

The government wastes millions, probably tens of millions, of dollars annually spying on and disrupting the anarchist movement. It wouldn't waste all that money trying to stop us if it wasn't worried that we might inspire resistance.

Even though most anarchists are dedicated to nonviolent direct action and many participate in useful projects such as infoshops, bicycle co-ops, and the sharing and growing of food, the police, state agencies, federal agencies, and military intelligence units in the United States routinely infiltrate anarchist groups, and government provocateurs have repeatedly attempted to entrap activists. For the most part, they've failed at that.

But unfortunately some activists have not only been arrested, but have been tried, convicted, and sentenced to years in prison.

The FBI and other law enforcement agencies can and do frame or entrap anarchists to devastating effect, so it is important to do all you can to reduce the possibility of being set up on phony "terrorism" or other charges. Not only could you be removed from the community for many years, your family and friends would suffer through your ordeals in court and through the pain of knowing you are in prison. Defense activities also siphon off huge amounts of energy, time, and resources from the good work of building a better world.

Still it is not always possible to avoid being the target of the authorities, so take precautions to limit the damage if the state seeks to silence you. Taking actions that you can be proud of may be the most important single thing you can do. Think of the consequences of your acts. How will you feel if someone is injured or killed because of something you did? Could your actions be used to discredit the movement? Could they add to the divisions, fear, and paranoia in the community?

Don't think that you can get away with risky, pointless actions. You're not clairvoyant. The government targets even the most peaceful groups through its use of informers and provocateurs, and surveillance is unrelenting and omnipresent. So what can you do beyond carefully considering your actions and doing only things you feel good about?

You can take some simple steps to reduce the possibility of being arrested and prosecuted on phony charges. When people talk or joke about taking up arms, trashing communities, or bombing or burning down some place, speak loudly about how you would never participate in any action that could injure someone.

The fact that we know that we are not considering acts of terrorism can cause us to make light of statements about arson, bombings, and rock throwing, but the FBI and Homeland Security have sent infiltrators to political meetings to talk about using violence or property destruction, or initiated conversations while being wired to record conversations. Months later, out-of-context statements can appear as evidence that anarchists were plotting acts of terrorism. When the cases get to court, prosecutors and the media can point out that the accused activists didn't object to the comments made by the informants, "proving" their guilt.

You can minimize the success of the state in harming you and your efforts by making it clear that you are not going to participate in acts of violence or destructive sabotage. (They're not the same: violence involves damage to people or animals; sabotage involves—sometimes, not always—damage to property.) If you are planning to damage property, consider making your intentions clear in advance by offering a public explanation of your actions. Examples could include pulling up genetically modified crops or dismantling the separation wall in Palestine, actions designed to stop an egregious harm. At the same time you can refrain from giving the exact time or location of your plans so that the authorities will have at least some difficulty blocking your actions. While you may still be accused of taking part in a "terrorist" plot, you will have much more popular support, and you'll make the authorities' "terrorism" accusations less credible.

You can make your positions clear in your literature, statements to the media, at meetings, social gatherings, and during informal conversations. If people are joking about using violence or talking about the virtues of acts that could injure or kill people, it is wise to make several statements making it clear that you will not engage in any kind of violent activity. Point out that you are dedicated to nonviolent direct action and that anyone considering any other strategies or methods should talk elsewhere.

It once was possible to use the defense of entrapment, but that is no longer the case. Vice News contributor Natasha Lennard's article, "The Line Between FBI Stings and Entrapment Has Not Blurred, It's Gone," makes this quite clear.

In her introduction to the Human Rights Watch report, "Illusions of Justice: Human Rights Abuses in US Terrorism Prosecutions," Andrea Prasow said that "Americans have been told that their government is keeping them safe by preventing and prosecuting terrorism inside the US . . . But take a closer look and you realize that many of these people would never have committed a crime if not for law enforcement encouraging, pressuring, and sometimes paying them to commit terrorist acts." While this report focuses on the entrapment and framing of people in the Muslim community, anarchists in the United States have also been targeted, as described in the report.

Natasha Lennard writes:

Since 9/11, Muslims in the US have been the focus of major counterterror stings. But other groups have been caught in the net where sting meets entrapment. A small group of self-identified anarchists in Cleveland were all convicted and sentenced to around 10 years in prison for allegedly plotting to blow up a bridge in Ohio. But an FBI infiltrator provided the target and the fake C-4 explosives. Rick Perlstein wrote of the case in *Rolling Stone*, "the alleged terrorist masterminds end up seeming, when the full story comes out, unable to terrorize their way out of a paper bag without law enforcement tutelage."

The case of entrapment in Cleveland provides concrete examples of what activists should watch out for. The FBI sent an informant, Shaquille Azir or "Kalvin Jackson," to the kitchen at Occupy Cleveland on October 21, 2011, seeking to build a relationship with some of the cooks.

FBI Special Agent Ryan M. Taylor filed Federal Complaint 1:12-mj-3073 regarding the matter. The government presented it at the defendants' May 1, 2012 arraignment; it details how the entrapment worked. It's a stark warning to anyone who might be a target of the FBI. In sections 8 and 9, the FBI admits to using a Confidential Human Source (CHS) and Undercover Employee (UCE) to encourage acts of terrorism:

8. The (CHS) Confidential Human Source hereinafter has been working as a source for the FBI since July 20, 2011. The CHS has a criminal record including one conviction for possession of cocaine in 1990, one conviction for robbery in 1991, and four convictions for passing bad checks between 1991 and 2011. The CHS is currently on probation in Cuyahoga and Lorain Counties for passing bad checks. Since July 20, 2011, the CHS has been paid approximately $5,750 for services and $550 for expenses, the CHS has not been paid since beginning her/his probation.

9. The (UCE) Undercover Employee has been employed by the FBI for over 15 years and has been working in an undercover capacity for 10 years. The UCE has received ongoing training in conducting undercover investigations and has participated in dozens of investigations in an undercover capacity.

Section 12 suggests the FBI was seeking anarchists to frame at Occupy Cleveland.

12. Based on an initial report of potential criminal activity and threats involving anarchists who would be attending an event held by a protest group, the Cleveland FBI directed the CHS to attend that event. On October 21, 2011, at approximately 6:30 pm, and while the CHS was attending the event, the CHS identified four suspicious males with walkie-talkie radios around their necks. Three of the four men had masks or something covering their faces; one male did not. The men were wearing black or dark colored shirts, had black backpacks, carried the anarchist flags and acted differently than the other people in attendance.

Section 29 shows that informant Shaquille Azir was recording meetings for the FBI and claimed that one of those targeted, Michael Wright, had talked of making smoke bombs from a recipe taken from the William Powell book titled *The Anarchist Cookbook* (*NOT* this *Anarchist Cookbook*).

(In a separate case, according to a terrorism complaint filed in Brooklyn in April 2015, FBI informants provided Asia Siddiqui and Noelle Velentzas with copies of the Powell book on November 2, 2014, circling the types of bombs the government thought would help build their case.)

29. On March 22, 2012, the CHS was provided a body recorder [and] consensually recorded a meeting between the CHS and WRIGHT. In sum and substance, WRIGHT described using an upcoming festival as an opportunity to create a civil distraction in order to commit a larger act of violence. WRIGHT also discussed making smoke bombs and other explosive destructive devices using the 'Anarchist Cookbook,' a book that describes the construction and use of weapons and explosives. The following are some of the relevant excerpts from that conversation:

Sections 97 and 98 show that phone calls and conversations were recorded a couple of days before the FBI-engineered May Day fake bombing:

97. On April 29, 2012, the UCE recorded a telephone call with WRIGHT. In sum and substance WRIGHT said that he would call the UCE around 1:30 pm to give the UCE the exact meeting location, however it was in the Warrensville Heights, Ohio area.

98. On April 29, 2012, the CHS was provided with a body recorder and consensually recorded a meeting with the UCE and WRIGHT, BAXTER, and HAYNE.

In Section 110 of the federal complaint, the FBI admits that the alleged criminal activity that they were investigating amounted to no more than "smoke grenades and destruction of signage on buildings in downtown Cleveland":

110. WRIGHT recruited BAXTER, C.S. and the CHS to participate in some form of direct action, initially involving smoke grenades and destruction of signage on buildings in downtown Cleveland;" Erick Trickey of Cleveland Magazine noted that defendant Connor Stevens expressed support for nonviolent direct action.

On a Saturday in April, about three weeks before his arrest, Stevens served dinner in Market Square with Food Not Bombs. He got talking with fellow volunteer Aidan Kelly about Ernest Hemingway's novel *For Whom the Bell Tolls*, in which an American joins the Republican side in the Spanish Civil War to fight a fascist uprising, and is assigned to dynamite a bridge. "I remember distinctly talking about his

ideas about pacifism," Kelly says. He and Stevens agreed that movements such as Food Not Bombs offered a better alternative for creating social change than violence.

Trickey writes of the first meeting of Stevens and co-defendant Brandon Baxter, a meeting like those you may have had if you travel in anarchist circles.

At Food Not Bombs last year, Stevens met another young anarchist, Brandon Baxter, as intense and passionate as Stevens was cerebral.

The 19-year-old Lakewood High graduate's influences weren't long-dead, bearded writers, but websites ranging from the far right (the conspiracy-minded InfoWars) to the far left (the Anonymous "hacktivist" movement). He embraced Food Not Bombs with gusto, screaming "Free food!" across Market Square when dinner was ready.

Yet the FBI claims that Wright downloaded Powell's version of the *Anarchist Cookbook* with the purpose of making a bomb, which would have been a good trick given that to all appearances Powell's book has never been sold in e-book format.

111. WRIGHT repeatedly asserted he downloaded the 'Anarchist Cookbook' in an attempt to learn how to make explosives including constructing plastic explosives from bleach and other household items; . . .

The complaint finally shows that the FBI was moving their own plot along by providing the defendants with phony C4.

112. When presented with the opportunity to purchase C4, WRIGHT and BAXTER met with an individual offering it for sale;

Michael Winter of *USA Today* reported that "Three self-described anarchists were sentenced to prison Tuesday for trying to blow up a highway bridge between Cleveland and Akron using dummy explosives provided by an undercover FBI agent."

Ed Meyer of the *Akron Beacon Journal* wrote that "U.S. District Judge David D. Dowd, Jr. rejected the government's insistence that the defendants get 30 years in prison and instead gave Douglas L. Wright 11½ years, Brandon L. Baxter nine years and nine months and Connor C. Stevens eight years and one month."

Both of Stevens' parents, James and Gail Stevens, lashed out at the government's actions.

"My son is guilty, and so are you!" James Stevens told federal prosecutor Duncan Brown at one point. Gail Stevens called her son "my hero," said she loved him with all her heart, and that he never would have acted as he did if not for the provocateur.

The entrapment of the young Occupy anarchists in Cleveland was the most dramatic attempt to discredit the Occupy movement. And it worked—with the help of some protesters who played into the hands of the police.

Efforts to re-energize the movement failed as the media reported on a wave of Occupy-related violence. Reuters reported:

> Occupy Wall Street protesters smashed windows in Seattle, fled police on scooters through the streets of New York, and clashed with officers in Oakland on Tuesday in a May Day effort to revive the movement against economic injustice with demonstrations around the United States. . . .

> New York police reported 10 instances of harmless white powder—apparently meant to raise an anthrax scare—being mailed to financial institutions and others . . .

> In Seattle, some 50 black-clad protesters marched through downtown, carrying black flags on sticks they used to shatter the windows of several stores including a Nike Town outlet and an HSBC bank before police moved them out of the area. Others smashed windows at a Seattle federal building, and swarms of demonstrators gathered in an open-air plaza.

May 2012 was not the first time authorities used an alleged May Day bomb plot to discredit anarchists. Chicago police, seeking to stop the movement for an eight-hour workday, attacked a peaceful rally in May 1886. A bomb was set off and police shot into the rally in what has become known as the Haymarket massacre. The bomber was never identified and the government provided no evidence linking them to the bombing, yet anarchists August Spies, Samuel Fielden, Adolph Fischer, George Engel, Louis Lingg, and Albert Parsons were accused of the bombing, convicted, and executed.

Historians James Joll and Timothy Messer-Kruse claim the evidence points to Rudolph Schnaubelt, brother-in-law of Michael Schwab, as the likely bomber. Howard Zinn, in *A People's History of the United States* also indicates it was Schnaubelt, sug-gesting "he was a provocateur, posing as an anarchist, who threw the bomb so police would have a pretext to arrest leaders of Chicago's anarchist movement."

Spies would later testify, "I was very indignant. I knew from experience of the past that this butchering of people was done for the express purpose of defeating the eight-hour movement."

That was in the 19th century. The government has been framing, imprisoning, and occasionally murdering anarchists ever since.

But you're not powerless. You can take some simple steps to protect yourself from being arrested, charged, and convicted of planning or participating in acts of terrorism. The FBI and Homeland Security have sent infiltrators to our meetings to talk about using violence. The authorities will often attempt to give the impression in affidavits or typed memos that someone other than their informant or undercover officer made statements advocating violence, and imply that everyone participating in the discussion supported its use.

One of the most successful strategies used by the FBI is to have those infiltrating joke about the use of violence. When the words they used become the text in memos or court filings, they're out of context, they no longer seem humorous, and can be presented as a serious conversation supporting the use of violence. Since those participating in such conversation consider the statements nothing more than an awkward attempt to be humorous or fit in with the group, no one thinks to make it clear that they don't intend to participate in a violent action. Months later, out-of-context statements can appear as evidence that anarchists were plotting acts of terrorism. Even if you state clearly that it is not appropriate to talk or joke about violence, you can still be arrested and tried, but you will greatly reduce that possibility if you do speak up.

Activists have been charged as terrorists after getting a ride home with people that turned out to be infiltrators. After dropping off their passengers, provocateurs and those they're setting up have burned down buildings or torched vehicles. The fact that you were seen getting into the informant's vehicle before the act of alleged terrorism happened can provide the evidence needed to accuse you of taking part. The FBI and their informants are not always honest, and may choose not to mention that you were not at the scene of the crime, even though they can honestly say you got into a vehicle with the arsonist. Sometimes federal prosecutors have been able to get convictions simply because the set-up activists were intimidated into not expressing their dedication to nonviolence, fearing that they would be accused of being "weak" and not serious about social change, the well-being of animals, or the environment. Both provocateurs and holier-than-thou true believers use such fears to manipulate people into saying or doing things they would never otherwise say or do. Don't let anyone manipulate you into silence. Don't let anyone manipulate you into saying or doing things that could land you in prison.

The first step is to make it clear that you are not going to participate in acts of violence or destructive sabotage. You can make this clear in your literature, statements to the media, at meetings, social gatherings and during informal conversations. If people are joking about using violence or talking about the virtues of acts that could injure or kill people, it is wise to make several statements making it clear that you will not engage in any kind of violent activity. Point out that you are dedicated to nonviolence and that anyone considering any other strategies or methods should meet elsewhere. To help protect your friends you might also point out that it is very unlikely that such plans could be concealed from the government. As you can see in the Cleveland case, otherwise innocent conversations can be recorded and provide support for prosecution.

Another step you can take is to include statements about nonviolence in your literature about any direct action you might be planning or supporting. On occasion, the media and prosecutors will claim that our literature didn't make any mention that our protests would be nonviolent, and use that as "proof" we are terrorists. If your group is planning an action, you can protect yourself by including explicit language about nonviolence in your publications. This can be difficult when working in coalition with groups that might not share our principles of nonviolence, but you could publish your own literature on the action. Don't be intimidated into remaining silent on the issue of violence. It isn't necessary to exclude reference to nonviolent direct action just because people are arguing in support of a "diversity of tactics." You may initiate a pledge of nonviolence for the campaign you are supporting and organize nonviolence training sessions. Nonviolent resistance is every bit as valid as other methods and is often more effective.

Nonviolent direct action, noncooperation, and nonviolent resistance can be very empowering. It takes courage to organize and participate in cam-

> "There is no greater fallacy than the belief that aims and purposes are one thing, while methods are another. This conception is a potent menace to social regeneration. All human experience teaches that methods and means cannot be separated from the ultimate aim. The means employed become, through individual habit and social practice, part and parcel of the final purpose; they influence it, modify it, and presently the aims and means become identical."
>
> —Emma Goldman, *My Disillusionment in Russia*

paigns of nonviolent struggle. Nonviolent struggle can build trust between participants and the public. Campaigns of nonviolent direct action and civil disobedience can be so effective that governments and corporations will try anything to push our movement into adopting violent tactics. That is one reason groups like Food Not Bombs have been the focus of infiltration and why the authorities rely on agents provocateur to reduce the impact of nonviolence, while sowing fear and alienation.

Don't let people intimidate you into silence. People can make comments about nonviolent activists being "wimps" or "pussies," that nonviolence never works, or that you are not really committed to change if you aren't willing to use sabotage or violence. You might even hear that nonviolence is racist because people of color "have to take up arms," and that white, first-world people have the luxury to use nonviolence. Infiltrators or government agents may be talking to some of your friends at cafes, clubs, or other public locations, promoting the idea that armed resistance or arson is the only solution. Honest discussion of all tactics and methods, including types of violence, is fine, but make it clear that you and your group are dedicated to nonviolence.

At the same time, it is not wise to make claims of infiltration or accuse someone of being an informant. It is best to not worry about infiltration and to stay focused on the work of your organization. Just take the simple precautions of asking that any discussions of violent tactics take place somewhere

31

other than at public meetings, make it clear you are dedicated to nonviolence; and make that plain in your publications and through organizing nonviolence trainings. If you do this, attempts to convict you on terrorism charges will likely fail, and the fear and mistrust that so often destroy movements will be defused. The government can use the fear of infiltration as a way of destroying trust in your community. Don't accuse people—just be careful about what you say and do.

You can make sure you and your friends will not fall prey to the government's efforts to disrupt your work. First, stay focused on the fundamentals of your project or campaign. Don't feel guilty about refusing to take violent action. Since the world is facing so many dire crises, it might seem rational to consider arson or other acts deemed violent by the corporate state, but these tactics often backfire. They can cause the public to withdraw any support they may have had for your cause. The use of violence also breeds distrust among activists, because of the secrecy involved. But as we have learned from Ed Snowden and other whistleblowers, it is nearly impossible to have secrets in the United States. According to the *Washington Post*, over eighty billion dollars is spent each year on government and corporate spying.

A campaign of violence would add to the disempowerment in our community and scare the public into greater support of the authorities. If you feel you must investigate tactics that include violent action, ask yourself whether such tactics will do more harm than good for you personally and for the cause you support. Are you really ready to live fearing capture? How will you feel if your friends spend their lives in prison while you're all portrayed as dangerous and crazy? Will your actions really inspire the public to rise up and save the earth? How will you feel if you kill someone or if one of your friends is killed? Can you really see yourself coordinating a campaign of bombings, arson, shootings? How will you feel spending the rest of your life in prison, seeing the stress this puts on your family and friends?

While it is possible you could spend decades in prison for taking nonviolent direct action, you are likely to feel more empowered and have wider support on the outside than if you were imprisoned for violent acts. Unlike people who are doing life in prison for bombings or shootings, if you are sentenced to a long prison term for organizing or participating in a campaign of nonviolent direct action and noncooperation, you have a much greater chance of

inspiring popular support, possibly achieving your political or environmental goals, and of leaving prison before your sentence is up.

In addition, mass nonviolent direct action based on a thoughtful strategy is more likely to be effective. Agents provocateur encourage drastic actions, knowing we are knowledgeable about environmental and economic threats. If pressured, you can remind your friends that many of the anarchists in prison were framed for "terrorist" acts and that as anarchists we are dedicated to nonviolent direct action.

Along with making it clear you are not going to be silent when people suggest using violence, you may want to organize nonviolence preparations, trainings or workshops with your friends or organizations. Suggest that your community study the history of nonviolent direct action in books by people such as Emma Goldman, Erica Chenoweth, Gene Sharp, Martin Luther King Jr., and others who experienced first hand the power of noncooperation and nonviolence.

Again, be concerned about jokes concerning violence. If people joke about armed revolution, bombings, rock throwing or other acts of violence, make it clear that you are dedicated to nonviolent direct action and ask them to stop. You might remind your friends that conversations and jokes about using violence have resulted in activists being framed and sentenced to long prison terms. Terms sometime decades long. The activists that are joking about violence or making statements about the need to use violence are not necessarily infiltrators or police agents, so don't make any accusations. They may have been influenced by someone they met or may have read some of the many books romanticizing violence. It is best not to worry and to stay focused on the work of your group. The government can use the fear of infiltration as a way of destroying trust in your community. Again, simply remind your friends that you are dedicated to nonviolent direct action and that we don't joke or talk about taking violent action.

While armed resistance has worked to overthrow governments and change the power structure of some countries, in virtually every case the system that resulted continued to use violence to retain its authority. That is the exact opposite of what anarchists are seeking: a society free of coercion, exploitation and domination. Nonviolent social change offers the clearest route there.

ANARCHISM VS. "LIBERTARIANISM"

The meanings of words often shift with time. The term "fulsome" provides an example. The 1940 edition of *Webster's Collegiate Dictionary* defines it as "1. Offensive, disgusting; esp. offensively excessive or insincere. 2. *Rare*. Lustful, wanton." And that's it. Today, the term's meaning has shifted. It's still occasionally used in sense 1 of the Webster's definition (never in sense 2), but it's usually used as a synonym for "plentiful," "ample," or "generous."

The meaning of "libertarianism" has undergone a similar extreme shift, at least in the United States. P.J. Proudhon used the term as a synonym for anarchism as early as the 1840s, and the term is still almost universally used in that sense in the rest of the world, where "libertarian" still means "anarchist," an advocate of stateless, egalitarian communism or socialism.

To cite a few of the almost innumerable examples of this usage, in 1895 Sebastien Faure and Louise Michel founded the most important French anarchist periodical, *Le Monde Libertaire* (Libertarian World), which is still publishing today. The primary Cuban anarchist group of the 1930s, '40s, and '50s (with thousands of members), was the *Asociación de Libertarios Cubanos*, and its youth wing was the *Juventud Libertaria de Cuba* (Libertarian Youth of Cuba). The Spanish anarchists of the *Confederación Nacional del Trabajo* (with over a million members in the 1930s) routinely used the words "anarchist" and "libertarian" as synonyms, as in the influential 1932 pamphlet, *El comunismo libertario* (Libertarian Communism), by Isaac Puente. The great Mexican anarchist Ricardo Flores Magón also used the terms as synonyms in the pages of *Regeneración* in the World War I era. And there exist to this day important anarchist publications titled *El Libertario* in both Venezuela and Uruguay.

Here in the U.S., the term "libertarian" was also commonly used as a synonym for an advocate of free, stateless socialism in the 19th century, but was also used extensively in a somewhat different sense by individualist anarchists such as Benjamin Tucker and Josiah Warren, who advocated mutualism (freely associating small holders and co-ops) rather than socialism. These usages remained relatively constant through the middle of the 20th century. Whatever their minor differences, though, essentially all libertarians considered the abolition of the state absolutely necessary. And essentially all rejected capitalism.

Ignoring this historical context, and recognizing the usefulness of the term, advocates of *laissez-faire* capitalism began using "libertarian" self-referentially in the 1960s. (They very likely knew of the then-standard meaning of the term "libertarian," but chose to ignore it.)

Even then, most of them—including, arguably, their two leading spokesmen, Karl Hess and Murray Rothbard—advocated abolition of the state, and tended to be absolutists on civil liberties. But they (at least Rothbard) did not want to get rid of police and prisons. In place of the state, Rothbard argued for a privatized repressive apparatus—though of course he didn't use that term—including private prisons.

Even that's too radical for today's "libertarians," who overwhelmingly support the state, and have seemingly forgotten that their early leaders rejected it.

Today, almost no one challenges the *laissez-faire* capitalists on their Orwellian use of the term "libertarian." Today, the Orwellian use is the accepted use. Most people don't even know that "libertarian" once had a very different meaning in the U.S. And things are getting worse.

Since their early days, U.S. "libertarians" have drifted steadily to the right. They now embrace the discredited, misnamed theory of social Darwinism (which is based on gross misinterpretation of Darwin's scientific theory) and advocate abolishing the social welfare functions of the state while retaining its repressive functions (the police, prisons, and military).

In their early days, U.S. "libertarians" were, by and large, reliable advocates of individual liberties.

> "True liberty is not a mere scrap of paper called 'constitution,' 'legal right,' or 'law.' It is not an abstraction . . . It is not a *negative* thing of being *free* from something, because with such freedom you may starve to death. Real freedom, true liberty is positive: it is freedom *to* something; it is the liberty to be, to do, in short, the liberty of actual and active opportunity."
>
> —Emma Goldman,
> *The Place of the Individual in Society*

No more. Today, some are outspoken opponents of reproductive rights, and advocate government interference in what should be private medical matters.

The term "libertarian" has now degenerated to the point where, in the U.S., it refers *only* to *laissez-faire* capitalists who embrace social Darwinism (as expounded by cult figure Ayn Rand), who embrace the repressive functions of the state, and who advocate state intrusion into the most intimate aspects of our private lives.

Comparing anarchists and *laissez-faire* "libertarians" on a few specifics is instructive. First, the similarities:

- Anarchists tend to be civil liberties absolutists.

- "Libertarians" tend to be civil liberties absolutists. As "libertarians" drift further to the right, though, one expects this commitment to lessen.

- Anarchists almost invariably oppose military adventurism.

- "Libertarians" by and large oppose military adventurism.

- Anarchists almost invariably support reproductive rights.

- "Libertarians" are divided on the issue; some (notably Ron and Rand Paul) advocate state intrusion into private medical matters, though one suspects that most "libertarians" still favor reproductive rights.

Now the differences:

- Anarchists reject the state, especially its repressive functions. By and large they don't object to its social welfare functions, which they see as ameliorating the worst effects of a grossly unfair distribution of wealth and income, thus increasing the freedom of the poor.

- "Libertarians" support the state, especially its repressive functions, and reject its social welfare functions. Many of them have social Darwinist views, see the misery of the poor as a good thing, and want to increase it by destroying what's left of the social safety net.

- Anarchists believe that the world's natural resources should be shared equally.

- "Libertarians" believe that the world's natural resources should be in the hands of those ruthless enough to seize them, and their heirs.

- Anarchists believe that wages should be equal, with perhaps additional pay for those doing dangerous or distasteful work.

- "Libertarians" believe that grossly unequal income is not only acceptable, but desirable—again due to social Darwinist views—and they have no problem with those doing no useful work receiving the highest incomes and those doing dirty, dangerous work the lowest.

- Anarchists believe that workers should democratically control their workplaces, their working conditions, and what they produce.

- "Libertarians" believe that workers should be content to live under a workplace dictatorship (their employer's) and have no say in either their working conditions or in what they produce.

- Anarchists by and large accept scientific theories and conclusions.

- "Libertarians," more and more, deny them.

This denialism is especially noticeable in the climate change controversy. Anarchists almost universally accept the scientific conclusion (backed by an overwhelming majority of climate scientists) that climate change, global warming, is real and is a terrible threat. More and more "libertarians" deny it. Some go further. Two of the leading funders of the climate-change-denial industry are the "libertarian" Koch brothers (heirs, whose money comes largely from fossil fuels).

> "The law says that your employer does not steal anything from you, because it is done with your consent. You have agreed to work for your boss for certain pay, he to have all that you produce. Because you consented to it, the law says that he does not steal anything from you.
>
> But did you really consent?
>
> When the highwayman holds his gun to your head, you turn your valuables over to him. You 'consent' all right . . .
>
> Are you not compelled to work for an employer? Your need compels you, just as the highwayman's gun."
>
> —Alexander Berkman, *What Is Anarchism?*

> "If a slave owner of our time has not an Ivan whom he can send into a privy to clean out his excrements, he has three rubles which are so much wanted by hundreds of Ivans that he can choose any one of them, and appear as a benefactor to him because he has chosen him out of the whole number and has permitted him to climb into the cesspool. . . . Slavery exists in full force, but we do not recognize it . . ."
>
> —Leo Tolstoy, *The Slavery of Our Times*

But "libertarian" climate change denial is hardly surprising. Climate change denial has absolutely nothing to do with libertarianism in its traditional sense (anarchism). What it does have to do with is *capitalism*. If the predominant conclusion of climate change science is correct (and it almost certainly is), that climate change is largely man made, that means that the *laissez-faire* "invisible hand" article of faith is spectacularly wrong on perhaps the most important issue of our time. For that article of faith to be correct, the unbridled pursuit of profit by the fossil-fuel energy companies could *not* lead to disastrous results the world over. Science indicates that it does, so out goes science. All of this is evidence that "libertarian" ideology in the U.S. is nothing but a minor variant of *laissez-faire* capitalist ideology, and one that grows increasingly indistinguishable from it with every passing day.

An August 2014 Pew Research poll supports this conclusion. Pew found that 33% of self-described "libertarians" opposed legalization of marijuana, 26% wanted to make homosexuality illegal, and a full 42% wanted to give police the power to stop and search anyone who, in the cops' opinion, *looks like* a crime suspect.

Since the 1960s, American *laissez-faire* capitalists have turned the meaning of the once useful word "libertarian" on its head. And, still, virtually no one challenges their gross misuse of the term. That's simply fulsome.

American "libertarians" are social Darwinists and capitalists, not libertarians in any real sense of the word.

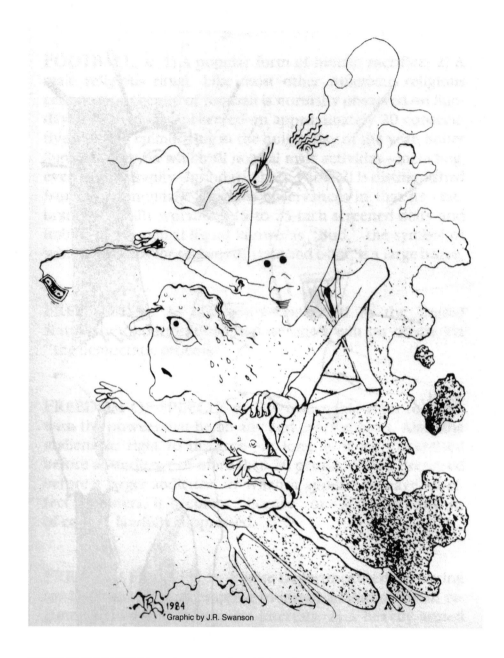

1984
Graphic by J.R. Swanson

FREE ENTERPRISE, n. A system in which a few are born owning billions, most are born owning nothing, and all compete to accumulate wealth and power. If those born with billions succeed, it is due to their personal merits. If those born with nothing fail, it is due to their personal defects.

—from *The American Heretic's Dictionary*

RECIPES

FOR SOCIAL CHANGE

WHAT WORKS, WHAT DOESN'T

Common Approaches to Social Change

We deal elsewhere with nonviolent direct action, the most effective means to social change. Here, we'll deal with the effectiveness (or lack of it) of various tactics and strategies, some of them involving direct action, others not involving it.

Boycott and Divestment Campaigns

Boycotts—refusal to do business with specific companies or refusal to buy certain classes of products or services—have a long history, going back at least to the boycott of British goods in America in the period leading up to the American Revolution.

More recent boycotts include the successful Montgomery bus boycott in 1955/1956, protesting segregation in public transit; the temporarily successful United Farm Workers grape and lettuce boycott in the 1970s, which led to the signing of a large number of contracts with agribusinesses; and the current boycott of Israeli goods. One of the more successful boycott movements, the Indian independence movement's boycott of British goods prior to the achievement of independence in 1947, had a second component: social boycotting (shunning) of those who broke the boycott.

There are both significant advantages and disadvantages to using boycotts as a strategy. One advantage is that they're legal in most parts of the developed world, and some parts of the developing world. So, legal risk is generally minimal (though sometimes there is physical risk).

A second advantage is that they're nonviolent, which makes it difficult for governments and corporations to stigmatize boycotters—though they'll certainly try to do so. A third advantage is that they're sometimes effective.

Another advantage is that boycott movements necessarily involve a wide swath of people, and anarchists will in all likelihood be a small minority within boycott movements. This provides a good opportunity to expose nonanarchists to anarchist ideas, and to see that anarchists can be helpful, cooperative people. Given the widespread misunderstandings of anarchism and anarchists, it would be a mistake to underestimate this opportunity.

Both an advantage and disadvantage of boycotts is that they're often narrowly focused and have limited aims. The disadvantage here is that even if a boycott succeeds, it will have reduced or eliminated some type of specific abuse, and will probably have done little to achieve fundamental political and social change.

The advantage of this narrow focus is that the goals of boycotts are often achievable. Boycotts do at times succeed, and there are few things more empowering that taking part in a successful campaign of *any* sort.

Divestment campaigns are similar in many ways to boycotts. The difference is that they focus on influencing institutions and individuals to sell their holdings in companies doing ecological, political, or social harm.

Divestment campaigns have several goals. One is to deny capital to corporate malefactors. A second is to lower the stock prices of criminal corporations, and so instigate a shareholder backlash that could influence a corporation to mend its ways. A third, though usually unspoken, goal is to use the campaign to gain media attention.

The most prominent current divestment campaign is that dedicated to having universities and philanthropic foundations divest their holdings in fossil fuel extraction companies, because of the catastrophic environmental damage those corporations are causing. One expects at least limited success for this campaign, whose beneficial effects will be multiplied if the institutions it influences put their money into renewable energy development.

Boycotts and divestment campaigns are essentially two sides of the same coin, and as strategies have similar advantages and disadvantages.

Co-ops

Both consumer and producer co-ops have a long history, dating back to at least the 19th century, when there were active co-op movements in both England and the U.S. The aims of those founding co-ops varied. The aims of some, especially consumer co-ops, were simply to reduce costs for their members. The aims of producer co-ops were sometimes more ambitious: many founders and members of producers co-ops (and some members and founders of consumer co-ops) saw them as a means of transforming the economy into a federation of co-ops.

There are both internal and external reasons this transformation never took place. One can look to such matters as capitalization and economies of scale, but other factors were and are at work.

Perhaps the most important of those factors is that co-ops exist within a capitalist economy, and they usually become co-opted; sooner or later they begin to act like typical capitalist businesses, distinguished only by ownership being spread out among their members rather than in the hands of individual owners or shareholders.

The wave of co-optation of food co-ops from the 1970s is a case in point. (I'm quite familiar with those co-ops, having worked off and on as a paid staffer and volunteer at one of those co-op for seven years.) Those who founded those food co-ops often had rosy visions of a cooperative economy gradually supplanting corporate capitalism.

Needless to say, that didn't happen. Instead, the 1970s food co-ops that survived, for the most part, have evolved into high priced health food stores with an uninvolved membership and a traditional management structure. (The last I heard, the co-op where I worked had followed such a path, and had branched out into selling high end wines, with some bottles selling for several hundred dollars.) This isn't the worst thing in the world, but it certainly falls short of revolutionary change.

Producer and service-provider co-ops can be both far better and far worse. At their absolute nadir, such co-ops can become simple vehicles for exploitation of nonmember workers. The taxi co-ops in some U.S. cities are a good (actually horrifying) example. Many have devolved to the point where the owner-drivers have become pure owners (who no longer drive), mercilessly exploiting non-owner drivers who often make less than minimum wage.

At best, producer and service-provider co-ops can and do operate along directly democratic, self-managed lines, and serve as models demonstrating that such an operating structure is viable. The rub is that such co-ops exist within the capitalist economy and are subject to the same relentless pressures as any other business.

One such problem is the pressure to expand ("expand or die," to quote a capitalist proverb). When co-ops do expand, they often hire nonmember workers, and this inevitably sets up a two-tier structure within their work force. Even when pay remains the same for members and nonmembers, nonmembers are normally the first ones fired when an individual co-op's business worsens or the overall economy slumps. As well, nonmember workers are just as powerless over their jobs as unorganized workers in any other business.

Beyond that, almost all co-ops above a certain small size adopt a traditional management structure. Some draw managers from their work forces and compensate management less lavishly than in typical corporations, but the fact remains that their workers are *managed*.

Another pressure on co-ops is that of keeping costs to the minimum, in order to keep their prices competitive. This pushes co-ops to buy from the cheapest sources possible, which often involves buying from suppliers who exploit labor and/or have dodgy environmental policies.

But within these limitations, co-ops can do good work. The example co-op advocates typically cite is the Mondragon Corporation, by far the largest and most successful co-op federation, which consists of 260 cooperatives worldwide, employing nearly 75,000 people, and with revenues in 2014 of nearly 12 billion Euros (equivalent to about $16 billion).

Within Mondragon co-ops, top management earns only three to nine times the wages of the lowest paid workers, and members own the co-ops. On the down side, not all workers are owners, competitive pressures to keep costs down are a constant, and there is still the traditional capitalist division between workers and management, even though managers are drawn from the work force in many co-ops and managers receive relatively modest compensation. In other words, the co-op movement typified by Mondragon is reformist, not revolutionary. It will not and, by its very nature, *cannot* lead to fundamental change.

One relevant piece of evidence that this is so is the origin of the Mondragon co-ops. They began in the 1950s in the Basque region of Spain, with the permission of Spain's government, headed by mass-murdering fascist Francisco Franco. The Franco dictatorship ruthlessly suppressed all forms of dissent, and anything else it deemed even remotely threatening. And it allowed formation of the Mondragon co-ops; it didn't see them as a threat.

This is not to say that co-ops are useless. Far from it. Within their limits, they can bring significant benefits to their members. But they're reformist, not revolutionary.

Even if it succeeded globally, the best the co-op movement could deliver would be "capitalism with a human face."

Education

"No ideas. No revolution."

—Crane Brinton

Educational work comes in many forms: books, bookstores, infoshops, discussion groups, web sites, videos, theater, music, graffiti, stickers, flyers, posters, informational picketing . . . The list goes on, and a lot of people spend a lot of time on such work.

But it can be frustrating; it's difficult to quantify the effects of educational work beyond the number of hits on web sites, number of books sold, etc. Because of this, some militant types criticize educational work as "useless," "all talk, no action," or even "cowardly." In their eyes, the only real revolutionary action lies in confrontation—in general, the more violent the better—with the authorities, especially the police.

Neglecting the condescending, reductionist, and macho nature of this all-action approach, and its conspicuous lack of success, let's look at whether it has any validity.

One reason that many people become impatient with educational work is that the immediate payoffs from doing it are few and far between, and it's often

> "What harm can a book do that costs a hundred crowns? Twenty volumes folio will never make a revolution. It is the little pocket pamphlets of 30 sous that are to be feared."
>
> —Voltaire

unglamorous. It's entirely possible to spend one's life in the background doing educational work and to have nothing tangible to show for it.

As an example, one of our friends has spent decades working as the unpaid, *de facto* manager of an anarchist bookstore. During that time, the store has sold hundreds of thousands of books and pamphlets, has served as a free meeting place for innumerable discussion and organizing groups, and has spawned many other projects. Yet the revolution hasn't happened in our friend's lifetime. So, have the thousands of hours he's spent doing unpaid educational work been a waste? Those who favor the all-action-all-the-time confrontational approach would say "yes." I'd say "no."

One obvious thing confrontational types overlook is that those engaged in educational work almost invariably advocate other kinds of political/ social change activities as well as education, and often engage in them. Virtually no one advances the view that educational work in itself is enough to bring revolutionary change.

Another obvious thing confrontational types overlook is that educational work (often in conjunction with nonviolent direct action and, sometimes, even electoral strategies) can lead to incremental reforms. Often these reforms are of the ten-steps-forward-nine-steps-back type, as with reproductive rights, and sometimes they come more suddenly, as with the accelerating movement to end drug prohibition. Again, virtually no one argues that such reforms will bring revolutionary change. Such reforms do, however, tend to make people's lives better in the here and now, and every step toward greater freedom tends to delegitimize coercive authority.

But the most obvious thing that those who dismiss educational work miss is that thought precedes action. In insurrectionary situations, one of the key questions—very probably *the* key question—is what ideas, what beliefs, are in the heads of the people in the streets?

> "Make no laws whatever concerning speech, and speech will be free; so soon as you make a declaration on paper that speech shall be free, you will have a hundred lawyers proving that 'freedom does not mean abuse nor liberty license'; and they will define and define and define freedom out of existence. Let the guarantee of free speech be in every man's determination to use it . . ."
>
> —Voltairine de Cleyre, *Anarchism and American Traditions*

Do they still hold the old beliefs in civil and religious authority? Do they still believe that such authority is "inevitable" and that they (and everyone else) should be subject to it? Do they still think that all that's needed is "better" people at the top? Do they still believe in hierarchy and competition-based economics?

Or have they rejected capitalism and religion but still believe in coercive authority, and simply want to give it to a new "revolutionary" government?

Or have they (at least a sizable minority) rejected hierarchy and coercion in all their forms and want to build a new society based on voluntary cooperation, mutual aid, egalitarian distribution of wealth and labor, and direct democracy?

These are crucial questions, and the answers to them in large part determine the outcomes of revolutionary uprisings.

Look no further than the Iranian "revolution" to see the results of a mass revolt in which a large majority of those taking part held reactionary beliefs, and still accepted religious, governmental, and capitalist authority. Look no further than the Russian revolution to see the results of a revolt in which the majority of those in the streets had little political consciousness or experience, but retained faith in authority, and so allowed the Bolsheviks to hijack their revolution.

Look to Spain (1936–1939) for a real revolution. There, the Spanish anarcho-syndicalists had engaged in decades of mass union organizing and educational work prior to the outbreak of the revolution. They abolished government and capitalism, and brought workplace democracy, community democracy, and egalitarian economics to millions of Spaniards in large regions of Spain. That they were stabbed in the back by the Spanish Communists and crushed by the combined forces of Spanish, German, and Italian fascism does not diminish their achievements.

And those achievements point to an important lesson: thought precedes action, and the content of thoughts determines actions.

Educational work in itself is not enough to produce revolution. But without it, no revolution will succeed.

Labor Organizing

Business (AFL-CIO-type) Unions

When Americans think of means to change, labor organizing tends to be well down on the list, if it's there at all. There are good reasons for this.

It's obvious that the business unions, the AFL-CIO unions, are not a means to fundamental social and political change. Rather, they're an obstacle to it. Their very nature ensures this, and their history amply demonstrates it. They're hierarchical organizations with entrenched, often highly paid bureaucracies that are in the business of selling their members' labor for top dollar (unless their hierarchies are only concerned with harvesting dues from their members, as occasionally happens).

The business unions have never challenged capitalism (or the state); rather they have always attempted to make themselves an integral part of it, ensuring "labor peace." One need only to look at the history of the American labor movement to confirm this. In the World War I and post-World War I period, when the largest genuinely revolutionary union in U.S. history, the Industrial Workers of the World, was being viciously persecuted and thousands of its members imprisoned for opposing U.S. participation in the war and the draft, or for "criminal syndicalism," the AFL unions sat on their hands. This complacent attitude was exemplified in a well known photo of AFL founder Samuel Gompers in formal attire dining at a banquet with the head of the U.S. Chamber of Commerce.

Over the coming decades, the business unions continued to sell out their members. One infamous example of this was AFL-CIO head George Meany's support for the Vietnam War, which pointlessly killed over 50,000 working class Americans and several million Southeast Asian workers and peasants. A famous Meany statement from the period perfectly exemplifies the reactionary attitude of the business unions: "Why should we worry about organizing groups of people who do not want to be organized?"

Today, AFL-CIO leaders mouth more progressive rhetoric, but the leopard hasn't changed its spots. The business unions are still hierarchically organized with well paid, out-of-touch executives, many are outright undemocratic, and they're still in the business of selling their members' labor.

And they're increasingly ineffective at even that. In 1940, 34% of the private sector workforce was organized; more than one in three workers belonged to a union. Things are different today. According to the Bureau of Labor Statistics, in 2014 the percentage of unionized private-sector workers was down to 6.6%—one in 15.

Why has the percentage of nongoverment workers fallen so far? AFL-CIO backers would (in part correctly) point to the laws passed since World War II that hamstring the union movement (notably "right to work" laws and the Taft-Hartley and other federal labor acts—laws which among other things prohibit secondary boycotts and allow the government to order striking workers back to work). AFL-CIO backers would also point to lack of enforcement of laws protecting workers who try to organize; because of that lack of enforcement, employers have fired organizers with impunity for decades.

But there's another reason too: the very nature of the business unions (hierarchical, often undemocratic, often corrupt), and beyond that their utter lack of an inspiring vision. Many invite noninvolvement of members—just pay your dues and leave the rest to us. To put this in other words, organizations with entrenched bureaucracies intent on self-preservation and having no goals beyond selling their members' work lives for the highest dollar simply are not inspirational

Where the business unions are effective is in serving as bad examples. Most people think that the oft-times corrupt, hierarchical, undemocratic, accommodationist, uninspiring AFL-CIO unions are the only type possible, even the only type that ever existed. And so they look down on and are resistant to joining unions of any type. (And, yes, other types are possible.)

While the AFL-CIO unions sometimes bring members better wages and working conditions, that comes at a price: by design they're a support for capitalism, not a challenge to it.

If you want fundamental change, don't look to the business unions. Don't waste your time and energy on these reactionary dinosaurs.

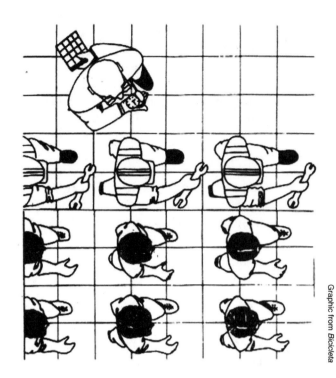

Graphic from *Bicicleta*

Revolutionary Unions

But is labor organizing ineffective as a means to fundamental change? No, it can be quite effective.

In the 1930s in Spain, revolutionary unionism of the IWW type, as practiced by the anarchist *Confederación Nacional del Trabajo* (CNT), did lead to a genuine revolution and social transformation in approximately half of Spain, including Catalonia, its major industrial region. That social transformation lasted approximately two years, until it was crushed by the anarchists' Communist "allies" and the combined military forces of Spanish, Italian, and German fascism. This, however, does not take away from the achievements of the Spanish anarchists. And it provides evidence that revolutionary labor organizing can lead to fundamental political, social, and economic change.

The hallmarks of such organizing are direct democratic control by members, horizontal structure, decentralization, unpaid officers, rotation of offices, and immediate recallability of all (unpaid) officers. And, importantly, having a motivating vision. That of the CNT was elimination of capitalism, elimination of government, and direct democratic control of the economy by those who work. To put this another way, the goal of the CNT was (and is) the achievement of freedom in both its senses, the positive ("the freedom to") and the negative (freedom from restraint). That's an inspiring vision.

Today, the CNT still exists and still pursues those goals, as do the other member unions of the IWA (International Workers Association). IWA unions and groups exist in Europe, South America, and Australia. Here in the United States, the IWW continues to work for emancipation, and is active in almost all states.

Labor Tactics

There are many labor tactics that can be used to effect social, economic, and political change. The one that most people will immediately think of is the strike.

Standard strikes: Walkouts take place for several reasons: for union recognition, for improvement of wages, benefits, working conditions, and (rarely in the U.S.) to further political or social goals. Business union strikes normally take place after negotiators have failed to reach agreement on a new contract. At that point, the union takes a vote of its membership and goes on strike if the membership votes for it.

The advantage of standard strikes is that they're sometimes effective in raising wages or improving working conditions. The disadvantages are that management has advance warning and can make plans to hire scabs (strike breakers). As well, under the Taft-Hartley Act, the president can order striking workers to abandon a strike, and imprison union leaders if they refuse to order their members back to work. A third disadvantage is that corporations have far more assets than workers, and often can simply wait out striking unions as their members become more and more financially desperate.

Still another disadvantage is political: standard strikes cede to shareholders ownership of the business and to management the right to manage it (and to manage the workers who keep it functioning). Standard strikes effectively recognize the legitimacy of private property. That the standard strike is virtually the only weapon in the arsenal of the business unions says much about them.

Wildcat Strikes: Wildcat strikes take place for many of the same reasons as standard strikes, though they can take place for other reasons, such as the unfair dismissal of workers. In contrast with standard strikes, wildcat strikes are spontaneous, there is no advance authorization vote, and they often take place against the opposition of the business union supposedly representing the workers.

Wildcat strikes have the advantage of allowing the company no advance notice. They also allow workers to challenge management over a wider range of issues than those typically covered in union-management negotiations. Still another advantage of wildcat strikes is that they're usually of short duration, which allows workers to conduct them without suffering economic calamity.

One disadvantage is that management can legally fire organizers of wildcat strikes, in fact all who take part in them, something supposedly illegal with standard strikes called by the business unions. However, the body responsible for enforcing these protections, the National Labor Relations Board, has been ineffective for decades, and employers routinely fire organizers with impunity. So, this disadvantage is one in theory, not in fact.

Another disadvantage is that there will be no strike fund available to wildcat strikers. However, since strike pay from the business unions is paltry, this is not a major disadvantage.

One variation on the wildcat strike is the "sick in," where workers call in sick. This can be just as effective as walking out, but to be effective it requires the participation of at least a sizable minority of workers, and without seeing others do it (as with strikes) participation can be lower than in a wildcat walkout.

All things considered, there's a lot to recommend wildcat strikes, and to a lesser extent sick ins.

Sit Down Strikes: Sit down strikes involve workers stopping work but refusing to leave their workplaces.

The advantage of a sit down strike is that it guarantees that a workplace will be shut down while the sit down continues. This gives strikers considerably more leverage than in a walkout, where the employer can bring in scabs and resume operations.

The disadvantages of sit down strikes are that they involve significant disruption to the strikers' lives, they can lead to considerable police violence if employers have police attempt to evict strikers, and there are often considerable logistical problems in getting food, clean clothes, and other essential items to strikers.

Slowdowns: Slowdowns are exactly what they sound like—the slowing down of work. They're normally informal actions spurred by specific abuses by management.

One variety is the work-to-rule slowdown. Many workplaces have so many rules that if workers followed them all strictly, work would grind to a halt, or very nearly so. By working exactly according to rule, workers can stop or drastically slow the work process without losing income by striking, and without giving management a convenient excuse to fire them.

Informational Picketing: This involves picketing an employer to bring pressure on them via the media and via solidarity actions by other workers, notably refusal to cross a picket line. With informational picketing, it's often advantageous to have nonemployees do the picketing in order to reduce the possibility of retaliation from management.

Boycotts: (see Boycotts, p. 39). Boycotts are often used in conjunction with strikes. They can be standard consumer boycotts, or they can involve delivery workers refusing to cross picket lines and thus impede or stop the work process if the employer has brought in scabs. Such delivery boycotts can be highly effective.

Workplace Occupations: Occupations take sit-down strikes a crucial step further. In them, workers take over the workplace and continue to operate it as their own. In some places, as in Argentina in the first years of the 21st century, workers have taken over abandoned businesses. In others, as in the wave of factory occupations in Italy following World War I, workers have taken over still-functional businesses.

Such occupations can be revolutionary, but not if they're done in isolation. Where there have been scattered, uncoordinated occupations, the occupied businesses are inevitably recuperated back into the capitalist economic system and end up operating as standard-issue co-ops.

But when takeovers occur in a coordinated manner, with the goal of transforming political, social, and economic life—that's revolutionary.

Public Space Occupations

The tendency of governments the world over to crush public space occupations, and their frequent brutality in doing so, is an indication of the effectiveness of such occupations.

Overseas, one need look back no further than 2011 to see the central role the Tahrir Square occupation played in the overthrow of the Mubarak regime (1981–2011) in Egypt, despite that regime's brutal attempts to break up the occupation. Another example is the Tiananmen Square occupation in 1989, and its murderous suppression by the Chinese government, in which the military killed at least several hundred, more probably several thousand, demonstrators.

One notable aspect of the Tiananmen occupation was its peaceful nature and the very moderate demands of the demonstrators. These things made no difference to the regime. It was frightened to death of the Tiananmen occupation, and chose to crush it with troops it brought in from outside the (Beijing) region, for fear that those based locally wouldn't shoot demonstrators.

Here in the U.S., suppression of public space occupations is also the rule, both currently and historically. One instructive example occurred in 1932, with the "Bonus Army" of over 40,000 unemployed World War I veterans and their families occupying public space and setting up an encampment in Washington, D.C.; they were demanding early payment of bonuses the government had promised them in 1924 for serving it during the war. The federal response? The government sent in the army (under the command of right-wing icon Gen. Douglas MacArthur) to drive them out and demolish the encampment, killing two people in the process.

More recently city governments in apparent collusion with the FBI, DHS, and corporate security firms shut down Occupy Wall Street encampments all across the country in 2011/2012 in what appeared to be a coordinated wave of attacks, sometimes with deliberate brutality. This was despite the peaceful nature of the encampments, the generally moderate demands of the protesters, and the fact that most of the city governments responsible for the police attacks were controlled by the supposedly progressive Democratic Party.

The Occupy movement, and its suppression, in Tucson is a case in point. (It was obviously not the most significant occupation; I mention it only because I directly witnessed it, and to a small extent took part in it.) The Occupy encampment here originally occupied Armory Park in the downtown area. Over its first few weeks, the encampment gradually grew. At its high point (when it was shut down), the Armory Park encampment might have held a hundred people staying overnight and two to three times that many during the day.

With that first shutdown, the city gave the encampment adequate notice. They evidently thought the occupiers would just disperse and go away. They were wrong. A new encampment sprang up almost immediately in a nearly unused, even smaller downtown park. When the city shut that encampment down, it gave almost no notice—two hours—before the cops moved in.

Finally, a third encampment sprang up on a strip of vacant land adjacent to still another park. The city shut it down in fairly short order, on transparently bogus grounds (blocking the sidewalk—an outright lie). There, the cops simply showed up, trashed the campers' belongings, and illegally arrested people.

Why were governments, city and federal, so frightened, so motivated to suppress Occupy encampments? The stated reasons for the suppression were obvious falsehoods. The authorities nationwide routinely cited public safety concerns, despite the fact that the encampments were self-policing (no drugs, alcohol, violence, or sexual harassment, etc.), and almost all of the relatively few problems were caused by homeless people attracted to the encampments because of free food (provided by supporters in the community) and a safe place to sleep; those causing problems were quickly invited to leave. (In the case of the final shutdown here in Tucson, the reason police cited [blocking the sidewalk] was blatantly false, as anyone driving by the encampment, which faced Stone Avenue, a major thoroughfare, could see—not that that stopped the media from repeating the cops' lies without comment).

The real reasons for the repression? The government and police had lost control of the spaces occupied by the encampments. Never mind that the encampments were textbook examples of free speech and free assembly for nonviolent political purposes, that they were democratically run, that they were self-policing, and that they were providing a safe place, a home, for the homeless. No. The fact that the cops and government were no longer in total control was intolerable to them.

As the encampments grew, the fear of the authorities grew. Their reaction was revealing: to hell with the right of free political speech, to hell with peaceable assembly. The authorities invented pretexts and shut down the encampments, often with a great deal of police violence (as in Oakland).

This explains the panicked reactions of the city and federal governments (whose FBI and DHS heavily infiltrated Occupy encampments). But what value did the encampments have beyond exposing the hypocrisy and lust for control of the authorities?

Great value. They gave participants an experience of direct democracy, no matter how imperfect, in stark contrast to the corporate-funded electoral farce. They gave participants many opportunities for voluntary cooperation, in contrast to the "normal" authoritarian manner of organizing work. And they helped participants overcome the disempowering isolation that is a plague in this country; there is strength in numbers—something almost impossible to appreciate as an isolated individual.

As well, the encampments politicized at least some of the homeless and spawned other political projects, notably the occupation of vacant and abandoned buildings. And they were gathering steam—attracting more and more participants—when the police shut them down.

In short, the Occupy movement provided its participants with a glimpse, no matter how limited and short lived, of what life could be like in a free society, and it showed real promise of fostering further, fundamental change. Future public space occupations will likely have similar promise, and will almost certainly face similar repression.

Sabotage

A reasonable definition of sabotage is that it's anything that causes physical damage or destruction to chosen targets and/or causes disruption to the normal operation of such targets.

Surprisingly, given the romantic notions that surround it, most sabotage is done for nonpolitical reasons. Rather, it's done on the job, and its perpetrators are workers who are simply fed up with low pay, lousy working conditions, meaningless work, bosses they hate, or all of the above. As Martin Sprouse puts it in his book, *Sabotage in the American Workplace*, workers engage in sabotage "as a direct method of achieving job satisfaction."

In contrast, very little sabotage is done for political reasons. But the two types can overlap, as with slaves in the pre-Civil War United States feigning stupidity, ignorance, or incompetence as a way of lightening their work burden. Though it probably was not a primary motivation, such sabotage helped to undermine slavery.

But here we'll consider only politically motivated sabotage.

Except in very rare circumstances, sabotage in and of itself is not sufficient to achieve political goals—*any* political goals. It's usually part of a broader campaign that can include civil disobedience, legal actions, and public education.

Because of this, it's very important that sabotage doesn't alienate unaligned people. It's essential that it be nonviolent, that it injure no one. Sabotage that injures or kills is a godsend for corporations and authoritarian politicians. They're already attempting to equate sabotage with terrorism. Don't make their job easier. Don't play into their hands.

Sabotage (sometimes) involves destruction of *things*. Terrorism involves destruction of *people* (or threats of it). Make this crystal clear if you engage in sabotage.

Because much sabotage is illegal (not all is), it can be quite risky. Prosecutors routinely and viciously persecute politically motivated saboteurs, and judges routinely hand down savage sentences to them for piddling crimes—20 years for torching an SUV, for example.

One consequence of this is that those who engage in sabotage in groups are often turned against each other. The FBI routinely infiltrates progressive groups, no matter how mildly reformist and nonviolent, and will not only use informers but also provocateurs who will urge the group to perform illegal actions. (For all practical purposes, the entrapment defense no longer exists in the United States.) In addition to this, provocateurs will often offer to supply money and logistical support for the actions they push. Sometimes they'll also use emotional manipulation, appeals to "ethical responsibility" or "moral duty," implying that they're ethical and courageous, and everyone else isn't—unless they do what the provocateur wants them to do.

Then if any members of the target group take the bait, the FBI will arrest them and, through threats of sadistic prison sentences, often turn at least one member who will then identify and testify against the rest, and sometimes implicate and provide false testimony against innocent others. This is not only tragic on a personal level, it's movement destroying.

Be very wary of anyone who urges illegal, especially highly illegal, acts, offers to supply money or other support for them, and attempts to emotionally manipulate you. (But be aware that not all who do these things are informers or provocateurs. Some true believers also urge illegal acts; some employ emotional manipulation; and some supply logistical support. If a person does one of these things, it's a warning sign; if they do two, it's a bells-and-whistles alarm; and if they do all three, get away from them as fast as your legs will carry you.)

Since the risks can be so extreme, we recommend that people do not engage in highly illegal sabotage in groups except under exceptional circumstances (under outright dictatorship, for example), and even then it should only be done as a last resort. It's far safer to engage in legally risky sabotage as an individual, and if you do that to tell absolutely no one about it. (Not telling anyone is difficult to do and takes a psychological toll—it's isolating—so think several times before engaging in solo sabotage.) Group sabotage should only involve legal forms of sabotage or the least risky forms of illegal sabotage.

Sabotage in the context of labor disputes is a somewhat different matter. There, a large part of the public is usually sympathetic to strikers, which makes it difficult for corporations and the corporate media to present saboteurs as mindless thugs or "outside agitators." That public sympathy also tends to dampen the viciousness of prosecutors, making labor dispute sabotage slightly less risky than sabotage motivated by environmental or animal rights concerns. Still, the risks are significant, and labor-dispute sabotage can be a double edged sword. Please think carefully about its possible benefits, drawbacks, and risks before engaging in it.

Sabotage in almost any context can take many forms, ranging from the highly illegal to the perfectly legal. On the illegal side, it can range from simply pulling out survey stakes or altering billboards to destroying equipment worth hundreds of thousands of dollars. On the legal side, one form involves going into a supermarket during a grocery workers strike, filling shopping carts with food, and leaving them in the aisles.

One grey area (quite probably illegal) activity some friends of mine took part in ages ago involved

McDonald's announcing plans to open a new Golden Arches in their neighborhood. About a dozen people went to another McDonald's a couple of miles away, ordered meals, ate them, and then took ipecac. They had a puke-in. After they vomited, they left a flyer asking that McDonald's not build the new outlet in their neighborhood. (One hesitates to call it a "restaurant.")

They only had to do this twice before McDonald's canceled construction of the new store. They evidently didn't have the stomach to call the cops and then see headlines screaming, "Customers Arrested for Vomiting in McDonald's."

A relatively famous example of sabotage took place at the New York Stock Exchange in the late 1960s. Abbie Hoffman and other Yippees—who normally would have been turned away simply because of their appearance—gained admittance after telling security, "We're Jews and we want to see the stock exchange." Once inside, they tossed dollar bills down to the trading floor from a balcony. Chaos ensued as traders clawed all over each other to get the money, and what Hoffman and company did was entirely legal.

If you decide to engage in sabotage, be creative, keep your risk to a minimum, have fun, and think carefully about public perception of your acts.

Simple Living

It's tempting to dismiss the concept of simple living solely because of its most fervent advocates, who have forsaken their materialistic lifestyles and now preach the virtues of voluntary poverty to everyone, the poor and working classes included (not that there's much difference between the two anymore). Some simple living advocates go so far as to claim that individual adoption of a "simple living" lifestyle in itself is enough to save the planet.

The bedrock "simple living" attitude is renunciation of materialism. This does seem as if it should lead to an increase in happiness, but research contradicts this. Some studies state that happiness increases with income up to a certain level, but doesn't increase above it; the studies place that level at $75,000 (Princeton University, cited in *Time*) to $161,000 a year (Skandia International). But a more recent University of Michigan study indicates that there's no upper limit—it posits that happiness increases as income increases, period. But even if the Princeton study is correct, $75,000 per year is far more than

the vast majority of people will ever make, not that "simple living" advocates seem aware of this.

One strongly suspects that many of them have never faced the day-to-day stress of being out of work, watching their bank account dwindle to nothing, putting off necessary medical treatment for lack of money, and worrying about not making the rent and ending up on the street.

Those who have been in such situations are all too familiar with how even small increases in income mean less stress and greater happiness. So, good luck on selling simple living to . . . damn near everyone, and especially to those who have experienced economic stress and the miseries that accompany it. To recommend "simple living" to people in such circumstances is, as Oscar Wilde put it, "grotesque and insulting."

Leaving its advocates aside, many simple-living practices do have value. (Both of the authors of this book follow many of them.) They include growing food locally, using alternatives to private cars, recycling, using recycled building materials, using environmentally friendly building practices (passive solar, etc.), using alternative energy sources, growing your own fruits and vegetables, and eating lower on the food chain.

These all make ecological sense, but there's huge corporate resistance to almost all of them. For example, extremely powerful corporate interests oppose the development of "green energy," and have been doing everything in their power to throttle it for decades, while they take billions in subsidies every year, and while they cite the relative paucity of alternative energy developments as evidence of alternative energy's "impracticality."

To put this another way, public energy policies (including massive subsidies) have kept fossil fuel and nuclear energy prices artificially low, while keeping alternative energy prices high—putting alternative energy (e.g., photovoltaics) out of the reach of most people. (This is changing rapidly, no thanks to government energy policies. New wind generation is now cheaper per kilowatt hour than new fossil-fuel generation, and photovoltaics are approximately on a par with fossil fuels.)

Next, let's consider food. Fruits and vegetables (foods low on the food chain) are sometimes more expensive per pound than meat, which is relatively cheap only because of huge subsidies to corn (cattle feed) producers and, to a lesser extent, "welfare ranching," in which cattle producers rent (and often seriously degrade) public lands for grazing at

> "*Meaningful action*, for revolutionaries, is whatever increases the confidence, the autonomy, the initiative, the participation, the solidarity, the equalitarian tendencies and the self-activity of the masses and whatever assists in their demystification. *Sterile and harmful action* is whatever reinforces the passivity of the masses, their apathy, their cynicism, their differentiation through hierarchy, their alienation, their reliance on others to do things for them and the degree to which they can therefore be manipulated by others—even by those allegedly acting on their behalf."
>
> —*As We See It*, Solidarity (British libertarian group)

incredibly low rates. Add to that the widespread use of unhealthy, subsidized ingredients, especially high fructose corn syrup, in cheap foods, and unhealthy, unecological eating patterns are the result.

Then take public transit (or don't take it). In most places in the U.S., it's miserably inadequate. Especially in the sprawled-out cities in the West, there's little alternative to owning a car if you need to commute to work and if you're not content to have a very restricted social life.

The list goes on. The end result of all this is that to a very great extent most people are locked into their present consumption patterns; they can't afford to pursue often more expensive, more time consuming "simple living" alternatives. And "simple living" does nothing to address the system that locks people into their economic circumstances.

Adoption of environmentally friendly, "simple living" practices by those who have the time or money to do so is fine, but such adoption will do nothing to combat the corporate capitalism that's destroying the planet. Even if "simple living" was universally adopted, it wouldn't fundamentally alter the existing political and economic structure. The best it could deliver would be a slightly less toxic form of capitalism.

Street Demonstrations

When many, probably most, people think of political protest, they think of street demonstrations. Some people probably think of them as the *only* form of political protest.

How effective are they? Many activists have noted the ritualistic aspects of street marches and have dismissed them as a waste of time, as simple political theater.

There's some reason to do so. In themselves, isolated marches, no matter how large, seem not to do much beyond "raising awareness."

As an example, I took part in an anti-war march in San Francisco in 1991 near the beginning of the first Gulf war. A quarter of a million people took part (with some estimates being higher). The march went from the ferry building to the civic center (about a mile). Market Street was completely packed and the march lasted about six hours. Apparent net result? Zero.

In fact, the only street protests that have ever succeeded have been those that occurred day after day, week after week, sometimes year after year. In the U.S., the anti-Vietnam War marches are the prime example. They ranged from small to massive, and took place for years in communities across the country. But they didn't exist in a vacuum. They occurred in a context of campus occupations, draft resistance, cultural upheaval, political music (Bob Dylan, The Fugs, Phil Ochs, Country Joe and the Fish, and too many others to mention), street theater (notably The Living Theater and San Francisco Mime Troupe), active, widespread radical political groups (SDS and the Black Panthers most notably), a burgeoning underground press with countercultural newsweeklies springing up in every major city and a lot of smaller ones, and a feeling, no matter how delusional, that *anything* was possible.

In contrast I took part in an anti-SB 1070 march in Tucson in 2010 with roughly ten thousand other people. A much larger number marched in Phoenix, with some estimates in the fifty thousand-plus range. There were a few other large marches in Phoenix during the first half of the year. Net result? Apparently zero, other than "raising awareness." The governor signed the bill, and following one final protest march, that was that.

But what about "militant" demonstrations involving property damage. Are they more effective? What are their advantages and disadvantages?

The one advantage in "militant" demonstrations is that they allow participants to blow off steam. It's very difficult see any other advantages, and there are a lot of drawbacks.

The first disadvantage of trashing stores/cars during demos is that it doesn't work, it doesn't achieve its alleged goal of inspiring an uprising in the community.

The second disadvantage is that it discourages nonviolence-oriented people (that is, *most* people, including most other demonstrators) from taking part in subsequent demonstrations.

The third disadvantage is that it makes it very easy for the corporate media to portray demonstrators as mindless vandals and to dismiss their causes.

The fourth disadvantage is that it tends not to distinguish between criminal corporations, small businesses, and the property of individuals.

The fifth disadvantage is that it invites brutal police violence, with resulting injury to innocent people.

A case in point is the Rodney King demo, which turned into a riot, in San Francisco in 1992. Both of us took part in it. It began as a massive peaceful demonstration, but quickly turned into a riot when a few "diversity of tactics" types began indiscrimately smashing cars on McAllister Street—class enemies tend not to drive ten-year-old Toyotas—and devolved into an orgy of destruction with no distinction between targets. A Bank of America branch was destroyed, but so was a small shoe repair shop, a limo was trashed, but so was a news kiosk, etc., etc.

The cops attacked, coming in swinging with many injuries resulting. In the midst of all this, a motorcycle cop nearly, and deliberately, ran me down (I had to leap a wall to escape) and another cop.targeted Keith, smashed in his face with a truncheon, and arrested him for assaulting an officer. Keith's facial injuries were bad enough that he had to have reconstructive facial surgery.

The end result of this demo/riot? Not a hell of a lot except a very large number of smashed windows. As I walked home that night along Market Street, I couldn't take a step for a good half mile without my boots crunching on broken glass.

Finally, it's important to recognize the difference between deliberate attempts by small groups to turn demonstrations violent and spontaneous uprisings. A case in point is the "White Night Riot" in San Francisco in 1979, sparked by right-wing Catholic supervisor Dan White's acquital—following his use of the infamous "Twinkie defense"—in the murder of Supervisor Harvey Milk and Mayor George Moscone. This was a spontaneous uprising, not one formented by a small minority. It was an outpouring of anger from the gay and left communities, and significantly focused on the symbol of governmental authority, city hall. The emblematic, inspiring photo of that uprising is of a deceased friend of ours smashing an uprooted parking meter through city hall's glass front door.

This was a spontaneous, cathartic mass release of anger at a blatant injustice. It might even have had some minor benefits. Those who took part in it felt good about it, and it did "raise awareness" (for whatever that's worth) of the injustice of the verdict and the evil of homophobia.

But again, there's a big difference between a small group engaging in violence at demonstrations, and spontaneous uprisings. And there's a huge difference between attacking government and corporate sites, and small shops and old cars.

The lesson of all this seems to be that isolated street demonstrations rarely succeed. Those that do are usually those whose participants repeat them over and over, gathering participants as time goes on (something property destruction and violence discourage) in the context of many other ongoing political, economic, and cultural resistance activities.

Vanguard Parties

Vanguard parties (i.e., any of the 57 varieties of leninist parties—marxist-leninist, maoist, stalinist, trotskyist, etc.) have a long and sordid history. Their goal is always the same: seizure of the state apparatus in the name of the people. The leninist term for this is the oxymoronic "dictatorship of the proletariat"—as if an entire class of people could somehow be a dictator. But no, the dictator is, of course, the ultra-hierarchical vanguard party itself, as the expression, somehow, of the "will of the people." (Transubstantiation perhaps?)

The Bolsheviks provide the most prominent early example of a vanguard party. The results of their power seizure are well known: over a hundred thousand prisoners murdered by the Cheka (secret police) under Lenin, over ten million more human beings murdered or starved to death under Stalin, a one-party state, suppression of civil liberties, elimination of independent unions, dictatorial control of workplaces by the party/state apparatus, gulags,

Graphic from *SRAF Bulletin*

of American leftists who traveled to Cuba to work in the cane fields in support of "the revolution.") At one point, Fidel himself showed up where they were working in the fields. My friend told me that he found the reaction of his fellow brigadistas sickening, that their reaction was like that of 14-year-olds at a Beatles concert. And this at a time when the Castro regime was still executing political prisoners in droves. (That regime is, of course, secretive about this; as a result, estimates of the number of those executed vary widely, from a low of a few hundred to a high of over 30,000.)

If you think a one-party state, suppression of civil liberties, government control of the media, suppression of independent unions, travel restrictions, replacement of capitalist bosses by "Communist" bosses, secret police, prisons, executions, a network of neighborhood informers, militarism, and a personality cult are a good tradeoff for the Cuban people in exchange for good health care, free higher education, and a guaranteed low-paying job, by all means support the Cuban dictatorship—and support a vanguard party here.

But if you want individual freedom, democratic control of communities and workplaces, voluntary cooperation instead of coercion, and equality in place of domination and submission, vanguard parties are an absolutely terrible idea. On a personal level, they're bottomless pits of self-sacrifice, and on a societal level they're catastrophes in waiting.

purges, show trials, secret police, personality cults, and the rise of a new party/government elite—a "new class" that assumed the power and privileges of the old elite.

Where vanguard parties have taken power since the Bolsheviks, the results invariably have been bleak, from the surveillance state of Honecker's DDR (East Germany), to the mass murder in Mao's China's early days, to its subsequent transformation from a leninist state to a fascist state, to the totalitarian nightmare of North Korea, where millions starve while the state lavishes the proceeds of their labor on a bloated military, nuclear weapons, and grotesque spectacles—all in the context of a "people's state" that is in effect a hereditary monarchy.

In fact, the record of vanguard parties that have seized power is so uniformly awful that there's little point in examining them at length. They're simply failures—all of them. Examining their ideologies, structures, and theories is of interest only as an exercise in forensic pathology.

At this point, some readers will say, "What about Cuba?" Well, what about it? Even after fifty-plus years of dictatorship, many American leftists still have a soft spot for the Cuban Communists. They've bought into the false dichotomy that the only choice is between U.S. imperialism and the "Communist" dictatorship. Their attitude seems to be, "Well, we wouldn't want that here, but it's for the best there, so, we support Fidel (now his brother Raul)." To put it mildly, this is paternalistic and smacks disturbingly of what one might charitably call hero worship.

Decades ago, a maoist friend told me about his experiences in Cuba as part of a Venceremos Brigade in the 1970s. (Venceremos Brigades were bands

Voting

What's the best route to social change? Many, probably most, people would say "voting." That's not surprising. Day after day, year after year, the schools, corporate media, and politicians of all stripes present it as the *only* route to change.

But is it? Because of if its very nature, voting *cannot* lead to fundamental social change. No matter whom you elect, no matter if you elect "better people," there will still be a government. There will still be some giving orders and others forced to take them—because of the threat, and often the application, of institutionalized violence (police, prisons, the military). If your goal is a noncoercive, free, and

egalitarian society, you cannot get there through voting.

A brief glance at the Western democracies confirms this. No one in his or her right mind would contend that centuries of electoral politics have brought anything approaching full freedom and equality to the US or the UK. The best that voting seems capable of producing is the social-democratic systems of the Scandinavian countries. But even there, you still have capitalism—an ecocidal system of economic inequality, with some giving orders and others forced to take them—overlaid by a veneer of social welfare measures.

> "He who declares the common will to be the absolute sovereign and yields to it unlimited power over all members of the community, sees in freedom nothing more than the duty to obey the law and to submit to the common will. For him the thought of dictatorship has lost its terror."
>
> —Rudolf Rocker,
> *Pioneers of American Freedom*

Of course, that veneer matters. It reduces—but doesn't come close to eliminating—the economic inequality inherent to capitalism. Publicly funded healthcare, education, childcare, food assistance, public transit, unemployment benefits, and retirement benefits all make the day-to-day lives of poor and working people in capitalist countries much more bearable than they would otherwise be. But at the same time, such social welfare measures are almost certainly at the outer limit of what electoral politics can deliver. Centuries of cumulative experience in dozens of electoral democracies strongly suggest this is so.

If you're content with that, fine. But don't pretend that that's freedom and equality. Even in the best social-democratic system, you'll still have ruling elites, you'll still have a relatively small number of politicians, bureaucrats, and capitalists giving orders and the vast majority of people forced to take them.

Given this, is voting a useless or worse-than-useless activity? No. It's silly to pretend that it is. The social welfare programs mentioned above are worthwhile, and were achieved in part through the electoral process. As well, initiatives and referendums—for example, on marijuana legalization—can clearly be of public benefit. One might also ask,

"The right of absolute and irresponsible dominion is the right of property, and the right of property is the right of absolute, irresponsible dominion. The two are identical; the one necessarily implying the other . . . If therefore Congress have that absolute and irresponsible law-making power which the Constitution—according to their interpretation of it—gives them, it can only be because they own us as property. If they own us property, they are our masters . . .

But these men . . . dare not be consistent, and claim either to be our masters, or to own us as property. They say they are only our servants, agents, attorneys, and representatives. But this declaration involves an absurdity, a contradiction. No man can be my servant, agent, attorney, or representative, and be, at the same time, uncontrollable by me, and irresponsible to me for his acts. It is of no importance that I appointed him, and put all power in his hands. If I made him uncontrollable by me and irresponsible to me, he is no longer my servant . . . or representative. . . . If I gave him absolute, irresponsible power over myself, I made him my master, and gave myself to him as a slave. And it is of no importance whether I call him master or servant . . ."

—Lysander Spooner, *No Treason*

ultimate futility of electoral politics and burn out. Believing that there are no other means to social or political change, they lapse into cynicism and inactivity. This cycle repeats decade after decade after decade.

But that's not to say voting is entirely useless. It can produce limited reforms. Recognizing its marginal utility, Howard Zinn once remarked that voting takes five minutes, so why not?

Just don't waste much time on it, and don't expect it to fundamentally change anything.

if voting is useless, why are theofascist Republicans so intent on denying black people, latinos, the poor, and young people the right to vote?

At the same time, belief that voting is the sole legitimate means of political change is harmful. It induces many idealistic young people to waste huge amounts of time on political campaigns. A great many, probably most, eventually recognize the

"As long as there are rich and poor, governors and governed, there will be no peace, nor is it to be desired . . . for such a peace would be founded on the political, economic, and social inequality of millions of human beings who suffer hunger, indignities, prison, and death, while a small minority enjoys pleasures and freedoms of all kinds for doing nothing. *On with the struggle!*"

—*Manifiesto del Partido Liberal Mexicano*, 1912

BASIC STEPS TO EFFECTIVE ORGANIZING

Affinity Group Formation

An affinity group is a group of five to twenty people that work together autonomously in a decentralized and nonhierarchical way on projects, protests, tasks, or other actions. Affinity groups make decisions using a consensus process in which every participant has equal ability to influence the decisions that affect the group.

To form an affinity group, talk with your friends and others you believe you would feel comfortable working with. You can organize an affinity group in preparation for a protest or campaign of direct action. Such an affinity group may last a few days or weeks, or even years.

You may also wish to organize an affinity group around a shared location, interest, background, gender, passion, or philosophy. Affinity groups can also form around an activity such as music, art, gardening, animal rescue, books to prisoners, squatting, water harvesting, or any other shared interest. Your local Food Not Bombs chapter is an example of an ongoing affinity group.

Your affinity group may choose a name that reflects the personality or interest of those participating. The group may hold regular meetings to make decisions about the actions and goals of its participants.

When an affinity group forms in preparation for a protest, participants may volunteer for tasks in support of those risking arrest: jail support, legal observer, medic, food and water supplier, pet caretaker, or anything else of use.

The formation of affinity groups that plan to work together for extended times can provide a solid foundation for future actions such as occupa-tions, blockades, boycotts, climate change protests, or other campaigns. Affinity groups can organize regular nonviolent direct action preparations and role plays. They can organize workshops on the use of the consensus decision-making process, first aid, or other skills useful during a protest or uprising.

The affinity group structure was used by the Clamshell Alliance, the Abalone Alliance, and other organizations during the anti-nuclear power campaigns of the 1970s and 1980s. Thousands of activists joined affinity groups that sent representatives to regional cluster meetings. Representatives of those clusters sent volunteers to participate in spokes council meetings to discuss the overall strategy and principles of the campaigns. Decisions that the spokes council meetings came to consensus on were discussed at regional cluster meetings. Those decisions consented to at the cluster meetings were added to the agenda of each affinity group for discussion. If the affinity groups reached consensus they would implement the decisions.

The affinity group structure was also used in the lead-up to the November 1999 Seattle protests against the World Trade Organization Summit (WTO). A coalition of affinity groups called the Direct Action Network asked participants to pledge adhere to nonviolence for the action. The Network also encouraged the formation of affinity groups and asked that everyone signing the pledge of nonviolence participate in a day of nonviolence training. Thousands of people signed the pledge and took the training before heading to Seattle.

Today, formation of ongoing affinity groups and a network of nonviolent direct action preparation facilitators would be a step forward for the anarchist movement. This network could help with nonviolent direct action preparation and also help facilitate workshops on consensus decision making and other skills necessary to an effective campaign.

Social activities are also important. Affinity groups can build solidarity and trust by taking hikes, attending concerts and other events, having parties, taking bike, skiing or canoe trips, organizing street performances, or taking part in any other enjoyable activity that could encourage a close bond among those in the group.

There is a long history of anarchists using the affinity group structure to organize worker collectives and resistance to political, economic, and religious domination. Anarchists first started using an affinity group-type model in 1868 when Giuseppe Fanelli traveled the Iberian peninsula organizing for the First International. Anarchists organized *tertulias* of friends that would meet in cafes to talk about art, culture and politics. The Anarchist Organization of the Spanish Region more formally adopted the *tertulias* structure in 1888, meeting in cafes and taverns to organize clandestine acts of resistance to the Spanish oligarchy.

The affinity group formation used by anarchists today started decades prior to the Spanish Civil War and Revolution of 1936 to 1939. When the war broke out, the Iberian Anarchist Federation (FAI) had an estimated 50,000 members organized into affinity groups and confederated into local, regional, and national councils. In a very real sense, the FAI provided the backbone for the Spanish Revolution—which succeeded in large parts of Spain for over two years until it was crushed by the combined forces of Spanish, Italian, and German fascism.

Public Outreach

You can have an impact on society. Often, the simplest activities, performed in a consistent, regular manner, can be a very effective way to encourage political, economic, and social change. A regular literature table can attract volunteers, support for your group's actions, and donations to support your work. The people inspired by talking with you at the table can become participants in your regular meetings, and can help make your group's meals, events, tours, protests, and gatherings more effective. One main reason movements like Food Not Bombs are as effective as they are is because they staff so many literature tables in locations where they reach peo-

ple who had no idea other anarchists exist in their area. Literature tables have helped to connect countless people to anarchist meetings, events, tours, and gatherings.

Literature Tables

It almost seems too simple, but, to repeat, a consistently appearing literature table is one of the most effective ways to inspire social change. The location and timing are important. For maximum effectiveness in reaching the public with information about anarchism, volunteer opportunities, current issues, and community projects, set up in a high visibility location at a time with the most traffic. This will allow you and other volunteers to meet and talk with as many people as possible. It's also good to find a location where you can hang a banner near or over the front of your table. In addition to regular tabling, you may want to table at concerts, lectures, and other public events.

A neat and orderly looking table is attractive, and people are more likely to stop, talk, and pick up literature than if your table is a mess. You can put out your own flyers, download flyers from websites, or collect literature from other organizations. Many will be happy to donate it. They will be excited that you will be reaching hundreds of people with their message. The volunteers in your group can ask people passing the table a question about their opinions, if they heard about an upcoming event, or if they would like to participate in your group.

Your literature table can also include a plate of cookies or other baked goods. Offering cups of hot cider or sun tea is another way to make your literature table inviting. You may want to include a volunteer sign-up sheet and attract visitors by handing each pedestrian a quarter-page flyer about upcoming events.

One indication of the effectiveness of literature tables is the effort the police put into trying to stop people from setting them up. Your banner and literature are often the first things the police take.

Food Not Bombs provides an example of just how threatening the state finds literature tables. Food Not Bombs activists in the United States have reported many cases where the police say they can share meals but are not allowed to distribute literature or display banners. However, Food Not Bombs is not a charity and is working to change the political, economic, and social systems that perpetuate hunger and poverty. The right to distribute literature is protected in the United States by the First Amendment. Don't let anyone discourage you from having literature and a banner.

Literature with your group's contact information is essential in helping your group build interest in your goals as well as in attracting volunteers. Groups that don't bring literature and a banner to their actions often struggle to recruit help, but those groups that do have literature and a banner are more often vibrant and find the flyers increase interest in their groups and their activities.

Your group can have a box of literature always ready to take to protests or other events. If your group has a well packed literature box always on the ready, you will never arrive at an event without materials to hand out.

Your group can keep your literature neat and inviting by packing the largest publications on the bottom of the literature box, then stacking the next largest literature, and putting the smallest items on top. If your volunteers place business cards on the bottom of the box and put the larger items on top, the literature will be bent or torn and may end up being too mangled to hand out. When you put your literature out, wrap one or two number 19 rubber bands around each stack. Rocks don't work as well. When a rock is lifted off a stack of flyers, the wind can blow some of them away. The authorities might also accuse you of intending to use the rocks as weapons. A stack of 100 flyers wrapped in one or two rubber bands will be heavy enough to keep the wind from blowing the flyers off the table. A large stack will also encourage people to take a copy.

At the end of each event, place the literature back into your box, large flyers first with each smaller size on top, with the banner folded on top. Then, the next time you need to table, your literature will be in good condition and it will just be a matter of adding your literature box to the items you are taking out to the street.

How to Organize a Meeting

Organizing a meeting for any purpose, from starting a Food Not Bombs group to planning a protest, concert, or political campaign, could be the most difficult, yet most important and useful skill described in this book. Meetings might not seem enjoyable or important, but well organized, regular meetings provide access to anyone interested in your group. If well facilitated, they also contribute to distributing responsibility and tasks, and can help reduce burnout. Meetings also provide a forum where new ideas, projects, and innovations can be proposed, formulated, and implemented. Meeting while cooking, sharing food, or doing other tasks is rarely as productive as when everyone's attention is focused. Using the consensus process will also inspire the best in everyone participating at your meetings.

Meeting Step 1: Time, Date and Location

Ask the venues you want to use if there is a time and day that would be best for your meeting. Then ask the people you want to work with if they can meet at those given times, dates, and locations. You may need to provide more than one option; then decide based on how many people can attend. A meeting may include an activity such as sign painting, though the less distraction the better. The most common venues include cafes, bookstores, libraries, student unions, and classrooms.

If you're working with homeless people, it might be best to meet in a park or plaza at a time that is after people get off work, but before the homeless need to return to their campsites or shelters.

Before setting meeting times, it would be best to check that your meeting doesn't conflict with other meetings or events that would draw away interest.

Meeting Step 2: Sample Agenda

You can have an agenda planning committee and request agenda items from everyone you are inviting. Give them a completed copy of the agenda a day or two before the meeting. This one step can make the meeting itself and consideration of each agenda item go more smoothly.

You can accomplish a great deal by sticking to the agenda. You can introduce an agenda item at one meeting and make the decision about that agenda item at one of the next meetings if you need to. Some agenda items may be discussed for many meetings before you come to the best decision. Rotate the tasks of facilitator, note keeper, time keeper and, if very organized, door greeters, vibe watchers and the many other possible roles at a meeting. Many groups fail to keep notes and this can cause confusion in future meetings. Your group may want to return the notes after each meeting to the same volunteer. If that volunteer moves or leaves the group, ask them to pass the notes on to another reliable volunteer.

Sample Meeting Agenda

This is for a Food Not Bombs meeting. You can adapt it for your group's needs.

- Date of the meeting
- Facilitator's name and phone number
- Note keeper's name and phone number
- Time keeper's name
- 7:00 to 7:10—Introductions, agenda review, and short description of consensus process
- 7:10 to 7:30—Food collection route and details
- 7:30 to 7:45—This week's cooks and kitchen
- 7:45 to 8:00—Servers and program at the distribution location
- 8:00 to 8:15—This week's clean up crew
- 8:15 to 8:30—Solidarity actions at which to provide food.
- 8:30 to 8:45—Literature discussion and planning: flyers, literature tables, web postings, etc.
- 8:45 to 9:00—Review of all communications the group has sent and received
- 9:00 to 9:15—Financial report, discussion of upcoming benefits
- 9:15 to 9:30—Critique the meeting and choose date, time and facilitator of next meeting

Meeting Step 3: Consensus Process

Using the consensus process to make decisions has made it possible for people to organize local groups without relying on a headquarters, directors, or a leader to start and maintain the group. Each decision is consented to by all the participants.

To arrive at consensus, each proposal is made with the idea that it will accurately reflect the goals and interests of the group, trusting that it will evolve and change as everyone adds their input. It may take several meetings to discuss a proposal before the group arrives at consensus. By using this process, participants are more likely to be committed to implementing proposals, because they're all invested in them. In contrast to Robert's Rules of Order, which most groups use, consensus produces no winners or losers, and there is no competition to win the most votes. Instead, the goal is to make a decision that is best for everyone participating.

Many groups start their meetings with the facilitator asking for everyone to introduce themselves and then asking for someone to give a brief description of the consensus process. Everyone is invited to participate fully in every meeting. Everyone is free to introduce agenda items and speak to those items. Everyone is also free to speak to every proposal.

The facilitator will introduce the agenda items, asking those making a proposal to explain the details. Then the facilitator will ask for comments and open the floor. Once everyone has spoken or when the time for a particular agenda item has been used up, the facilitator can ask for five, ten, or fifteen more minutes to continue to discuss the agenda item or suggest the group move to the next item. When the additional time is up, the facilitator will ask that the proposal be re-stated, and then ask the group if anyone feels they need to stand aside because they can't support the proposal, but won't block it, because their opposition is not based on the proposal being contrary to the values and goals of the group.

If anyone feels the proposal is contrary to the values and goals of the group, they can block the proposal. The facilitator can ask those blocking what would need to change so that they would lift their block. Those changes should become an agenda item and should be placed on the next meeting's agenda; a committee might be organized to re-work the proposal.

Even after all this, it is possible the block will not be lifted and the group will not come to consensus. Most proposals are never blocked, but these things do happen.

Sticking to the time set aside for each agenda item shows respect for the group, even though some proposals might remain on the agenda for meeting after meeting. Because the process honors everyone's opinion and time, the decisions are likely to be implemented effectively.

It can be very helpful to rotate facilitators from meeting to meeting to reduce the possibility of any one volunteer feeling that they are being seen as the leader or becoming a *de facto* leader. The more all volunteers participate in making decisions, the more dedicated everyone will likely be implementing them. Groups can organize their own workshops to study the use of consensus in the effort to nurture everyone's participation skills.

However, some individuals simply do not want to facilitate. It's good to talk with them about the advantages of rotating facilitation, but if they still

Consensus Flow Chart

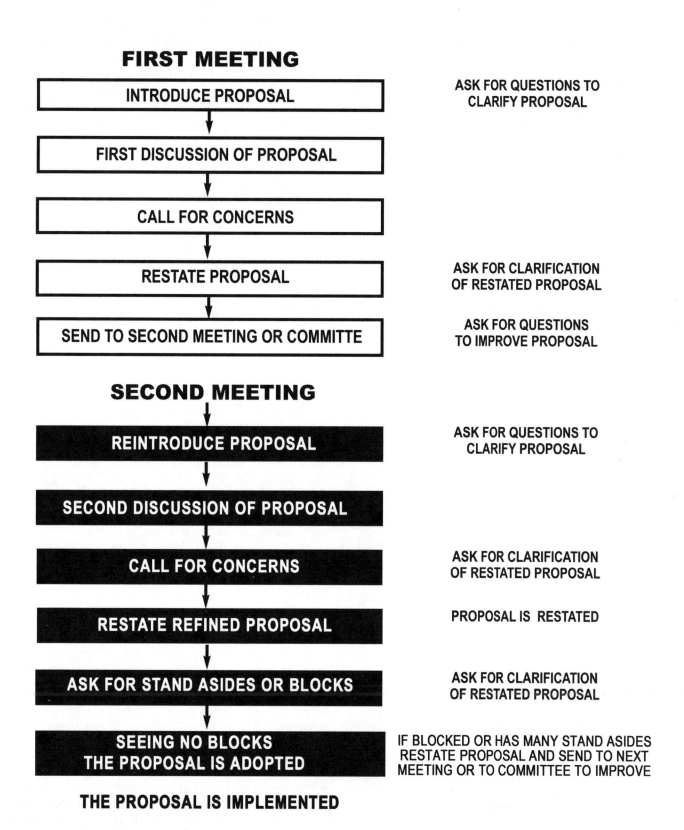

FIRST MEETING

INTRODUCE PROPOSAL

ASK FOR QUESTIONS TO
CLARIFY PROPOSAL

FIRST DISCUSSION OF PROPOSAL

CALL FOR CONCERNS

RESTATE PROPOSAL

ASK FOR CLARIFICATION
OF RESTATED PROPOSAL

SEND TO SECOND MEETING OR COMMITTE

ASK FOR QUESTIONS
TO IMPROVE PROPOSAL

SECOND MEETING

REINTRODUCE PROPOSAL

ASK FOR QUESTIONS TO
CLARIFY PROPOSAL

SECOND DISCUSSION OF PROPOSAL

CALL FOR CONCERNS

ASK FOR CLARIFICATION
OF RESTATED PROPOSAL

RESTATE REFINED PROPOSAL

PROPOSAL IS RESTATED

ASK FOR STAND ASIDES OR BLOCKS

ASK FOR CLARIFICATION
OF RESTATED PROPOSAL

SEEING NO BLOCKS
THE PROPOSAL IS ADOPTED

IF BLOCKED OR HAS MANY STAND ASIDES
RESTATE PROPOSAL AND SEND TO NEXT
MEETING OR TO COMMITTEE TO IMPROVE

THE PROPOSAL IS IMPLEMENTED

don't want to do it, don't pressure them; simply pass them over when their turn comes up, and gently bring the matter up again in a month or two.

Other individuals are terrible facilitators (don't keep the discussion on track, let motormouths ramble on, don't attempt to include everyone in the discussion, etc.), and some of them don't even realize it. In such cases, one solution is to have them share the task with a good facilitator if they're open to it. If they aren't, it's often necessary to bring up points of order to keep discussions on track.

Spokes Councils

It's sometimes necessary to coordinate with other affinity groups or a coalition of groups. The group seeking coordination on a particular matter invites the other groups to send two or more representatives to a spokes council meeting to review the proposal, seek consensus, and send the proposal back to each group to address at their next meeting. Then the individual groups can adopt the proposal or send an adjusted proposal back to the next spokes council meeting. If the spokes council meeting comes to consensus, the proposal is sent back to the groups to adopt and implement.

A number of activists have proposed that anarchist projects and collectives organize regular regional and global gatherings with a spokes council meeting as a regular feature to help coordinate inter-group actions and communication. With so many anarchist groups active in almost every area of the world, inter-group coordination could be very effective in bringing about social change.

The wave of uprisings in early 2011 showed just how important it is to use consensus and the need to develop a strong culture of inclusive decision-making. As oppressive systems fall under popular pressure, our movement can fill the resulting power vacuum with an already well established democratic community-based structure.

Organizing an Event

Event planning is one of the most often used and important skills in any social change group. Your group can have monthly, weekly, or even daily events, or host them on a random basis. If your group implements the following steps, your events will be well attended and likely have the impact you desire.

Event Step 1: Venue

Start by contacting all possible appropriate venues. They may include cafes, concert halls, the public library, a loft, an occupied building, or outside in a park, plaza, or in front of a corporate or government office. Agree on a date and time for both the event and preparation.

Depending on your expectations of the event, you might want to set the date and location as far in advance as possible. Large events such as gatherings or festivals should be announced more than a year in advance to give adequate time to plan and promote the event. For most events, such as concerts and benefits, it is best to allow six to eight weeks from the time your group confirms the date, talent, and venue, so your announcements can be listed in monthly publications. If there is a particularly important publication, you may want to base the date of your event on the deadline of that publication, setting it for a week or two after publication.

It's a good idea to have several people visit a venue before scheduling to use it. You may need to bring your talent as well when you check it out. A circus or performance using fire may need a large open space or require special arrangements with the fire department. Find out the details about rent of the venue, including when the deposit is required, and see if you can't get the venue to waive the rent. It may have a contract or require insurance. Ask the manager if they have the equipment required, or if you will need to provide things like video projectors, lights, or a sound system. Write down the manager's name, phone number and e-mail address, and send her or him an e-mail confirming the dates and times. Remind the manager of the event two or two-and-a-half weeks before the event.

Event Step 2: Talent

Talent can consist of bands, artists, athletes, magicians, a speaker, poets, films, skill sharing, group singing, puppeteers, dancers or dancing, game facilitation, or anything else you think appropriate. You may want to invite someone to record the event. Your talent may require sound or lighting equipment. Send the talent and other participants, such as sound companies, an e-mail to confirm the date, time and location of the event. Also confirm details such as how much they will be paid, what equipment they will provide or may need, and when they will arrive to set up. Remind all the talent about the event one week and also the day before the event. You may even want to give them a call the morning of the event. Give copies of your posters and flyers to your talent. Invite them to schedule interviews, or set them up yourselves. You may join them at radio programs so you can talk about the activities of your group and the talent can talk about their group and the upcoming performance, and if they're musicians play a song live or as a recording.

Event Step 3: Promotion

As soon as you have the date, time, location and talent, it is time to draft a public service announcement (PSA). Keep the PSA short enough to be read on the radio in either 30 or 60 seconds. Read it out loud and time it. The text of your PSA can be adapted for your flyers, e-mails, and announcements on websites. Send an e-mail of the PSA to the local media and your group's contact list, and give a hard copy to any radio station managers or DJs you know or who you think would be sympathetic.

Ask a volunteer to design a flyer and post copies announcing the event all over town. Make a poster (11"X17") if appropriate. Your volunteers can start posting flyers as soon as your group knows the details and can make them. Make and hand out small quarter-page or half-page flyers at concerts or other events. Make sure you have posters in as many store windows and flyers on as many bulletin boards as possible. It's not a bad idea to return to every location a week before the event to make sure your flyers and posters are still up, and repost them as necessary. You can also have a stack of flyers on your table at other events and regular tabling sessions.

Call your local media and make sure the event is listed. Call your local radio stations and ask them if they might like to interview you and the talent on some of their programs. There may be music or feature writers at your local paper that would be interested in interviewing someone from your group or some of the talent. You might call in to local talk shows, tell them about the projects you are working on, and mention that listeners can find out more at your next event, sharing the date, time and location on air. Venues might have a space or schedule where they announce upcoming events, and some communities have a place where groups are allowed to hang banners announcing events. Volunteers can visit each media office and hand a copy of

the flyer and public service announcement directly to the staff. Volunteers could also visit the offices of other community groups and invite them to set up a literature table at the event and ask them to post a flyer or send an announcement of the event to their e-mail list.

When you mail the announcement to your group's list, you can end the post with a request to those receiving it to forward it to their lists. You can ask the venue and talent to e-mail their lists and add the event to their websites. Volunteers can also ask to announce the event at other groups' meetings, during concerts, or at rallies and protests.

You may want to send out your PSA several times starting as soon as you have the date, venue and talent, a month before the event, two weeks before and during the week of the event. Always call the media to make sure they have your PSA in hand. Media outlets can get over a hundred PSAs each day and unless employees are directed to yours it may be lost in the chaos. If you are friendly, they will probably make a point of putting your PSA at the top of the pile. This can be a great way to alert your community not only about the event you are announcing, but also about your group.

The following is the format most organizations follow for their public service announcements. PSAs should normally be a single page and should start with "For Immediate Release" centered and in large type near the top of the page.

PSA Format

FOR IMMEDIATE RELEASE
Date (including year)

CONTACT:
The name of your group
Name of person to contact
Phone number to contact
Email address to contact
Website

TITLE OF THE EVENT
Talent (who will do what)
Day and time of event
Location of event
Cost of event, even if free

After this, you'll have the body of your PSA. Include a very short description of the event, details about the talent, and a short statement about your group. Your PSA should never be longer than one page double spaced, and you should end it with the three number signs as shown below.

(Note that the ### is often centered and is the formal way used to end the basic PSA or section intended to be read or listed. You can add supporting information after the three number signs designed to supply details for longer articles or as background on the issue, talent, or your group.)

Event Step 4: The Event

Once you have the date, time, location, and the talent, it is a very good idea to record the contact information of everyone involved, including phone numbers and e-mail addresses. It's also a good idea to make sure at least two people have this data. Someone in your group can call the venue and talent a week before the event and the day before, making sure they all remember the details. You might want to confirm the time when you plan to arrive to set up. Your group may organize committees to implement the various tasks or simply have "bottom liners" responsible for each task.

Two or three people can be responsible for setting up and staffing a literature table. You will also need volunteers to collect tickets or donations at the door. You might want to hand each guest a flyer about upcoming events and your group's contact information. Make sure to have a sign-up sheet at your literature table. Hang your largest banner in the back of the stage above the heads of the performers.

You may want to have a volunteer stage manager who meets the talent, provides them with the schedule, is responsible for making sure each performer is ready to perform, and makes sure the groups get on stage and off stage on time. The stage manager can also be the master of ceremonies (MC), though it's better to have a separate stage manager and MC, especially at large events. At such events it's also often helpful to have stage hands to help with equipment and props.

Your group might want to provide food at the event, and will need volunteers to collect, cook and share the food during the event. This might be a full meal or just desserts and drinks. If you do this, you'll need a time and location for cooking in advance of the event. Make arrangements with the management of the venue to make sure it is possible for your volunteers to arrive early to set up the literature table, food, props, and banners.

As the event comes to its end, your group can start to clean up the venue, picking up trash and collecting the recycling. As soon as everyone leaves, be prepared to sweep and possibly mop the floor of the venue. Pack up all the equipment and help load the items in the appropriate vehicles. Pack up your literature box with the large flyers on the bottom and smallest items on the top. Don't forget your banner.

You can design and print an event planning checklist to make sure each task is assigned and completed, and you can keep that list with the notes of your meetings and other reports, flyers, and news clippings so new volunteers can see what you have done (so they don't have to reinvent the wheel) and will have contact information for future events. Plan to critique the event at your next meeting.

Organizing a Tour

Tours are a great way to build the movement and encourage support for protests or campaigns. If you are in a band, theater group, circus, or puppet show you could organize a tour featuring your group and encouraging people to participate in a future gathering or protest. You could invite bands to join the tour and invite local Food Not Bombs chapters to provide food and literature at the events. They could also promote your tour's appearances, help schedule radio and newspaper interviews, post flyers, and announce your appearances at other concerts and events. The following are the main steps in organizing a tour.

Tour Step 1: Create a Theme

When you consider organizing a tour, it is helpful to consider your message and goals. Some tours are designed to build interest in a future campaign or mass action. Other tours are designed to encourage interest in an organization or project.

When planning appearances, make an outline of the presentation and designate who will do what and for how long. Your outline might include an introduction, a first speaker or act, a DVD or PowerPoint presentation, music, and puppets, banners, handouts, or other props. The elements of each presentation should be organized to move your audience to action. Try to choose a title that is memorable, catchy, and describes the intention of the tour. In addition to a title with impact, you might want to include a subtitle, descriptive paragraph, and troupe name (if there is one). These elements can be used in all your materials from your initial letters to host organizations and venues, to your public service announcements, flyers, and website. This part of the process of organizing your tour should be fun and creative.

Tour Step 2: Proposed Schedule and Route

Before contacting groups with your proposal, consider mapping out your route, being sure to give yourself adequate time to travel from one venue to another. You might consider a tour of one month and plan to appear every other evening. This would make it possible to have fourteen or fifteen events in fourteen or fifteen different communities. You might want to have more than one event in some of the locales and stay several days in those places. It's generally good to always arrive before noon the day of your event so you can staff a literature table or speak with the media to promote the event. Taking these things into consideration, write out an itinerary with the dates and cities. Traveling from one community to another in order of their locations is, obviously enough, the most efficient way to plan a tour.

"By definition, an anarchist is he who does not wish to be oppressed *nor wishes to be himself an oppressor*, who wants the greatest well-being, freedom and development for all human beings. His ideas, his wishes have their origin in a feeling of sympathy, love and respect for humanity: a feeling which must be sufficiently strong to induce him to want the well-being of others as much as his own, and to renounce those personal advantages, the achievement of which would involve the sacrifices of others."

—Errico Malatesta, *Volonta*, June 15, 1913

Tour Step 3: Send a Proposal to Possible Hosting Groups

E-mail and/or physically mail the proposed title, theme, and elements of the event, with the proposed date(s) of when you intend to hold the event in their communities to anarchist groups, other types of organizations, or the management of venues to see if they would be interested in hosting your presentation or performance. You could provide a list of all cities and dates to everyone you contact so they can have an idea of your route and, therefore, understand why a particular date works best for an appearance in their community.

Include questions about what they would be able to do if they wanted to host you. Ask if the proposed date would work or if another date would be better. You could also ask if they would they be willing to post flyers around the community to advertise the event and tour, make arrangements for a venue, contact local media, or help with other details. You could ask if they would have a place for you to sleep, take a shower, or park your vehicle.

Suggest some of the ways hosting your event could benefit their organization, venue, or community. Ask that they respond by a certain date, and let them know if they choose to host the event that you will provide them with a letter of confirmation, publicity, and the other materials necessary for a successful event.

> "The calloused hands of the fields and of the factories must clasp in fraternal salute because, truly, we workers are invincible; we are the force and we are the right. We are tomorrow."
>
> —Emiliano Zapata,
> *A los obreros de la república ¡Salud!*

Tour Step 4: Confirm Dates and Venues

Ask each hosting organization or venue to confirm with an e-mail or letter stating that they are willing to host the presentation on the agreed date(s). Try to get these letters of agreement as soon as you can so you can start to publish the tour schedule in e-mails, posters, and on your website. Request the starting time, complete name, address and contact information for the venue so it can be correctly listed on the publicity. Venues may have a website that you can also list in your promotional material.

Tour Step 5: Promotion of the Tour

Start by writing a public service announcement. (See the sample above under planning events.) Create a contact list of local community groups and media in each city or town you have scheduled. You can post PDFs of your publicity materials on the tour's website, include them as attachments in your e-mails, and ask the recipients to print out copies and post them in their cities. Your hosts can also e-mail their lists, post the information on their websites, and post flyers around town. They could also e-mail, call, and visit their local media. Ask them to arrange radio and newspaper interviews.

Tour Step 6: Logistics

In the weeks before you head out on the tour, practice your presentation and collect and pack your props, literature, equipment, and anything else you'll need. It's often helpful to print up business cards and bring sign-up sheets to collect the names, phone numbers, and e-mail addresses of those attending your events.

Pack the appropriate amount and type of clothing. Estimate the cost of transportation, food, phones, materials, and equipment. You'll need maps of the area you plan to be traveling through or a smartphone. Create a written list of dates, addresses, and contact people with their phone numbers and e-mail addresses.

Confirm that you will have places to sleep and confirm other details before heading out on the tour. Your hosts may provide food, but you will also need to provide for yourself at times.

If traveling out of the country, make sure you have applied for proper visas and that your passport is current. Determine if you'll need vaccinations or if you'll need to bring mosquito netting, heavy clothing, or other special items. Make sure you have enough medicine (in properly labeled containers) or other items that may be difficult to obtain while on tour. You may need special adapters for electricity or need to have translators and literature in the local language(s). Call or e-mail each host a week before you are scheduled to arrive and the day before your event. Arrange the time and location of where you will meet your host once you arrive in their community. Consider bringing small gifts for each host and those who provide housing or other support.

Tour Step 7: After the Tour

Send thank you cards to everyone that helped with the tour. Take all items such as posters, photos, and other artifacts and create a scrapbook. You may want to write an account of the tour or organize an event to report back to your community. It's a good idea to record logistics or plans created during the tour. Make contact with those that signed the contact list.

Organizing a Gathering

Gathering Step 1: Propose a Gathering at your Group's Meeeting

Gatherings can be valuable in many ways. It is inspiring to meet activists from other communities and discover their solutions to common issues. Gatherings also provide the chance to organize inter-group actions and to share skills. The principles and projects common to many groups and organizations were initiated at gatherings.

Include the proposal for a gathering at your group's next meeting and talk about the reason and theme of the gathering, dates, and other details you might want to propose to other groups. Include the geographic scope of the gathering in your proposal. Consider workshops, topics, and the focus of the gathering that would be most beneficial to those you plan to invite. You might consider having a gathering during the days or weeks preceding a large protest or other event.

You should choose a date that is at least a year in the future for world or international gatherings, and you'll need almost that much time for regional gatherings. The more time everyone has to prepare, the better the event will be organized, and the more everyone will get from participating.

Inter-group coordination of a global community as large as the anarchist movement could inspire positive social change in a way that would otherwise be very difficult to achieve. (We have a video of the 1995 International Food Not Bombs gathering on the Food Not Bombs website at www.foodnotbombs.net/videos.html.)

Gathering Step 2: Contact other Groups

Once your group has come to consensus on the focus, theme, dates, and location of the proposed gathering, your group can ask other groups if they would be interested in participating; to make things more transparent your group could e-mail them a questionnaire about participation. You could also include the questions on a website detailing the proposed theme, dates, and location of the gathering. You might ask if other groups would support the proposed gathering and, if so, what workshops, topics, entertainment, and additions or changes they might suggest. Also ask about participants' needs for housing, transportation, or anything else. Ask that the other groups respond by a certain date.

Gathering Step 3: Develop the Structure and Schedule of the Gathering

As you start to receive responses to the proposal, you can organize committee meetings. Your group could have finance and fundraising, program, venue, housing, food, transportation, documentation, healthcare, childcare, and outreach committees. At first, most of your volunteers may be on almost every committee, but before long you'll start getting more volunteers as news of the gathering inspires interest.

The finance committee can develop a budget and start organizing benefit concerts and other fundraising events.

The program committee can contact the other groups to make sure they respond to the questions you sent, and it can start work on the framework of the daily schedule.

The venue committee can secure a place to have the gathering. It could be a large facility like a school, place of worship, or community center, or it could be a collection of spaces.

The housing committee can write a letter requesting housing for certain nights, and then make a list of all places offered. The list should include the names of those offering places to stay, their addresses, phone numbers, e-mail addresses, and number of people they can accommodate.

The transportation committee can base its actions on the responses to the questionnaire about transportation needs.

The food committee can draft a letter requesting food donations, create a list of possible food sources, and arrange for a large kitchen located at or near the venue.

Gathering Step 4: Outreach

The goal of outreach for a gathering is to attract as much interest from other groups and individuals as possible. The more input the participating groups have in forming the focus and agenda of the gathering, the more support they'll provide. After your group e-mails and posts the proposal for the gathering, you can call each potentially participating group to remind them to discuss the proposal and ask them to return the completed questionnaire by the deadline for responses. You can e-mail an announcement of each planning meeting, including its agenda, to all participating groups and invite them to respond in person or by e-mail. Also remind them that they are free to make proposals or modifications.

You'll need to put up a gathering website with updates on housing, programs, transportation, healthcare, childcare, and other matters. Ask a volunteer to design a poster announcing the gathering, its dates, location, focus, workshops, entertainment, and contact information. E-mail a PDF to participating groups so they can print it and have copies on their literature tables and post it at other activist sites. If it's attractive enough, you might want to

"We declare ourselves the enemies of every government and every state power, and of governmental organization in general. We think that people can be free and happy only when organized from the bottom up in completely free and independent associations, without governmental paternalism . . .

Such are our ideas as social revolutionaries, and we are therefore called anarchists. We do not protest this name, for we are indeed the enemies of all governmental power, since we know that such a power depraves those who wear its mantle equally with those who are forced to submit to it. Under its pernicious influence the former become ambitious and greedy despots, exploiters of society in favor of their personal or class interests, while the latter become slaves."

—Mikhail Bakunin

use the image from the poster on t-shirts and other items.

Gathering Step 5: Creating the Program

The program committee schedules workshops, discussions, and the agenda for the meeting of the whole. You could propose a discussion about an urgent issue where inter-group cooperation would be important, or you could propose a theme you think would help other groups. The committee can start to outline the programs by first making a tentative daily schedule. For instance, opening the morning with a moment of silence or meditation, then breakfast, a morning meeting of the whole, morning workshops, lunch, afternoon workshops, breakout meetings, dinner, and an evening event.

The breakout meetings might be used to develop proposals for agenda items at a final afternoon ple-

nary or meeting of the whole. At it, all those attending the gathering could try to come to consensus on the details of each proposal. The proposals would then be sent back to all participating groups for discussion and decisions.

The workshops could include proposals directly related to the focus of the gathering, and others could involve skill sharing or issues with a less direct connection. The program committee could reserve space for discussions of proposals at the meeting of the whole or plenary held the final day. This plenary could take an afternoon or an entire day. The goal of such meetings is to come to consensus on future actions or other proposals.

As soon as the committee knows what workshops and meetings will be held, it can produce a schedule with the days, times, and workshop or meeting names, facilitators, their contact information, and the locations. This schedule should be published in the program guide. The facilitator of each workshop or meeting can also provide a paragraph or two describing it for inclusion in the guide. If the program committee is well organized, it might be possible to publish the schedule and description weeks or even a month or more before the gathering. Copies then could be mailed to the participating groups and posted on the gathering website, providing additional time for everyone to discuss and contemplate the issues to be addressed at the gathering.

Gathering Step 6: Venue, Food, Housing, Transportation, Healthcare, and Childcare

The venue committee will secure a place to have the gathering. This could be one large facility such as a school, place of worship, community center, or it could be a collection of spaces. Make a list of all possible venues and include the contact person, their phone number, and the venue's physical address. Then make an appointment to visit each venue and meet with the people responsible for providing access. Ask about the cost and requirements necessary for securing the use of the facility. Ask if it will be available during the dates of the gathering and if insurance will be required.

If you are able to use the venue, have one of your volunteers be responsible for staying in contact during the gathering with the staff person responsible for the venue. That volunteer should talk with the staff person a month, a week, and a day before the gathering about access to the venue.

A venue should have at least one large room, so everyone can participate in a meeting of the whole, and smaller rooms for workshops. It's generally good if the venue has space for camping and is near public transportation. It should be accessible to everyone and free of distractions such as noise, extreme temperatures, or high winds. The venue committee should make sure there are enough seats, toilets, video projectors, chalk boards, and large sheets of paper with markers.

The housing committee should write a letter to the community requesting lodging for certain nights and make a list of all places offered. The list should include the names of those offering places to stay, their addresses, phone numbers, e-mail addresses, and the number of people they can accommodate. Volunteers should be on hand at the convergence space as the participants arrive, so they can direct them to their housing. Each participant should be given a page with the name, address, and phone number of the person offering them housing. The sheet should, ideally, also include directions and a map to the housing. The housing committee might be able to secure school dorms, group camping, or a gymnasium. Ideally, the committee will send housing details to the participants in advance of their arrival. This notification should indicate if the participants need to bring their own sleeping bags, camping mattresses, or other items.

The transportation committee should consider and deal with the answers from returned questionnaires about transportation needs. If you're holding a world or international gathering, the committee may need to assist potential participants with visa applications. The committee might write a visa letter inviting the participants, using their full names and addresses, to attend the gathering on specific dates for the purpose of working with other volunteers toward the goal of the gathering. The visa letter would also state the name, address, and phone number of the person responsible for hosting the applicant. A travel itinerary or plane, train, or bus ticket may be required. In some countries you can provide a letter about your gathering to the office that issues visas so they will have this information at the airport when people arrive.

Your group will need to have food available, and may want to start collecting nonperishable bulk goods as soon as you have agreed to host the gathering. You can also request that participating groups bring food. The food committee can draft a letter requesting special food donations and create

"People can accept that anarchy may not mean just chaos or confusion, and that anarchists want not disorder but order without government, but they are sure that anarchy means order which arises spontaneously and that anarchists do not want organization. This is the reverse of the truth. Anarchists actually want more organization, though organization without authority. The prejudice about anarchism derives from a prejudice about organization; people cannot see that organization does not depend on authority, that it actually works best without authority.

A moment's thought will show that when compulsion is replaced by consent there will have to be more discussion and planning, not less."

—Nicolas Walter, *About Anarchism*

a contact list of all possible food sources. The committee might need to find a large kitchen located at or near the venue. Or it may be possible to organize an outdoor field kitchen. If you don't have enough cooking gear to cook for the entire gathering, you might ask participating groups to bring some of their cooking equipment. The committee should encourage anyone who wants to help in the kitchen. It will be a great place to talk informally, and you shouldn't have any trouble finding people to help.

Many gatherings will organize a healthcare committee. If so, the committee should designate a room or tent as the healthcare clinic. The clinic could provide water, aspirins, bandages, and simple first aid. You might ask individuals, political groups, or businesses in the community to donate services. The healthcare committee could also contact local emergency rooms and ambulance companies to let them know you will be having the gathering, telling them the location and number of people you expect will attend.

It is really helpful to offer childcare. Choose a safe place a short distance from the rest of the gathering so children can be loud yet not too far from their parents. Organize games, collect children's books to read out loud, provide costumes for dress up, balls for sports, and work with the kitchen to have snacks and meals for the children before the adults.

Gathering Step 7: Convergence Center and Orientation

As soon as you've set a date, find a place for your convergence center. This could be a room near the entrance of the gathering, or if the gathering is held in a number of locations it could be a space in an easy-to-locate building near public transportation. But try to have your convergence center at the same place as your gathering. If you have to use spaces in different places, try to have them near to public transit, and make sure to provide transit maps to out-of-towners. Remember, many of the people participating will not be familiar with the host city, so make their first destination, the convergence space, easy to find. The convergence space is where you will greet participants and provide them with the program guide, directions to housing, and information about other logistics. It's a very good idea to have a notice board there to post information about rides to and from the gathering, announcements of special workshops, and meetings and events not in the program.

Gathering Step 8: Workshops and Meetings

As host group you'll receive many workshop and meeting proposals. You might not be able to accommodate all of them on the schedule. Even so, you'll have to schedule at least some workshops in the same time slots, but do your best not to schedule workshops at the same time that you know will be of interest to the same people. You might want to schedule important meetings that address the focus of the gathering or issues that require the participation of volunteers from all participating groups in their own time slots with no other workshops or other distractions scheduled opposite them.

Anarchist gatherings have offered workshops on vegan cooking, social media use, biodiesel, com-

> "A map of the world that does not include Utopia is not worth even glancing at, for it leaves out the one country at which Humanity is always landing. And when Humanity lands there, it looks out, and seeing a better country, sets sail. Progress is the realization of Utopia."
>
> —Oscar Wilde, *The Soul of Man Under Socialism*

posting, organic gardening, water purification, train hopping, wild food collection, giant puppet making, event planning, consensus decision making, silk screening, stencil making and graffiti, racism and sexism in the movement, weaving, sanitation and food safety, free radio, nonviolent direct action, and nonviolence training. Workshop topics can also include campaigns to stop mining or logging operations, sovereignty rights, efforts to stop genetically engineered food, or protection of animals threatened by hunting or habitat destruction. The subjects of workshopsare limited by organizers' imaginations.

Meetings on topics concerning interaction between groups could be one of the most important features of any gathering. The meeting of the whole or spokes council meeting near the end of the gathering should consider the ideas generated during the meeting of the whole, and make sure they are e-mailed to all participating groups and posted on the gathering website. Each group can review the proposals and seek consensus on their implementation. The gathering proposals might be modified, changed, or blocked by one or more local groups and returned to a future gathering for further consideration before they are implemented.

Gathering Step 9: Closing and Critique

Gatherings often end with a closing circle with all participants offering a brief critique of the gathering, what could have been better, and what they believe was successful. Participants could also provide a short recap of the essential points or decisions addressed during the gathering.

Revolutionary Nonviolence Direct Action Campaigns

There is a long, proud history of nonviolent direct action. As governments and corporations become more sophisticated in the use of violence and disinformation to resist change, they are providing an opportunity for nonviolent direct action to be more effective than ever. Governments and corporations are so fearful of the potential of nonviolent resistance that they are working to create the illusion that nonviolence can't succeed and that nonviolent direct action is the same as passivity.

Nonviolent direct action is far from being passive and is often the most effective strategy we have to respond to the global economic, political, and environmental crises. There has never been a more important time to develop and implement well planned campaigns of nonviolent direct action.

Campaign Step 1: Identify and Analyze the Issue

Before starting any campaign, you'll want to announce the holding of regular organizing meetings by posting flyers and e-mailing organizations and friends about your intentions. Early meetings can identify the issue and analyze it, and identify the groups, companies, and individuals that would support or oppose your position. Consider why the public would either favor or disfavor each position related to the issue and investigate the relationship of each party to it. You might want to "follow the money" and investigate who would benefit and who would be harmed economically if your campaign succeeded.

It's often wise to use a public opinion survey to collect opinions and data. Avoid asking leading questions. You can find a list of sociology or other college departments that might be of help in developing your survey from the American Association for Public Opinion Research by visiting their site at www.aapor.org, and you might find graduate students in those department who'd be willing to help. There are similar organizations in many other countries that can provide access to graduate students.

College departments and grad students can be of use in other ways, including help in understanding the deeper aspects of the issue you're concerned with. You can use the information they supply in articles, posters, petitions, and talking points. You can analyze the data collected in your public opinion surveys to see how people view the issue, determine the amount of support or opposition that already exists, and craft your message to sway public opinion. This information can also help you identify the strengths and weaknesses in your opponent's position.

While collecting responses to your survey, determine what would motive your opponents to change their position. Can pressure be exerted against the people funding your opponents? Could supporters of your opponents be concerned about losing an election? Is it possible that negative publicity could threaten a corporation's bottom line?

As you collect this information, your group will become clearer about the strategy and message of your campaign. Your group might have a set of goals that need to be achieved before concluding the campaign, such as ending certain policies or an end to a war or an environmentally damaging commercial practice. As your campaign continues, your tactics might change, or your group might determine that your opponents have modified their practices enough that you can claim victory and end the campaign.

The more clear and specific your demands, the more likely it is that you can build support and win concessions. Goals such as world peace, save the environment, or love everyone are so vague as to be almost meaningless. How exactly do you want to achieve world peace? Only when you get down to specifics do demands become meaningful. A real step toward "world peace" would be to organize a campaign to convert a weapons facility to manufacturing solar panels. A campaign to pressure Congress into cutting funding for a new generation of nuclear weapons could succeed, and if it did it would inspire confidence that we could take more steps toward ending militarism. Organizing a campaign to stop the clear cutting of an area of forest with specific owners and boundaries, or blocking the construction of a nuclear power station provides your group with a clear, understandable goal. Being clear about specific goals is a necessary first step toward success.

Campaign Step 2: Outlining the Campaign and Strategy

In many situations, building public support is essential in changing government policies or corporate behavior. Many successful campaigns start with a period of education. Produce literature and put up websites to explain the issue. Your group might organize a teach-in or public forum, inviting people from all sides of the issue to participate. Your group could organize other educational events such as lectures, puppet shows, documentary screenings, or putting up regular literature tables outside groceries, in public squares, and at events.

A petition is also a great tool and, in some cases, is all that is needed to have an impact. Petitions are a simple way to involve the public, build a contact list and show your opponents that you have popular support. Once you have an impressive number of signatures, you can contact the media and organize a public event where you deliver the petitions. Sometimes this is all that's needed to achieve your goal, to get a government or corporation to mend its ways. Even if your opponent fails to respond favorably to the petition, it will build support for you and your goals, and will provide a public-support base for your actions. Most campaigns employ an educational component during the entire effort, even as the group escalates its tactics.

Your opponent's failure to change, after being presented with a substantial number of signatures, can provide your group with a solid foundation for the next more drastic action in your campaign. Increase the severity or militancy of your tactics by measured degrees.

After the appeal by petition, consider a picket outside the opponent's office, factory, or other recognizable and highly visible location. Your group may announce that you intend to return until your demands are met, or for one month, at which time your group will call for a boycott, strike or other escalation of tactics. The more deliberate and measured the increase in pressure, the more public support you can gain.

Offer a way for your opponent to change its policies or position while preserving its dignity. If your opponent understands this, you are more likely to succeed at getting them to change. This can be a very difficult position to maintain, particularly if your opponent is ruthless, violent, and dishonest. If your opponents cause your group to perceive them as lacking dignity, your struggle could become protracted and the members of your group could feel justified in taking actions that could erode their sense of self-respect. The powerful routinely present themselves as so unreasonable and disrespectful that their opponents believe them to be so evil that any action is justified in resisting them. If they succeed in provoking you to violence or other ill-advised tactics, your group will lose its sense of dignity and provide your opponent with an excuse to employ violent repression. If the community sees that your group is being respectful and taking persistent dignified action, even though it is facing violence, dishonesty, and even prison and death, you will undermine the power of your opponent and draw popular support. It is often at the point when an opponent is most brutal and unable to undermine the self-respect and dignity of your group that the opponent realizes it must capitulate to the demands of your campaign.

If you suddenly and dramatically escalate your tactics, it can sometimes cost you support. So take care not to escalate your tactics until it is clear to the public that your next, escalated actions are justified.

Campaign Step 3: Discipline and Persistence

If your group can maintain a disciplined dedication to nonviolence, you are likely to attract support from the general community, and your participants are less likely to lose enthusiasm for the campaign. Your group can maintain self-discipline by organizing nonviolent preparations in advance of each new escalation in tactics. Your group might even start the campaign with a day of nonviolence preparation, even though you don't expect the campaign to escalate to an action that will require nonviolent direct action. Your campaign may last months, years, or even decades before achieving its goals. While the crises we are facing are very serious, and it doesn't seem that we have much time to change the direction of society, it's necessary to understand that the change we need requires determination and time to be successful.

Types of Nonviolent Direction Action

Governments and corporations have systematically discouraged protests and made great strides in erasing the knowledge of nonviolent direct action. Textbooks might mention Dr. Martin Luther King, Jr. and his speeches, but there is little about the dynamics of the nonviolent direct action used to end segregation. We've included a list of books in the appendix to help you study the history, tactics, and methods of direct action used throughout history. (We'd particularly recommend the works of Gene Sharp.) In our effort to change society so that everyone has freedom and the food they need without fear of going without, we recommend the following as being some of the most effective methods.

Marches and Funeral Processions

The first step to organizing a march is to announce the date, time, and place to gather. The location, such as a government or corporate office, could be chosen because of its relationship to the issue being addressed. A rally can be organized at the meeting point, and you can have speakers as people gather. You might want to provide materials so people can make their own signs and banners during the speeches. Have the march leave on time; it's disrespectful to those who arrive on time to delay it for stragglers. There should be a banner at the very front of the march stating the essential point of the action.

You may end up blocking streets if you have a great many participants, but it can be valuable to let traffic pass so the public can see your message. On the other hand, if you have many supporters, the disruption of traffic can also have an impact. The key is to reach the public through other methods so the disruption is not attributed to construction or

"Wherever you turn you will find that our entire life is built on violence or the fear of it. From earliest childhood you are subjected to the violence of parents or elders. At home, in school, in the office, field or shop, it is always someone's authority which keeps you obedient and compels you to do his will.

The right to compel you is called authority. Fear of punishment has been made into duty and is called obedience.

In this atmosphere of force and violence, of authority and obedience, of duty, fear and punishment, we all grow up; we breathe it throughout our lives. We are so steeped in the spirit of violence that we never stop to ask whether violence is right or wrong. We only ask if it is legal, whether the law permits it.

You don't question the right of the government to kill, to confiscate and imprison. If a private person should be guilty of the things the government is doing all the time, you'd brand him a murderer, thief, and scoundrel. But as long as the violence committed is 'lawful' you approve of it and submit to it."

—Alexander Berkman, *What Is Anarchism?*

obstruction by anti-social elements. The route of the march should probably be determined beforehand and pass by buildings, factories, or other locations related to the issue.

If someone is killed during your struggle, your group might organize a funeral march. Even if no one has died during the campaign, but people are dying or could die if your actions fail, your group can organize a symbolic funeral march which should end at a location that is central to the issue.

Vigils and Tent City Protests

Many times the strongest and most effective action can be a vigil, tent city protest, or public space occupation. Occupation protests ended the rule of Arab dictators in 2011, inspiring a global wave of occupations. If there is one main location such as government or corporate offices that decision makers frequent, you might consider organizing a vigil and tent city protest. You can start by simply standing outside the facility with banners, signs, and literature. Your vigil might start out being just an hour once a week at the entrance of the facility, then escalate to one hour every day, to all day, and then, if there has been no movement by those your protest is directed against, you might consider a twenty-four hour vigil and tent city protest. The power of this type of action is in its persistence.

Governments and corporations have little tolerance for this type of powerful protest. Your group may need to slowly introduce more elaborate props until you are able to set up the first tent. These props can be a literature table, large banners, giant puppets, flags and cardboard images of tents, or symbols representing the intention of the vigil.

Provide literature to all those passing. Your largest banners and signs should clearly announce the reason for your protest. Vigils with many messages often have much less impact than a focused vigil.

Your group may want to sponsor a nonviolence training for participants. There may be times when the police are called in to suppress the vigil, and your group will want to be prepared for arrest. Returning to the site after being driven off by the authorities can be very powerful. You may need to return with banners and signs and replace your larger tents and structures once you have retaken the space.

Your group will want to offer regular events during the vigil such as concerts, poetry readings, street theater, and other performances. There may be an appropriate time such as shift change or lunch breaks where the event will have the most impact. It's a good idea to hold special events on the weekends to encourage less committed people to show their support.

Many vigils post a sign announcing the number of days of the action. Your vigil might include people who are fasting, and they might wear signs saying how many days since they last ate. Fasting can be very dangerous, though, so it is wise to enlist the support of nurses or doctors to monitor the well-being of those who participate in a fast.

As vigils escalate into occupations, Food Not Bombs groups can provide meals on site, and has provided food at several successful tent city actions, including the 100-day action during the Orange Revolution in Kiev; a 600-day farmer's tent city protest in Sarajevo; and the Occupy Wall Street movement in dozens of cities.

As the global economic, environmental, and political crises grow more urgent, we might consider organizing more tent city protests as they have been very effective in the past.

Site Occupations

After trying other tactics, it might be necessary to consider an occupation. Your group might choose to occupy an office, school, factory, or a construction, mining or logging site. With the foreclosure crisis and increase in homelessness, the occupation of abandoned housing or land can be a very appropriate tactic.

Your group could choose to occupy a building because of its symbolism; you might take over the offices of a government official, corporate executive, or school administrator. Your strategy could involve an element of surprise or you could publicly announce the occupation beforehand.

Even "unsuccessful" occupation attempts can ultimately bring about change. The Clamshell Alliance occupation attempts at Seabrook Nuclear Power Station in New Hampshire influenced the power company to mobilize a costly defense of the plant site, likely contributing to its being the last nuclear power station to go online in the United States, and the reluctance of other power companies to construct new nuclear facilities.

Homes Not Jails is another "occupy" movement, and it takes over abandoned buildings in plain sight. Dressed as construction workers, activists break open the front doors of empty, foreclosed houses. Once they've put their new locks on the doors, they invite homeless families to meet them at the house the next morning, when they unlock the front door, let the new occupants in, and help them clean and repair the house, while pretending to be the management. At the same time, strategic buildings that cannot be repaired with the meager resources of

Homes Not Jails can be occupied on symbolic dates, with banners hanging from the windows to pressure the authorities to provide housing instead of jails to those living on America's streets. It's often helpful to have a support group outside the occupied facility that contacts the media, builds community solidarity, promotes the goals of the occupation through handing out flyers and holding vigils outside the offices of decision makers, and provides material assistance to those inside. Pre-planning sanitation and access to water and food is important.

San Francisco police disrupting a free Food Not Bombs meal in Golden Gate Park on Labor Day in 1988

Your group can also organize legal support before the action. With proper support, it's possible for occupations to survive days, weeks, and even, sometimes, years.

One cautionary note is that if the purpose of a housing occupation is purely to provide housing rather than call attention to the housing crisis, it's best not to call attention to the occupation until and unless it's discovered. One of us had a friend who discovered a long-unoccupied house in a sparsely settled, working class area of Phoenix, moved in, had the utilities turned on, stayed there for five years, and was never discovered. He left only because he decided to leave town.

Blockades

Disrupting the business or activities of those engaged in dangerous, unjust, or cruel policies may require an escalation to a blockade of an entrance to a factory, office, retail establishment, construction site, or logging or mining road, slowing or stopping the operations. Your group might organize large numbers of participants to arrive at a location, filling the streets or entrances with so many people that it would be difficult or impossible for the opponents to continue their operations.

The blockaders could simply stand or sit in the way. A standing group might plan to sit when facing repression. Your strategy might include linking arms or locking one another to gates to slow the resumption of normal operations. Sometimes activists use heavy materials such as old cars, logs and concrete to block access. In some instances involving logging, activists have halfway buried old cars in the middle of logging roads. Locking yourselves to entrance doors, tractors, or other implements can also be effective. A support team can speak with the media, coordinate with lawyers, and provide blockaders with food, water and other needs.

Risking Arrest Sharing Free Meals

When Food Not Bombs members were first arrested for feeding the hungry, observers suggested that this was America's Salt March, referring to the marches organized by Gandhi in India. When a state or corporation attempts to stop a basic activity like feeding the hungry or gathering sea salt, it can provide your community with an opportunity to expose larger truths. Nonviolent noncooperation with orders contrary to basic acts of survival can be a powerful way to inspire resistance.

Instead of letting the police walk off with our food, we can simply hold on to our containers of soup, salad, rice, beans, pasta and bread, and risk arrest. Your group can also divide the food into two small portions that you expect the police to seize, and a large portion that can feed everyone that comes to eat after the police have seized the smaller portions. Your group can also make temporary banners for each expected act of police interference. The banners are often the first item taken by the authorities, and the police might arrest volunteers for sharing food without a permit and take the food. Your group can return with another small amount of food and temporary banner, and the police might interfere again. After the second wave of arrests and confiscations, your group can return with the rest of the food, your regular banner and literature, and proceed to feed everyone with little concern that the police will make more arrests that day. If they do return and seize your food and banner, then your group will know that it must divide the food further and make more temporary banners. Your group can take video and photos of the arrests and confiscations, which can help in court and in publicity.

It is helpful to organize legal support people who work with your lawyers and follow those arrested through the system. They can speak with the media, the lawyers, and the public while those arrested are in custody. They can also contact employers, water gardens and house plants, and feed and walk pets. Each court appearance is another opportunity to share food outside the courthouse. If volunteers are convicted and sentenced to jail, it is possible to continue the pressure by sharing meals every morning outside the courthouse, informing the public that the court had the audacity to jail people for feeding the hungry. This can undermine the authority of the legal system and influence judges to release the imprisoned food sharers.

Anarchist Relief Efforts

Food relief isn't often considered a form of nonviolent direct action, but the ineptness of governments in responding to emergencies has sometimes made it necessary for anarchists working with everyday people to fill the void. In doing so, we highlight the real priorities of the authorities.

You might live in an area prone to hurricanes, tornados, cyclones, earthquakes, floods, blizzards, fires, drought, or other natural phenomenon that could require an emergency response. Your community might face a political or economic crisis, presenting your group with an opportunity to provide assistance. You can prepare for disasters by organizing benefit events to buy bulk rice, beans, oats, flour, and other dry goods. It can also be helpful to have a few large propane stoves, although your group can cook on fires fueled by scrap wood, coal, or other

flammable materials. You might include disaster relief as an agenda item at meetings and discuss plans for preparation and implementation of local relief efforts. Try to imagine cuts in communication, water, power, and other resources. Your group might want to store fresh water, solar electric generating equipment, bulk dry goods, CB radios, and first aid equipment. Consider organizing classes in first aid, water purification, and sanitation.

Anarchist groups can sometimes respond to crises at times when larger institutions are not able to. Relief organizations, such as the American Red Cross, sometimes find it difficult to provide assistance and will sometimes refer survivors to the locations of Food Not Bombs or other anarchist groups' meals. In the first few months after Hurricane Katrina in 2005, we received dozens of calls from people seeking food, telling us that the American Red Cross directed them to us. Large institutions may be required to follow government regulations and have legal liability issues. Their hierarchical command structure can also slow down their ability to respond quickly to disasters. Anarchist groups are often local, flexible, and free from restrictions.

In 1989, the San Francisco Bay area was hit by a huge earthquake. San Francisco Food Not Bombs was preparing its regular dinner when the earthquake rolled through the city. Gas and electricity were suddenly cut off. Fortunately, the volunteers had propane stoves and were prepared to cook outside. They collected all their equipment and drove down to Civic Center Plaza where the group had already planned to share dinner. They set up their tables and stoves and finished cooking. Grocery stores and produce markets lost power to their walk-in refrigerators, and some called Food Not Bombs to retrieve their perishable food. Hundreds of additional people showed up for dinner that night. The police had arrested the servers the day before, but this time they joined the line of hungry, shaken San Franciscans seeking food. The American Red Cross finally arrived in the wealthy Marina District three days after the earthquake. Until then, San Francisco Food Not Bombs provided meals to hundreds of people. Food Not Bombs also provided meals to the survivors of the 1994 Northridge Earthquake in Southern California and to survivors of the 2010 earthquake in Chile.

In August 2005, Food Not Bombs volunteers learned that a hurricane threatened the Gulf Coast of the United States. As soon as the hurricane was named, they posted a Katrina page on their website

Common Grounds Collective in New Orleans

Your group can make a huge impact by preparing to respond to local disasters. Anarchists groups are one of the few entities that can respond swiftly to ease the suffering of survivors. Our rapid response can encourage community self-reliance and provide an example that mutual aid, horizontal structure, decentralization, and other core principles of anarchism are a good substitute for corporate and government domination.

and started an e-mail conversation on their listservs. Hartford, Connecticut Food Not Bombs packed its blue school bus with food and equipment and drove to New Orleans. Houston Food Not Bombs prepared to feed the refugees and also left for New Orleans. Tucson Food Not Bombs sent a bus load of food, volunteers, and equipment.

In New Orleans, volunteers organized contact lists of drivers, food collections, and volunteers. The Katrina website was updated many times a day with details of kitchen locations and other logistics. Hundreds of anarchist volunteers mobilized, traveling to the Gulf to set up kitchens, free survivors from the attics of their homes, and provide food and support to communities ignored by the government and institutional relief organizations. Survivors saw all this: anarchy in action.

While Food Not Bombs helped to provide immediate relief, the focus of post-Katrina anarchist relief efforts in New Orleans was the Common Ground Collective, which set up a free clinic, provided help with food and housing, and survives to this day as several separate co-ops and collectives.

Another outstanding example of anarchist relief efforts was Occupy Sandy, an outgrowth of the Occupy Wall Street movement. When hurricane Sandy struck New York and New Jersey in October 2012, the Red Cross was again slow to respond. Occupy Sandy stepped in and set up food and clothing distribution centers in affected areas. Occupy Sandy continues to operate and, among other things, continues to help residents in areas that were flooded with mold remediation.

Food Not Bombs-inspired projects

Food Not Bombs has inspired a number of other do-it-yourself projects. These projects share many principles with Food Not Bombs including a critique of the economic system, dedication to collective decision making, and a desire to provide a direct service or perform a task that introduces the public to our philosophies of nonhierarchical, decentralized social organization that encourage self-reliance and independence from corporations and government. The most widespread projects are Food Not Lawns, Homes Not Jails, Indymedia, Really Really Free Markets, and Bikes Not Bombs.

Food Not Lawns

Anarchists have been converting abandoned lots to organic gardens for decades, at times creating spiral gardens, using rubble to build spiral mounds that provide micro climates. It starts with volunteers calling for a work day and party—through word of mouth and flyers—at an abandoned lot, bringing rakes, shovels and other tools and free meals for gardeners and interested neighbors. They remove garbage from the lot, recycling what they can. Once it's cleared, they turn the soil, dig in the beds, and start composting scrap organic matter from the cleanup. The next events include the planting of flowers, vegetables, and fruit trees. After that a watering schedule will probably need to be implemented, and the community might start holding weekly weeding sessions and periodic planting and harvesting parties.

Anarchists recovered lots in several California communities in the late 1980s and early 1990s. They also helped revive the famous garden in People's Park in Berkeley. New Brunswick, Canada Food Not Bombs started a community garden and produced a documentary detailing the progress and joy of organic gardening. Many other chapters also started local gardens, some on recovered land and others in cooperation with local schools and community centers.

In the late 1990s, Eugene Food Not Bombs volunteer Heather Flores and her friends were working in their community garden. Truck loads of sod passed them daily on their way to become lawns in Las Vegas, Los Angeles, and Phoenix. Heather was already inviting the community to help in the community garden, and she brought the garden surplus to the Food Not Bombs meal. Seeing trucks of lawn heading to the desert as thousands of people were going hungry was too much to bear. Food Not Lawns was born.

Soon Food Not Bombs groups were starting Food Not Lawns gardens, and there are now Food Not Lawns gardens in over 200 cities. Peterborough, Canada Food Not Bombs started a garden that inspired a weekly column in the local paper. And Heather Flores wrote the book, *Food Not Lawns*, providing a detailed plan on how to bring your community together to plant their own Food Not Lawns organic garden.

Occupy the Farm in Albany, California is a great example of anarchists uniting with the community to reclaim land that was slated to become a shopping mall. Thousands of local people occupied property that had been part of the University of California's agriculture program. The university decided to sell it to Whole Foods and other developers, but the community occupied the property and planed vegetables in a bold effort to stop the paving of this fertile land. Even though the university repeatedly forcibly evicted the gardeners, the occupiers returned after every eviction, frustrating the plan to develop the property. Whole Foods eventually abandoned their plans to build on the land, instead moving to an already developed property nearby. The campaign to use the land for community organic agriculture continues.

Homes Not Jails

Housing foreclosures are at record highs in many parts of the world; multitudes of people can't even consider buying a house, and many millions live outside, unable to afford shelter of any kind. Housing crises are nothing new, and neither are efforts to protect people through direct action. In the 1930s, during the Great Depression, it was common for banks to evict people from their homes, moving household furnishings to the curb, and for activists and neighbors to reopen the house and move the people and all of their household goods back in.

The United States faced another foreclosure crisis in the 1990s. City governments started programs designed to drive the homeless out as hundreds of buildings stood empty. Laws against panhandling, sleeping outside, and sitting on sidewalks were introduced. In San Francisco, the mayor started his "matrix" program confiscating homeless people's blankets and other belongings. Many were arrested for "quality of life" crimes such as sleeping in parks.

One evening, people arrived at the Food Not Bombs meal in Civic Center and told us that they had been evicted from a low cost hotel across the street from the Glide Memorial Church soup kitchen, and now had no place to live. We also learned that the mayor would be celebrating Thanksgiving with a photo opportunity serving turkey to the hungry at Glide. We talked with the San Francisco Tenants Union about organizing an action to protest the evictions and the hypocrisy of the mayor. Activists broke into the empty hotel the night before Thanksgiving and brought food, water, blankets and banners. When the mayor arrived for his photo-op, the activists emerged from the hotel windows with banners. One said "Homes Not Jails."

We asked several families if they would be interested in free housing. They were. We suggested that we all meet at a social service office near an empty building. From there, the whole group walked through the Tenderloin to their new home. The Homes Not Jails activists had put their own lock on the front door, so the families slipped in quickly once the door was unlocked.

After that success, Homes Not Jails started riding bikes through the city, writing down the addresses of abandoned buildings. They then took the addresses to the tax office at City Hall to find out who owned the structures. If a family owned the building, it was taken off the list, but if the building was in foreclosure and banks were wrangling over the mortgage, that building was listed, and volunteers would arrive with crow bars, bolt cutters, and locks and hasps, and put a new lock on the door. Then at dinner Food Not Bombs would ask if anyone wanted a free place to live. Those interested were instructed to meet Homes Not Jails activists at 9:00 am the next morning. Once everyone had arrived, the Homes Not Jails volunteers, dressed in hard hats with tool belts, would unlock the door and let everyone in. They would also bring cleaning supplies, paint and tools to help make the abandoned house livable, and would also give the new tenants a lease to show the police if they happened to question the legality of their occupancy.

According to the book, *No Trespassing*, by Anders Corr, San Francisco Homes Not Jails had locks on hundreds of buildings throughout the city, and nearly 100 homes were occupied at times. If a family lost their place, Homes Not Jails helped them move to one of the other locations.

Following San Francisco's lead, Homes Not Jails groups started in other American cities. Boston Homes Not Jails began on Thanksgiving 1995 and organized four public takeovers in two years. There have been a number of Homes Not Jails groups in Washington, D.C. One of them started in June of 2000, taking over a building at 304 K Street NE in February 2001. Three activists were arrested but found not guilty by a jury. Asheville Homes Not Jails started organizing actions in the winter of 2002. Homes Not Jails entered a new phase of action in response to the foreclosure crisis that started in 2008.

San Francisco Homes Not Jails continues to occupy property as the housing crisis drags on. On April 4, 2010, Homes Not Jails took over the former home of Jose Morales at 572 San Jose Avenue in San Francisco's Mission District. The 80-year-old Mr. Morales spoke about his 14-year struggle to stay in the home he had lived in for 43 years. Food Not Bombs provided the food for the occupiers and their supporters. On July 20, 2010, San Francisco Homes Not Jails occupied the Hotel Sierra, a 46-unit building in the Mission that had been abandoned for over a year.

Bikes Not Bombs

In 1979, Carl Kurz traveled to New England from Austin, Texas to participate in the actions to stop the Seabrook Nuclear Power Station in New Hampshire. After arriving, he started working at the bicycle repair collective in Cambridge, Massachusetts. Food Not Bombs co-founder Mira Brown also was into bike repair and soon Carl and Mira were talking about how they could use their shared knowledge for social change.

At the time, the U.S. government had an embargo targeting Nicaragua, making delivery of items such as food and fuel difficult; at the same time the Reagan administration waged the brutal Contra War against the new Sandinista government. Mira and Carl decided they could resist the embargo by sending bike parts to Nicaragua. They called their project Bikes Not Bombs and started collecting old bikes, frames, wheels, and other parts. By 1984, Carl was traveling to Nicaragua with bicycles and setting up workshops throughout the country teaching bike assembly and repair. Bikes Not Bombs delivered hundreds of bicycles to Nicaragua and trained Nicaraguans in how to build and maintain this form of clean, fuel-free transportation.

Bikes Not Bombs set up a workshop in Boston in 1990 and started providing bikes to low-income children. They also trained over 16,000 young people in bike safety and organized projects in Central America, Africa, the Caribbean and New Orleans, donating over 25,000 bikes to people in those places. Since then Bikes Not Bombs collectives have sprung up all over the United States.

Bikes Not Bombs volunteers use consensus decision-making, volunteer their time, and share bikes for free. Some Bikes Not Bombs chapters offer bicycle repair while others organize free bike repair clinics. Once a local Food Not Bombs chapter is established, the volunteers often add projects such as Bikes Not Bombs, Food Not Lawns community gardens, Homes Not Jails, Really Really Free Markets, Indymedia Centers and low powered FM radio stations to their effort to build a sustainable future.

This model of building collectives can create a foundation for long term social change. Bikes Not Bombs provides the transportation aspect of our decentralized DIY (Do It Yourself) community. If we can organize local Bikes Not Bombs collectives, grow some of our own food in community gardens, share items at Really Really Free Markets, report our

own news via Indymedia, and house our friends in Homes Not Jails buildings, we can go even further. This kind of change is not easy for corporate or government interests to co-opt, and is one of the most powerful ways for us to replace the current failing political/economic system.

Indymedia

There's no point in citing the malfeasance of the corporate media other than to mention that its lackeys regularly and respectfully provide a platform for climate change deniers, government shills selling unnecessary wars, and corporate criminals trying to convince us that it's fair that the 400 richest Americans own as much as the bottom 150 million of us combined. Clearly, an antidote is needed.

That antidote grew in part out of the second international Food Not Bombs gathering in San Francisco in 1995, where several computer programmers decided to use the Web to post news of the gathering to the world. They set up an Internet connection in the convergence center and announced the founding of the DIY media project, Indymedia. Its first task was to post a daily newsletter about the gathering to the Food Not Bombs listserve, which had been developed by volunteers in Toronto. Volunteer James Ficklin produced the documentary, *Food Not Bombs International Gathering '95*, showing volunteers working at the first Indymedia Center in the convergence center near United Nations Plaza.

Activists started Indymedia centers in a number of communities soon after the San Francisco gathering. Programmers in Australia designed self-publishing software so activists could upload reports in text, photos, sound, and video. By 1998, volunteers were putting up Indymedia websites in many major cities of North America, Europe, and Australia. An Indymedia Center was organized on November 24, 1999 to cover the protests against the World Trade Organization in Seattle. The network of Indymedia centers started to grow after Seattle, and two years later, there were 89 Indymedia websites reporting from 31 countries and the Palestinian Territories. Temporary IMC centers started to be a regular feature of most anti-globalization protests, social forums, and other large actions. On occasion, the police would attack the Indymedia Centers. Police shut down the satellite feed from the IMC coverage of the Democratic National Convention in Los Angeles on August 15, 2000 and violently attacked volunteers at the IMC center at the G8 Summit in Genoa, Italy in July 2001. Indymedia video was used in the trial of the activists charged during the protest. On October 27, 2006, New York-based Indymedia journalist, Brad Will, was murdered while covering the strike and occupation in the city of Oaxaca, Mexico.

Each Indymedia center is collectively organized. The volunteers have various policies on the content, but generally, unless postings are clearly racist, sexist, homophobic, or otherwise extremely disrespectful, anyone can post text, images, photos, sound files, or video. Some collectives monitor their sites more closely than others, but each site posts clear guidelines that provide as open access as possible. There is a central site that posts news from all over the world and provides access to local Indymedia sites organized by region. That site also focuses attention on specific sites covering prominent protests, uprisings, and other major events. News, in seven languages, is linked to the central site. If there's not already an Indymedia center in your community, you can start one.

The Really Really Free Market

The first Really Really Free Market was organized around 2001 by Food Not Bombs volunteers in New Zealand taking the 1960s Haight Ashbury Free Store concept to their local park. The volunteers organized areas of free clothing, music albums, furniture, appliances, books, and other items across the lawn. Christchurch Food Not Bombs held "markets" four times a year and provided free meals at the events. The idea soon spread to Food Not Bombs groups in Asia. The Jakarta Really Really Free Market drew

> "I shall continue to be an impossible person while those who are now possible remain possible."
>
> —Mikhail Bakunin, Letter to Ogarov, June 14, 1868

people from islands all over Indonesia. Volunteers not only provided free goods, they also offered free haircuts and medical attention.

The first Really Really Free Market in the United States was held during the protests against the Free Trade of the Americas Agreement summit in Miami in 2003, providing a unique contrast to the exploitative trade policies advanced at the summit. A Really Really Free Market was also held in Raleigh, North Carolina in solidarity with the Miami action. After the Free Trade of the Americas Agreement Summit in Miami, many groups added Really Really Free Markets to their activities. North Carolina Food Not Bombs even started including a Really Really Free Market at every meal. There have also been Really Really Free Markets held in memory of volunteers who have died in anti-globalization actions in other parts of the world.

Really Really Free Markets are great outreach events, and you and your friends can hold one. To make the day even more interesting, ask local bands to play music and encourage other entertainers to participate. The Really Really Free Market is becoming a popular response to materialism, promoting sharing and the ideals of the free society.

Free Radio

Free (pirate) radio has been around for many decades, and Food Not Bombs volunteers have taken part in many free radio projects. But free radio has largely been rendered obsolete by the Internet, as it's easier, safer, and cheaper to reach people on the 'net than by radio. At the same time, it's probably easier for the government to shut down the entire 'net than a dozen mobile FM stations. And free radio stations can also be an invaluable resource in emergency situations when other forms of communication are unavailable. So, we recommend that activists learn to operate and maintain free radio stations.

It's gotten quite cheap and easy to put a station on the air. Prices have fallen so far that there's no point in building a kit or building a transmitter from scratch rather than buying a ready-made transmitter. One good source of information and transmitters is Free Radio Berkeley. Another good source for transmitters and other gear is eBay.

There's a plethora of technical information on pirate radio on the Internet, and there's little point in going into detail about it here, so we won't. We'll restrict ourselves to one very important matter.

How To Get Away With It

Piracy is illegal. If you're busted, the government can seize your equipment, drag you through the courts, fine you thousands of dollars and, theoretically, throw you in jail, although we've never heard of that happening to anyone in the U.S. (In some other countries, the risks are far higher.) So, it makes sense to take every possible precaution to avoid The Knock (on your door from the FCC).

The ideal way to maximize a station's listenership is to broadcast 24 hours a day on a set frequency with high power and an efficient, permanently mounted antenna. Attempting such operation as a pirate, though, would be suicidal.

At the other extreme, you could go on the air with a very lower power (under 100 mw) transmitter, which would be legal under FCC rules and regulations. If you would be satisfied with a broadcasting radius of a couple of blocks, that would be the way to go. In fact, in cities with high population densities, such as San Francisco and New York, such an approach makes a certain amount of sense.

For those who wish to reach large numbers of people with their broadcasts, the trick is to find as safe a compromise as possible between the two approaches. In general, when making safety vs. coverage decisions, it's best to err on the side of safety. Your audience might be small if you operate safely, but if you're busted, *nobody* will hear you.

Here are a few steps you can take to protect yourselves. They may seem excessive, but by following some of them ages ago I avoided arrest and so did my co-conspirators; since then, others I know have saved themselves major headaches by following them.

1) First the obvious: If people don't need to know about your operation, don't tell them about it.

2) Another obvious one: Don't broadcast your location or phone number. Broadcasting a false location is not an effective subterfuge, but there's no reason to make the FCC's job any easier.

"[N]o revolution can be truly and permanently successful unless it puts its emphatic veto upon all tyranny and centralization, and determinedly strives to make the revolution a real revolution of all economic, social and cultural values. Not mere substitution of one political party for another in the control of the government, not the masking of autocracy by proletarian slogans, not the dictatorship of a new class over an old one, not political scene shifting of any kind, but the complete reversal of all these authoritarian principles will alone serve the revolution. . . .

Revolutionary methods must be in tune with revolutionary aims. The means used to further the revolution must harmonize with its purposes. In short, the ethical values which the revolution is to establish in the new society must be *initiated* with the revolutionary activities of the so-called transitional period. The latter can serve as a real and dependable bridge to the better life only if built of the same material as the life to be achieved. Revolution is the mirror of the coming day; it is the child that is the man of tomorrow."

—Emma Goldman,
My Further Disillusionment in Russia

3) If you're soliciting comments from listeners, use a disposable e-mail address you access via proxies and change regularly. Do *not* use your own e-mail or physical address, even if it's only a p.o. box.

4) Separate your studio and transmitter sites. It's a hell of a lot easier to hide a transmitter and uplink receiver than a complete studio. Use an uplink transmitter (from your studio or a remote location) with a highly directional antenna. This makes it very difficult for the feds to find you, even if they find your (FM broadcast band) transmitter.

To make their job even harder, if you live in a mountainous area, hide your (weather-proofed) FM transmitter, antenna, uplink receiver, its antenna, and some solar panels and a battery pack in a very inaccessible area that has a line of sight to both your intended coverage area and to your uplink antenna. (Here in Tucson, Radio Limbo did this and operated for *years* before the FCC tracked down their transmitter. They lost it and all of the associated gear, but were never busted.)

5) If you're operating from a fixed location, hide your transmitter and antenna. With your transmitter, at least set it up so that it's very easy to disconnect rapidly, so you can move it to a pre-arranged hiding spot.

There are a number of steps which you can take to hide your antenna. One is to make your antenna out of very thin wire (#20 or #22 for low-power, FM-band operation), to use nylon fishing line for your guy wires, and to make your antenna insulators from clear plexiglass or plastic and as small as possible.

6) Go mobile. It's a hell of a lot harder for the FCC to track down a moving car, motorcycle, or bicycle than a stationary target. Portable operation (driving up the side of a mountain and setting up there for a short period, for example) will also make it harder for the feds to track you down. The disadvantages of this method are that mobile antennas tend to be less efficient than fixed antennas and that the FCC does not need a search warrant to bust you if you're engaged in mobile or portable operation.

7) Have at least one lookout (preferably two or three, with binoculars) watching for suspicious vehicles if you're operating from a fixed or portable location. Your lookout(s) and transmitter operator should either use cheap "burner" phones or cheap CB walkie talkies, should use coded messages, and should use the less popular CB channels if using walkie talkies. It's also a good idea to have a police receiver and to scan the police frequencies while you're on the air (though the FCC will probably not use police frequencies).

8) Operate sporadically. Maintaining a regular schedule (especially if you're always on the same frequency) makes it easy for the FCC to lay for you.

> "It is true that the professional thief is also a victim of the social environment. The example set by his superiors, his educational background, and the disgusting conditions in which many people are obliged to work, easily explain why some men, who are not morally better than their contemporaries, finding themselves with the choice of being exploiters or exploited choose the former and seek to become exploiters with the means they are capable of. But these extenuating circumstances could equally be applied to the capitalists; but in doing so, one only demonstrates more clearly the basic identity of the two professions."
>
> —Errico Malatesta, *Il Pensiero*, March 16, 1911

9) Operate for short periods of time, especially in cities with regional FCC offices and "cars in town." If the FCC is on to you, they can track down your transmitter in as little as 10 or 15 minutes using direction-finding equipment. So, keep your operating periods short, especially if you're operating from a fixed location. If you're using mobile operation, you can get away with longer transmissions without too much danger.

If you follow all of the preceding advice, your chances of being busted by the FCC won't be much higher than your chances of being struck by lightning or eaten by hogs.

Graphic by
J.R. Swanson

SELF-MADE MAN, n. A businessman with a fortune of $10 million who began life
under the handicap of inheriting a mere $1 million.

—from *The American Heretic's Dictionary*

STOLEN PROPERTY
AND HOW TO RECOVER IT

"Property is theft!"
—Pierre-Joseph Proudhon

Opposition to property ownership, with its inherent domination and exploitation, is a core principle of anarchism. At the core of property ownership is its inherent inequality, the hierarchy of those who control property versus those who do not.

Indigenous peoples tend to consider property in the same way as anarchists. On September 23, 1875, Sioux Chief Crazy Horse responded to U.S. military claims to the areas inhabited by native peoples, saying that, "One does not sell the land people walk on."

This points to what anarchists mean when we denounce private ownership of property: private ownership of land, factories, mines, railroads—in short, everything necessary to maintaining economic life. We're not talking about your toothbrush, guitar, or your house (though we think no one should own more than one house while others go without).

The English Civil War and the execution of King Charles I in January 1649 set the stage for one of Europe's most notable challenges to private property at St George's Hill, Weybridge, Surrey.

On April 1, 1649, Gerrard Winstanley and some friends, the Diggers, started to cultivate vegetables on St George's Hill. The group's agent Henry Sanders notified the newly created "Council of State" at Surrey that a group of people had started to cultivate the pastures on St. George's Hill. Sander's letter to the council said they had invited "all to come in and help them, and promise them meat, drink, and clothes."

Winstanley and the Diggers were inspired in part by Acts 4:32 of the Bible "No one said that any of his belongings was his own, but they all shared with one another everything they had." The Diggers also occupied vacant or common land in Buckinghamshire, Kent, and Northamptonshire that same year.

Winstanley and 14 others wrote a pamphlet, *The True Levellers Standard Advanced*, that stated:

> And hereupon, The Earth (which was made to be a Common Treasury of relief for all, both Beasts and Men) was hedged in to In-closures by the teachers and rulers, and the others were made Servants and Slaves: And that Earth that is within this Creation made a Common Store-house for all, is bought and sold, and kept in the hands of a few, whereby the great Creator is mightily dishonored, as if he were a respector of persons, delighting in the comfortable Livelihood of some, and rejoycing in the miserable povertie and straits of others. From the beginning it was not so.

Winstanley's Digger colonies were destroyed in 1650 by goons in the pay of landowners. Winstanley never attempted to repeat the experiment, though he continued to advocate common ownership of land.

Pierre Jospeh Proudhon is often credited as the first to use the terms "anarchism and anarchist," and he was the first anarchist to mount a sustained assault on property ownership, which he did n his 1840 book, *What Is Property? or An Inquiry into the Principle of Right and of Government*. Historian George Woodcock says of Proudhon's views:

> He did not attack property in the generally accepted sense but only the kind of property by which one man exploits the labour of another. Property in another sense—in the right of the farmer to possess the land he works and the craftsman his workshop and tools—he regarded as essential for the preservation of liberty, and his principal criticism of Communism, whether of the utopian or the Marxist variety, was that it destroyed freedom by taking away from the individual control over his means of production.

Reclaiming Stolen Property

Anarchists have taken direct action to reclaim land for everyone's use not only by taking over buildings or pasture, but by occupying entire cities and regions. The Paris Commune (1871), Free Territory in Ukraine (1918–1919), Shinmin district of Manchuria (1929–1930), Catalonia (1936–1939), Chiapas (1994 to present), and the current struggle and occupation of parts of Kurdistan are examples.

Anarchists including Louise Michel, Elie and Élisée Reclus, and Eugène Varlin, participated in the formation of the Paris Commune in 1871, helping liberate the city from the Third French Republic. This was one of the first large scale occupations supported by anarchists. The commune set up nine commissions and by common agreement had no mayor, president, or director. All church property was confiscated for use by the Commune. George Woodcock writes: "[A] notable contribution to the activities of the Commune and particularly to the organization of public services was made by members of various anarchist factions, including the mutualists Courbet, Longuet, and Vermorel, the libertarian collectivists Varlin, Malon, and Lefrangais, and the bakuninists Elie and Élisée Reclus, and Louise Michel." The commune was brutally crushed after only two months by the Versailles government.

One of the earliest successes in liberating an entire region was the Free Territory of Ukraine, home to nearly seven million people. The Revolutionary Insurrectionary Army of Ukraine coordinated by Nestor Makhno fought in the Russian Civil War against the Russian White Army, the Bolsheviks, and other forces seeking control of Ukraine. The Nabat Confederation of Anarchist Organizations at its first General Assembly on November 12–16, 1918 formed The Free Territory and implemented the anarchist economic principles of Peter Kropotkin and the educational concepts of Spanish anarchist Francisco Ferrer.

According to Makhno, in his 1936 book *Russian Revolution in Ukraine*:

> The agricultural majority of these villages was composed of peasants, one would understand at the same time both peasants and workers. They were founded first of all on equality and solidarity of its members. Everyone, men and women, worked together with a perfect conscience that they should work on fields or that they should be used in housework . . . The work program was established in meetings in which everyone participated. Then they knew exactly what they had to do.

Anarchist participation in the liberation of entire regions has not been limited to Europe. In the late 1920s, anarchist Kim Chwa-chin organized the formation of The New People's Society in Manchuria after fighting against the Japanese occupiers; the Society consisted of the Korean Anarchist Federation in Manchuria and the Korean Anarcho-Communist Federation. The New People's Society occupied the Shinmin district in 1929, organizing a federal structure at the village level that coordinated regionally. The participants also set up executive departments in the areas of agriculture, propaganda, finance, military defense, health, youth, and education, They resisted both Japanese occupation and the Korean capitalist system. The autonomous region of Shinmin faded away as pressure from the conflict between Russia, Japan, and China escalated, and after. Kim Chwa-chin was assassinated in 1930 while repairing a rice mill operated by the Korean Anarchist Federation.

Anarchists of the anarcho-syndicalist *Confederación Nacional del Trabajo* or CNT and Iberian Anarchist Federation (FAI) were primarily responsible for the liberation of half of Spain at the outbreak of the Spanish Civil War. On July 21, 1936, in resistance to a fascist coup d'etat, anarchists and socialists called a general strike, put down with arms the military uprising, and occupied Barcelona and other cities and regions of eastern Spain. The CNT took advantage of its already existing structure (with over a million members) to reorganize the economy in Catalonia, Aragon, Andalucia, and other provinces based on the anarchist principles of leaderless direct democracy and workers control of the means of production. Historian Burnett Bolloten, author of *The Grand Camouflage* and *The Spanish Revolution*, writes that workers took over "railways, streetcars, buses, taxicabs, shipping, electric light and power companies, gasworks and waterworks, engineering and automobile assembly plants, mines, mills, factories, food-processing plants, theaters, newspapers, bars, hotels, restaurants, department stores, and thousands of dwellings previously owned by the upper classes."

The anarchist website libcom.org states:

> The anarchist philosophy had been absorbed by large layers of the downtrodden peasants and the outbreak of revolution was the opportunity to put these ideas into practice.

Collectivisation of the land was extensive. Close on two-thirds of all land in the Republican zone was taken over. In all between five and seven million peasants were involved. The major areas were Aragon where there were 450 collectives, the Levant (the area around Valencia) with 900 collectives and Castille (the area surrounding Madrid) with 300 collectives.

The EZLN or Zapatista Army of National Liberation (*Ejército Zapatista de Liberación Nacional*) occupied areas of Chiapas, Mexico on January 1, 1994. The Zapatistas adopted the principles of "horizontal autonomy and mutual aid." They also implemented "health, education, and sustainable agro-ecological systems," and sought to "promote equitable gender relations via Women's Revolutionary Law, and to build international solidarity through humble outreach and non-imposing political communication." The EZLN is still putting these principles into practice in parts of Chiapas.

There is also notable anarchist influence in the effort to liberate Rojava Kurdistan. In July 2012, the anarchist-influenced People's Protection Units (YPG) of the Kurdistan Workers Party (PKK) took control of the towns of Kobanê, Amuda and Afrin on the Syrian/Turkish border. The YPG declared the towns and other areas an autonomous region, and helped establish a federation in November 2014 even as the Islamic State was fighting to take Kobanê.

After a four month long battle, a militia of women and men drove the Islamic State out of Kobanê, retaking the city in January 2015. Mehmûd Berxwedan, a member of the General Command of the YPG told journalist Ersin Çaksu that on "the 19th of July, Rojava Revolution began in Kobanê. . . . [T]here are two forces that have successfully emerged in Syria. One is us and the other is ISIS. Now it is up to who will defeat who. There are two roads. Either it will be the path of the gangs and of the occupiers or the path of democracy. This is a test. For that reason ISIS amassed all their forces and together with the support of foreign states [Saudi Arabia and some Gulf states] attacked Kobanê with such strength."

Abdullah Öcalan, the leader of the PKK, was introduced to the writings of American anarchist Murray Bookchin while in prison on the Turkish island of İmralı. Subsequently, he rejected his Marxist-Leninist philosophy and adopted many of the principles of anarchism expressed by Bookchin.

Channel 4 News in England interviewed Kurdish activist Memed Aksoy, who explained how he "en-

"Renting, the collection of rents, and the relations of landlords and tenants are, respectively, among the most humiliating, vicious and deplorable interactions that the human race, to its sorrow, has devised.

For the landlord, all healthy striving has ceased; like a sluggish python digesting a deer, the propertied class swells and snores, its pudgy thumbs hooked in rolls of foul-smelling, unwashed fat. Unearned income breeds complacency; complacency breeds mental stultification; and this last evokes greed for more unearned income.

Landlords have no rights—they forfeit them by engaging in a criminal enterprise, for which seizure of dwellings by those who actually live in them, and complete discontinuance of paying of 'rents,' are the only remedies."

—Fred Woodworth, *Rent: An Injustice*

visioned a Kurdish region taking shape comprising autonomous areas in Turkey, Iran, Iraq and Syria based on Bookchin's idea of "libertarian municipalism":

There has been a great push in the past 10 years to do away with the nation-state mentality of the old PKK and develop cadres to have a democratic, ecological, gender-equal mentality," he explained.

Eight autonomous regions are proposed for North Kurdistan. Organizing the people from the "bottom-up" in an upside-down pyramid, there are currently street, neighborhood, town and city assemblies; each one sends representatives to the Democratic Society Congress.

There are currently three autonomous regions (cantons) in West Kurdistan (Syria) and each one has a parliament, a prime minister, ministers and its own defense force. These regions employ a barter economy where possible and have formed communes at all levels to solve their problems.

The Charter of the social contract in Rojava includes this in its preamble:

We the peoples of the areas of self-administration of Democratic Kurds, Arabs and Assyrians (Assyrian Chaldeans, Arameans), Turkmen, Armenians, and Chechens, by our free will have [decided] to materialize justice, freedom and democracy in accordance with the principle of ecological balance and equality without discrimination on the basis of race, religion, creed, doctrine or gender, to achieve the political and moral fabric of a democratic society in order to function with mutual understanding and coexistence within diversity and respect for the principle of self-determination of peoples, and to ensure the rights of women and children, the protection defense and the respect of the freedom of religion and belief.

The articles of the Charter show anarchist influence. For example, "Personal liberty is inviolable and no one may be arrested; women have the right to exercise political, social, economic, cultural and all areas of life; everyone is [to have] free access to information, knowledge and artistic activities; every human being has the right to seek asylum and refuge, and he may not be returned without his consent; . . ."

Local Reclamations

Going from the international to the local, in the past few decades anarchists have participated in several urban reclamation experiments. One of the best known is Christiania. The founding of the autonomous Fristaden Christiania community at an abandoned fort in Copenhagen began on September 4, 1971, when people from the area tore down the fences of the military base and occupied it. Danish journalist Jacob Ludvigsen proclaimed later that month that "The Forbidden City of the Military" had been "conquered by civilians." Christiania is thriving to this day.

Christiania's mission statement says:

The objective of Christiania is to create a self-governing society whereby each and every individual

holds themselves responsible over the well-being of the entire community. Our society is to be economically self-sustaining and, as such, our aspiration is to be steadfast in our conviction that psychological and physical destitution can be averted.

In the U.K., residents of Freston Road in London declared their independence from the United Kingdom on October 31, 1977, as "Frestonia," proclaiming that 1.8 occupied acres in the Notting Hill and North Kensington areas of West London were a sovereign region of the British Isles. This declaration was inspired by the 1949 comedy *Passport to Pimlico* and a visit to Christiania by Freston Street activist Nick Albery. Frestonia issued its own postage stamp, which the British Postal Service honored, and the Clash recorded their fifth album, "Combat Rock," at Era Studios in Frestonia in 1982. Unfortunately, the "nation" of Frestonia has vanished with time.

Hakim Bey's Temporary Autonomous Zones (TAZ) concept became popular with anarchists and their allies in the '80s. Starting in 1980, the first Food Not Bombs collective in Boston and subsequently groups in other cities formed temporary autonomous zones, taking over city squares or sidewalks for several hours where they would perform plays, puppet shows, exhibit arts and crafts, stage concerts, show DIY movies, and share free vegan meals. The participants would disappear almost as quickly as they had arrived, leaving the streets as they had found them.

A popular street squat or Temporary Autonomous Zone was called Reclaim the Streets. The first Reclaim the Streets party took place on May 14, 1995 at Camden High Street in North London. Activists borrowed the tactics used to direct people to raves. Reclaim the Streets organizers announced parties a few hours before they started, so those interested could pick up directions outside a tube stop or store front.

The Beautiful Trouble website describes the first Reclaim the Streets action:

The event began with two cars crashing into each other. The drivers jumped out in theatrical road rage and began to destroy each other's vehicles with hammers. Meanwhile, 500 people emerged from the subway station into the traffic-free street that the crashed cars had blocked, and started the party, dancing, sharing free food, and meeting new friends.

Occupying abandoned buildings is based on the same anarchist principles as those underpinning the occupation of land, cities, and regions. Many occupied buildings provide not only housing, but a community gathering place.

One of the first books to help popularize housing reclamations was *Cracking the Movement: Squatting beyond the media*, which described takeovers in the Netherlands. It stated, "Squatting was originally nothing more than breaking open a door."

Cracking the Movement continues:

> Moving into living space without the required permits was considered a fairly normal thing to do. It was done in connection with family or neighbors and caused little stir because it had been happening since the 1960s, and according to some even as early as 1945. No one got excited, except the future residents of the house. No police or mass-journalism stepped in. Everything usually quieted down again quickly.

> [T]hings changed in the late 1970s, in that people began to squat without direct relations in or with the neighborhood, that too remained hardly sensational. Though sometimes fifty buildings slated for demolition were broken into in a few months [prior] and newly refurbished for habitation, the press still couldn't get excited about it. It had little interest in the squatters, and ditto the other way around. Insofar as squatters in a neighborhood engaged in publicity, it consisted of self-copied information and posters. Squatting stood for nothing; it did not present itself as a social protest begging for attention. It was not a resistance, fight or reaction, but the beginning of something new: the insight that, apart from the political belief in rules, concrete problems can be solved practically.

Many anarchists have participated in reclaiming dwellings, ranging from abandoned single-family homes to defunct factories, warehouses, and institutions. In Catalonia, a former leper hospital became Can Masdeu, an occupied social center, residence, and community garden in Collserola Park on the hills above Barcelona. The hospital, which had been abandoned for over 50 years, became famous in 2002 when occupiers nonviolently resisted eviction with residents and supporters locking themselves to entrances. The authorities retreated after three days, and there have been no further attempts at eviction. Today, anywhere from 100 to 300 people participate in an open house every Sunday, with public participation in activities related to ecology, activism, and self-sufficiency.

Graphic from *The Match!*

Vienna, Austria is known for its lively reclamation culture. The best known occupied site is Ernst-Kirchweger-Haus, an "international, multi-cultural, anti-fascist centre," named after Nazi concentration camp inmate and anti-fascist resistance organizer Ernst Kirchweger, who was murdered during a protest against far-right leader Taras Borodajkewycz in 1965.

Anarchists are occupying buildings in solidarity with one another from Iceland to Poland. Vatnsstigur 4 in Reykjavik was first occupied on April 9, 2009 during the global financial crisis.

Catharine Fulton, in *The Grapevine of Iceland*, reports:

> The Freeshop at Vatnsstigur 4 is open for business… well for now, at least. Yesterday the group that successfully squatted the vacant building for nearly five days over Easter weekend (before being forcefully evicted by police on April 15th) resquatted and re-established the Freeshop for five hours before authorities shut them down. Being "persistent bastards," as one gentleman distributing flyers

for the Freeshop aptly put it, the group opened shop again around 16:30 today.

Yesterday's squat was not just about sticking it to the man here in Iceland, the man in Poland was a target as well. "Today is a solidarity squat with the squat in Rozbrat, in Poland," explained one young man as he used a Sharpie marker to sketch a skeleton onto a discarded cupboard door. "There has been a squat there since 1998 and there are plans to have it evicted. So we're showing solidarity today and also just showing [the authorities] that this can't go on, just taking houses from people and throwing people out."

Poland aside, the state of things in Reykjavík is still at the core of the group's concerns. "We just need to show people that we can bring life to a dead town . . . Laugavegur is in the death throws and it really, really pains my heart to walk down the street and see the boards they put across the windows," the Sharpie-wielding man elaborated, adding that he plans to paint on the boards to liven things up. "I just want to make this house colourful and fun. Even though we can't stay inside, we're going to show that we can leave our mark and let people know that we're not going to stop."

The Rozbrat community in Poznan, Poland is a hub for anarchist experiments. The warehouse complex in which it was located had been seized by a businessman after the fall of communism, but the new "owner" abandoned it and fled the country after making a questionable business deal. Local anarchists investigated the facility in 1995 and started organizing concerts at the location in the summer of 1996. The Scottish punk band Oi Polloi played at Rozbrat, and Food Not Bombs started to cook at Rozbrat a year later, taking its free meals by foot to the central train station.

Rozbrat.org states:

In 1997 Anarchist Federation started their activity at Rozbrat. . . . Meetings called the Liberation Feasts were initially a forum for both solving the problems of Rozbrat itself and the outer activity. The Anarchist Federation created the Anarchist Library in 1997, and in 2000 the Anarchist Club, where weekly meetings of AF still take place. In 2001 another room was adapted for initiative "Lame Mule" (Polish: Kulawy Muł), where recitals, poetry evenings, discos and lectures take place. The back of [the] "Lame Mule" [space] was transformed into the Gallery, that is open for all kinds of independent artists. With time, a technical structure and a management

system based on self-governance was being created. In 2005, a new cafe bar next to the Gallery was created, it is a chillout zone. All the time, we are creating and improving the infrastructure. With small steps we are developing the place engaging ourselves in it.

The Brixton district in South London was home to one of the most successful and long-lasting occupations. The 121 Center at 121 Railton Road was a focal point for anarchists and allies from 1981 to 1999, hosting "a squatted autonomous centre, serving the local community as as a bookshop, cafe, gig and rehearsal space, printing facility, office and meeting space." It was also home to a Food Not Bombs collective that shared food in central Brixton. It also housed the anarcho-feminist magazine *Bad Attitude*, Brixtion Squatters' Aid, a chapter of the prisoner support group Anarchist Black Cross, and the anarchist queer group AnarQuist.

According to a report by "Tom" on urban75.org, "The premises also hosted punk gigs ('Dead by Dawn'), regular women's cafe nights and a monthly Queer Night, hosted by AnarQuist serving up everything from sumptuous vegan banquets to film nights to live cabarets to zine-making to glittery glammed-up disco parties. "

In January 1999 the Lambeth Council won a court decision granting the authorities possession of the 121 building. The occupiers mobilized, organizing an "invasion" of Lambeth Town Hall with a Drink-In in protest of a new council law against drinking alcohol on the streets, billboard improvement, wheat pasting of protest flyers, and the publication of the *South London Stress*, with news and calls to protest the closure of 121 Railton. Urban75.org states:

As the eviction date grew closer, the squatters barricaded themselves into the building, which was decorated with banners and paint. On 10th April 1999, the occupiers held an all-day street party directly outside the building to celebrate 86 days of resistance, attended by over 500 people. Encountering no police resistance, the road was blocked off with barricades, sound systems brought out and the street resonated to the strains of an eclectic DJ mix, from hip-hop to roots reggae to the Clash.

The 121 has been an anarchist centre under different guises for 18 years. Now officially waiting for eviction from the council it has held out with a combination of round the clock occupation and enough "front" to keep the bailiffs at bay.

"The equal right of all men to use of land is as clear as their equal right to breathe the air—it is a right proclaimed by the fact of their existence. For we cannot suppose that some men have a right to be in this world and others no right.

The recognition of individual proprietorship of land is the denial of the natural rights of other individuals—it is a wrong which must show itself in the inequitable division of wealth. For as labor cannot produce without the use of land, the denial of the equal right to the use of land is necessarily the denial of the right of labor to its own produce. If one man can command the land upon which others must labor, he can appropriate the produce of their labor as the price of his permission to labor . . . The one receives without producing, the others produce without receiving. The one is unjustly enriched, the others robbed."

—Henry George, *Progress and Poverty*

The Evening Standard reported that "Six sheriff's bailiffs, assisted by a specialist armed police force, entered the 121 Centre in Brixton's Railton Road shortly after 6.30 am and successfully removed the seven remaining illegal residents. . . . Occupants had organised a highly efficient campaign from inside the three-story building with the use of a website and newsletter circulated among supporters, who included anarchists, hunt saboteurs and other radical issue campaigners."

In 1964 the Amsterdam student magazine *Propria Cures* published an article under the headline "Red a pawn" which reported on the first organized housing takeovers in the Kattenburg district. Nearly a decade after occupiers started reclaiming abandoned housing in Amsterdam, the movement took over abandoned businesses in other Dutch cities. The Utrecht community ACU is known for its home brew Oki Doki beer and the Oki Doki Hostel. The garage Autocentrale Utrecht was first occupied by members of group Federal Crack in 1976. Collective members set up a concert venue, food co-op, movie house, bicycle repair shop, and initiated the popular street festival Le Guess Who? with live music and dancing.

One of the most popular venues in Prague is the Milada community, taken along with other buildings as the communist government fell. Milada hosts concerts, workshops, Food Not Bombs, and a free internet system.

Italy is home to many anarchist occupations. These include Villa Vegan Squat, Ripa dei Malfattori, Corvaccio Squat and Rosa Nera in Milan, TeLOS in Saronno, El Paso, Asilo Occupato, Barocchio Squat and Mezcal Squat in Turin, Libera in Modena, Al Confino Squat in Cesena, Giustiniani 19 Squat and Mainasso Occupato in Genova, La Riottosa Squat, Villa Panico and Cecco Rivolta in Florence, Bencivenga Squat, L38 Laurentino Squat, Ateneo Occupato, ZK Squatt and Torre Maura Occupata in Rome, Spazio Anarchico Occupato Gaetano Bresci in Catania, Z.A.M Zona Autonoma Milanese and many others.

Mexico City's best known building reclamation is Chanti Ollin. Anarchists occupied the five-story structure near the city center in 2003. Residents and supporters work with the Zapatista movement, house a bicycle building and repair center, and host concerts, lectures, and organizational meetings. Many travelers stay at Chanti Ollin when attending protests in Mexico City. The police raided Chanti Ollin in January 2015 arresting 10 people. The space was reoccupied a few days later.

ABC No Rio is one of the best known occupied sites in the United States. Anarchists and local activists took over the closed school at 156 Rivington Street on New York City's Lower Eastside in 1980. It became home to the Thompson Square Park Food Not Bombs meal. It has also hosted many concerts, silkscreening projects, and organizing campaigns to support local gardening and free radio. Collective members were very active during the 1989 Thompson Square Tent City protest. ABC No Rio continues to support the local community on the Lower Eastside of Manhattan.

These are but some examples of successful local reclamations.

The takeover and occupation of vacant buildings will continue as long as capitalism continues to reduce masses of people to homelessness. It's the most direct way to fight this social and economic tragedy.

FOOD

THE FOOD CRISIS

"Bread, it is bread that the Revolution needs!"
—Peter Kropotkin

Food policies may be the most important question of our time. Food policies impact the climate crisis, civil liberties, trade, poverty, species extinction, public health, civil unrest, migration, hunger, and war.

The primary problem is the system of industrial animal agriculture. Its purpose is to produce maximum profits for investors and to centralize control of food production. Feeding people is a distinctly secondary concern. Anarchists reject this because of their belief that "food is a right, not a privilege."

Anarchists have been concerned with alleviating hunger since the advent of anarchism in the mid 1800s, but it was Peter Kropotkin's 1892 book, *The Conquest of Bread*, that helped make the right to food a core theme of anarchist philosophy. Kropotkin writes:

> The soil is cleared to a great extent, fit for the reception of the best seeds, ready to give a rich return for the skill and labour spent upon it—a return more than sufficient for all the wants of humanity. The methods of rational cultivation are known.

> Every clod of soil we cultivate in Europe has been watered by the sweat of several races of men. Every acre has its story of enforced labour, of intolerable toil, of the people's sufferings. There is not even a thought, or an invention, which is not common property, born of the past and the present. By what right then can any one whatever appropriate the least morsel of this immense whole and say,"This is mine, not yours?"

The Food and Agriculture Organization of the UN 2006 report, "Livestock's Long Shadow," says "livestock production is one of the major causes of the world's most pressing environmental problems, including global warming, land degradation, air and water pollution, and loss of biodiversity. Using a methodology that considers the entire commodity chain, it estimates that livestock are responsible for 18 percent of greenhouse gas emissions, a bigger share than that of transport." Animal agriculture adds 7,516 million metric tons of CO^2 into the atmosphere every year.

Worldwatch Institute's Robert Goodland and Jeff Anhang's 2009 study, "Livestock and Climate," reports the impact of animal agriculture may be even greater: 32,564 million metric tons of CO^2 annually, or 51 percent of total emissions. (The US environmental Protection Agency reports that transportation is responsible for 13% of global greenhouse gas emissions, industry is responsible for 19%, and energy production is responsible for 26% of all climate damaging emissions, which implies that the amount produced by animal agriculture is higher than the roughly 10% specified by the UN FAO, though not as high as the roughly 50% specified by Worldwatch—a very large amount by any reckoning.)

The climate crisis, due in part to animal agriculture, is the principle cause of unprecedented droughts (notably in the Plains States and California, America's breadbaskets). In addition, animal agriculture uses a disproportionate amount of fresh water. A Center for Science in the Public Interest study states that feed grown for livestock (mostly heavily subsidized corn and soy beans, but also sorghum, millet, and alfalfa) accounts for 56% of fresh water consumption in the United States. Estimates of the amount of water used to produce one pound of beef vary widely, from about 100 gallons up to 2,500, but one thing all estimates agree on is that it takes far more water to produce beef than any vegetable. (Pork and chicken production are also water intensive, though less so than beef.)

The world produces enough food to feed everyone if food were distributed equally. There is an abundance. In fact, in many countries, every day in every city, far more edible food is discarded than is needed by those who do not have enough to eat. Yet nearly a billion people go hungry every day.

Consider this: Before food reaches your table, it is handled by farmers, distributors, wholesalers, and retailers. Much perfectly edible food is discarded for a variety of business reasons at every step. In the average American city, approximately 10 percent of all solid waste is food. This comes to an incredible total of 50 billion pounds per year, or about 160 pounds per person annually.

Over $100 billion worth of edible food per year is discarded in the United States. The situation is similar in many countries in Europe as well as in Australia, New Zealand, Japan, and Canada. With the exception of Africa and parts of Asia, where poverty is so great that little edible food is discarded, it is possible to recover large amounts of wasted food in every community.

Estimates indicate that only four billion pounds of food per year could completely end hunger in the United States. A 2008 study by the Food Ethics Council in England argues that excessive consumption of food by people in wealthy countries is increasing food prices for people in the developing world, and that by utilizing the millions of tons of edible food that is thrown away each year in just the U.S. and U.K., more than a billion people could be lifted out of hunger worldwide. In the U.S. alone, 50 million people are "food insecure" and 20 million are "very food insecure"—that is, hungry, missing at least some meals—and approximately a third of them are children.

Clearly, an abundance of food is going to waste. To recover it and use it to feed people, three things are needed. First, the food must be collected. Second, it must be organized or prepared in a form appropriate for consumption. Third, the food must be made easily accessible to those who are hungry.

It's no accident that this is not already happening. We do not have a democratic say in how food is produced or distributed. Everyone would choose to have enough to eat, but in hierarchical economies where the threat of job loss allows owners to keep wages low, the intentional withholding of food helps increase its price, and consequent profits. A policy of scarcity is essential to political and economic control, and an underclass results from policies that encourage domination and violence.

In our society, it is acceptable, simply business as usual, to profit from others' suffering and misery.

Kropotkin writes about the political roots of hunger and the failure of revolutions to make the basic need for food a priority. There are always high-minded debates about "freedom," "political power," and "democracy," but rarely a plan to address the needs of those going hungry.

He notes:

Great ideas sprang up at such times [social upheavals], ideas that have moved the world; words were spoken which still stir our hearts, at the interval of more than a century. But the people were starving in the slums.

Famine was abroad in the land, such famine as had hardly been seen under the old regime (of monarchs and capitalists).

Kropotkin was not a pacifist, but in *The Conquest of Bread* he describes the futility of using violence to enforce access to food.

"The Girondists are starving us!" was the cry in the workmen's quarters in 1793, and thereupon the Girondists were guillotined, and full powers were given to "the Mountain" and to the Commune. The Commune indeed concerned itself with the question of bread, and made heroic efforts to feed Paris. At Lyons, Fouche and Collot d'Herbois [municipalities] established city granaries, but the sums spent on filling them were woefully insufficient. The town councils made great efforts to procure corn; the bakers who hoarded flour were hanged—and still the people lacked bread.

Kropotkin goes on:

Then they turned on the royalist conspirators and laid the blame at their door. They guillotined a dozen or fifteen a day—servants and duchesses alike, especially servants, for the duchesses had gone to Coblentz. But if they had guillotined a hundred dukes and viscounts every day, it would have been equally hopeless.

By focusing on toppling those in power while ignoring the need to replace the old order with a nonhierarchical system involving the people in deciding how to meet the basic needs of the community, revolutionaries helped sow the seeds of their own demise, a lesson anarchists should remember today as community after community descends into chaos.

The Arab Spring provides a recent example of the failure of activists to build a sufficient infrastructure. It would have taken years of preparation to replace authoritarian institutions with a culture of mutual aid and social equality. That preparation did not happen. Even though hunger was the spark that ignited the uprisings in North Africa, the Arab Spring failed to end that hunger. The power vacuum created by overthrow of the old authoritarian rulers was filled with a series of new authoritarian rulers equally prepared to use force to maintain control.

Kropotkin continues:

This picture is typical of all our revolutions. In 1848 the workers of Paris placed "three months of starvation" at the service of the Republic, and then, having reached the limit of their powers, they made, in June, one last desperate effort—an effort which was drowned in blood. In 1871 the Commune perished for lack of combatants. It had taken measures for the separation of Church and State, but it neglected, alas, until too late, to take measures for providing the people with bread. And so it came to pass in Paris that elegantes and fine gentlemen could spurn the confederates, and bid them go sell their lives for a miserable pittance, and leave their "betters" to feast at their ease in fashionable restaurants.

At last the Commune saw its mistake, and opened communal kitchens. But it was too late. Its days were already numbered, and the troops of Versailles were on the ramparts.

Let others spend their time in issuing pompous proclamations, in decorating themselves lavishly with official gold lace, and in talking about political liberty!

Be it ours to see, from the first day of the Revolution to the last, in all the provinces fighting for freedom, that there is not a single man who lacks bread, not a single woman compelled to stand with the wearied crowd outside the bakehouse-door, that haply a coarse loaf may be thrown to her in charity, not a single child pining for want of food.

95

The industrial agriculture industries promote the belief that hunger is caused by the scarcity of food, and that the only solution is to increase productivity and reduce trade barriers. But it is clear that we can and do grow more than enough food to feed everyone. The solution to world hunger is to end corporate control of agriculture.

The myth that hunger is caused by scarcity brought DuPont scientist, Norman Borlaug, the "Father of the Green Revolution," to prominence. Industrial agribusiness boosters credit his Green Revolution with saving over a billion people from starvation. They claim that hunger was reduced by the introduction of high-yield varieties of grains and hybridized seeds, improvements in irrigation, synthetic fertilizers, and chemical pesticides.

Borlaug created the World Food Prize in 1986 in conjunction with the General Foods Corporation. Today the World Food Prize is sponsored by entities such as the Bill and Melinda Gates Foundation, Dupont Pioneer, John Deere Foundation, and Monsanto.

Some of those receiving the $250,000 award are leading figures in industrial agriculture. For example, the three recipients of the World Food Prize in 2006 helped open the Brazilian Cerrado to animal agriculture. According to the World Wide Fund for Nature, the Cerrado is the "biologically richest savanna in the world." Laerte Ferreira at the Federal University of Goias in Goiania, whose institute has been mapping and tracking deforestation in the Cerrado since 2002, reports that around 50 percent of the Cerrado or 250 million acres has already been converted to agriculture, mostly cattle pasture and soybean cultivation for animal feed. Over 70% of Brazil's beef cattle production is carried out in the region. Conservation International reports that 40% of this vast ecosystem is currently being used for grazing and charcoal production. The August 26, 2010 edition of *The Economist* published an article, "Brazilian agriculture: The Miracle of the Cerrado," saying that, "As a result, Brazil has become the world's second biggest soybean exporter and, thanks to the boom in animal feed production, Brazil is now the biggest exporter of beef and poultry in the world."

Charles H. Rivkin, Assistant Secretary, Bureau of Economic and Business Affairs under President Obama, wrote an opinion piece titled "Feeding our Growing Planet by Opening More Markets" that appeared in the *Des Moines Register* on October 16, 2014. Rivkin proclaimed that the solution to feeding the world will come from those sponsoring the World Food Prize and their innovations in genetically engineered seeds, chemicals, and the lifting of trade restrictions and tariffs. In other words, solutions that will maximize the profits and control of the companies sponsoring the prize.

Rivkin writes:

Right now, more than 800 million people are chronically undernourished. While that figure has gone down by more than 100 million over the last decade, we will still have to increase world food production by 60 per cent if we are going to meet the demands of nine billion people by the year 2050—the estimated world population for that year. Not only that, we'll have to respond to other food-security challenges, such as the effects of extreme weather, famine, as well as economic and political instability. [Food-security challenges caused directly by the policies being promoted by those sponsoring the World Food Prize.]

Rivkin continues:

Secretary [of State, John] Kerry has long recognized that 'economic policy is foreign policy.' And that's why my bureau—the Economic and Business Affairs Bureau of the U.S. Department of State—is doing everything it can to support American agriculture, from opening markets to advocating for American business interests from our many embassies around the world....

One of our most ambitious efforts ever to open markets in Asia and the Pacific region is the Trans-Pacific Partnership Agreement (TPP). Working with eleven countries in the Pacific region, out trade negotiators are aiming for an agreement that will sharply lower tariffs and technical barriers to trade, liberalize investment, and set high-standard trade rules.

We are also working to improve food security, in part through promoting biotechnology. While there is considerable political debate about the subject, we believe it's critical that more countries develop improved, science-based regulatory frameworks, so they can develop crops and plants that are responsive to changing conditions. We are also involved in projects aimed at reducing post-harvest loss and promoting responsible agricultural investment.

Apparently passage of the Trans-Pacific Partnership (TPP) is so important to U.S. "national security" that U.S. Defense Secretary Ashton Carter announced on April 6, 2015 that, "In fact, you may not expect to hear this from a Secretary of Defense, but in terms of our [readiness] in the broadest sense, passing TPP is as important to me as another aircraft carrier."

Hunger and even famine are not always caused by natural disasters, droughts, insect infestations, blights, or the inability to grow enough food. More often hunger and starvation are caused by government or corporate policies. In many cases vast amounts of food are exported for sale from countries where people are hungry. Frances Moore Lappe, Joseph Collins and Peter Rosset's book, *World Hunger: 12 Myths*, states, "There is enough food; . . . hunger is not necessary; . . . hunger is a social creation; hungry people [are] a social phenomenon, and consequently one that depends on us and that we can change."

Hunger myths include that there is not enough food; nature's to blame; there are too many mouths to feed; it's a question of food vs. our environment; the Green Revolution is the answer; the free market can end hunger; free trade is the answer; more U.S. aid will help the hungry; we benefit from *their* hunger; and it's a matter of food vs. freedom.

A 1991 edition of the anarchist paper *Workers Solidarity* features an article by sociologist Eileen O'Carroll titled "Why half the world's children go to bed hungry." It begins by saying that "It's hard to know how anyone can consider capitalism a viable system when looking at the situation of the less developed countries... [I]t seems unreal that people are going hungry. A recent UN report estimates that 30 million people face starvation. Yet beef, butter and wine mountains rot in European warehouses, farmers are ploughing crops back into the land."

During the Irish potato famine, Sir Charles Edward Trevelyan served under both Peel and Russell in Great Britain's treasury, and had prime responsibility for famine relief in Ireland. He famously wrote, in a letter to his friend Thomas Spring Rice, that the famine was an "effective mechanism for reducing surplus population" as well as being "the judgement of God."

Irish leader John Mitchel noted in 1848:

> The English indeed, call that famine a dispensation of Providence; and ascribe it entirely to the blight of the potatoes. But potatoes failed in like manner all over Europe, yet there was no famine save in Ireland. The British account of the matter, then, is, first a fraud; second a blasphemy. The Almighty, indeed, sent the potato blight, but the English created the famine.

Thomas Gallagher points out in *Paddy's Lament* that during the first winter of famine, 1846–47, as perhaps 400,000 Irish peasants starved, landlords exported 17 million pounds sterling worth of grain, cattle, pigs, flour, eggs, and poultry—food that could have prevented those deaths. Throughout the famine, as Gallagher notes, "there was an abundance of food produced in Ireland, yet the landlords exported it to markets abroad."

The idea that economic and political policies rather than inability to grow enough food are the cause of hunger and famine is supported by Kropotkin in *The Conquest of Bread*:

> In Russia for instance, the peasant works sixteen hours a day, and half starves from three to six months every year, in order to export the grain with which he pays the landlord and the State. To-day the police appear in the Russian village as soon as the harvest is gathered in, and sell the peasant's last horse and last cow for arrears of taxes and rent due to the landlord, unless the victim immolates himself of his own accord by selling the grain to the exporters. Usually, rather than part with his livestock at a disadvantage, he keeps only a nine-months' supply of grain, and sells the rest. Then, in order to sustain life until the next harvest, he mixes birch-bark and tares with his flour for three months, if it has been a good year, and for six months if it has been bad, while in London they are eating biscuits made of his wheat.

Hunger today in the United States is also staggering. As mentioned above, the U.S. Department of Agriculture (USDA) reported in 2008 that nearly 50 million Americans lived in "food insecure households," with a third of them being children. So, in "the richest country on earth," more than one in five children are "food insecure."

The USDA reported that 17.3 million people lived in households that were considered to have "very low food security." That means one or more people in the household went hungry over the course of the year because of the inability to afford enough food. This was up from 11.9 million in 2007 and 8.5 million in 2000.

Race has a huge impact on hunger in the United States, with 25.7% of black households and 26.9% of hispanic American households experiencing food insecurity—far higher rates than the national average.

The Agriculture Department says 39.7 million people, or one in eight Americans, were enrolled in the food stamp program during February 2010. By February 2012, the number stood at 46.22 million. And that's still not enough to eliminate "food insecurity" in this country.

Global poverty and hunger are also increasing. The World Food Organization reports:

• 1.02 billion people in 2009 do not have enough to eat. That's more than the combined populations of the USA, Canada, Australia, New Zealand, and the European Union.

• 25,000 people (adults and children) died every day in 2009 from hunger and related causes.

• The number of undernourished people in the world increased by 75 million in 2007 and 40 million in 2008, largely due to higher food prices from speculation and the high cost of seeds and chemicals resulting from introduction of genetically modified seeds and plants that have forced many farmers into bankruptcy.

• 907 million people in developing countries were hungry during 2009.

• More than 60 percent of chronically hungry people of the world were women or girls in 2009.

• Every six seconds a child died because of hunger and related causes in 2009.

Clearly, the majority of people going hungry today are not the stereotyped homeless wandering America's streets or starving Africans. Hungry people are children and single parents (mostly women), the working poor, the unemployed, the elderly, the chronically ill, and those on fixed incomes (such as veterans and people with physical and mental challenges). All of these people find themselves in the clutches of oppressive poverty even while trying to improve their condition. With the global economy in a state of crisis, many people who thought of themselves as middle class just a few years ago are now finding that they must rely on soup kitchens and food banks to feed their families. Each month, more and more people in the United States and other wealthy countries are forced to choose between paying for rent, utilities, medicine, or food.

In the less developed world it's worse. According to the World Food Organization, in 2013 25,000 people died every day from starvation.

Food is so important that its increased cost sparked the Arab Spring. Millions could relate to Tunisian produce vendor Mohamed Bouazizi when he torched himself out of frustration in December 2010. The crisis that impelled Bouazizi to his drastic act started three years earlier.

The price of staples nearly doubled in 2007. Droughts, floods, and other extreme weather events reduced harvests worldwide, especially in the U.S. Plains States. The situation in Russia, one of the world's largest wheat exporters, was bad enough that its government banned the export of wheat in 2010. Floods reduced rice cultivation in Asia, driving up the cost of another staple for billions of people.

Many governments subsidized the cost of staples, especially flour, as in Egypt, in order to reduce popular discontent. But many governments were forced to increase their prices so drastically that many of the world's poorest people found themselves paying half or more of their income just to eat.

The housing crisis in the United States also affected the price of food. When the US housing market crashed, speculators turned to the one thing everyone needs, food, driving up its cost, while at the same time the US government subsidized the production of corn ethanol—for use in cars!—again, driving up the cost of food.

Authors Marco Lagi, Yavni Bar-Yam, Karla Z. Bertrand, and Yaneer Bar-Yam of the New England Complex Systems Institute in Cambridge, Massachusetts, studied the impact of speculation on increased food prices. In their 2011 study, "The Food Crisis: A Quantitative Model of Food Prices Including Speculators and Ethanol Conversion," they report:

Claims that speculators cannot influence grain prices are shown to be invalid by direct analysis of price setting practices of granaries. Both causes of price increase, speculative investment and ethanol conversion, are promoted by recent regulatory changes/deregulation of the commodity markets, and policies promoting the conversion of corn to ethanol.

Forbes columnist Jesse Colombo noted, "While the late-2008 Global Financial Crisis resulted in a 48% plunge in commodities prices, they staged a quick and powerful recovery, rising 112% from the depths of the crisis to a mid-2011 peak that surpassed the prior 2008 peak by over 10%." For example, corn prices increased by 348%, wheat by 275%, and oats by 300% from 2001 to 2011, with the sharpest increases following the collapse of the US housing market in 2007 and 2008.

Corporate control of food production is adding to the crisis. Agro-giant Monsanto made the bold move of doubling the price of Roundup in 2008 and jacking up the price of seeds in 2009, notably soybeans by 42%. Other seed companies followed suit. Monsanto states, "Without the ability to patent and profit from our efforts, there would be little incentive to develop the technology that thousands of farmers use today" (that is, Roundup and "Roundup-ready" GMO seeds). Monsanto executive Robert Fraley was quoted in *Farm Journal* as saying, "What you're seeing is not just a consolidation of seed companies, it's really a consolidation of the entire food chain."

Philip H. Howard from Michigan State University has written:

Since the commercialization of transgenic crops in the mid-1990s, the sale of seeds has become dominated globally by Monsanto, DuPont and Syngenta. In addition, the largest firms are increasingly networked through agreements to cross-license transgenic seed traits.

Sadly, instead of helping to end hunger, the food industry is driving farmers off their land. Contracts that force farmers to buy seeds and chemicals every season have forced many into bankruptcy, often causing these proud stewards of the land to kill themselves. I witnessed one such suicide on September 10, 2003, during a protest against the World Trade Organization. I stood a few yards away from 55-year-old Lee Kyang Hae, the president of South Korea's Federation of Farmers and Fishermen, when he climbed the chain link fence separating the delegates from the public and stabbed himself to death. Song Nan Sou, president of the Farmers Management Association spoke out, saying, "His death is not a personal accident, but reflects the desperate struggle of 3.5 million Korean farmers."

On March 19, 2014 the Associated Press reported that "More than 100,000 farmers commit suicide in India every year while under insurmountable debts." In 2008, Prince Charles spoke at a Delhi conference, stating that the use of genetically modified crops had become a "global moral question." He denounced the biotech industry, saying, "the truly appalling and tragic rate of small farmer suicides in India, stem[s] . . . from the failure of many GM crop varieties."

"Not man as such, but man in connection with wealth is a beast of prey. The richer a man, the greater his need for more. We may call such a monster 'the beast of property.' It is the lash of hunger which compels the poor man to submit. In order to live, he *must sell— 'voluntarily' sell—himself* every day and hour to the 'beast' . . ."

—Johann Most, *The Beast of Property*

In a November 2, 2008 *Daily Mail* article, Andrew Malone wrote about Indian farmers and their struggle to pay for chemicals and genetically modified seeds:

Official figures from the Indian Ministry of Agriculture do indeed confirm that in a huge humanitarian crisis, more than 1,000 farmers kill themselves here each month. Simple, rural people, they are dying slow, agonizing deaths. Most swallow insecticide— a pricey substance they were promised they would not need when they were coerced into growing expensive GM crops.

Ending world hunger is possible. According to the UN Food and Agriculture Organization, 72% of the food that people eat comes from small farms and gardens. Activists such as Vandana Shiva, Raj Patel, and Ronnie Cummins, as well as groups like La Via Campesina, Food Not Lawns, The Cornucopia Institute, Food First!, and the Organic Consumers Association are organizing to increase the percentage of food cultivated by women and independent farmers. While their efforts are starting to make a difference, there's still a tremendous amount of work left for us to do.

While the focus of hunger-alleviation groups is mainly on human suffering, all creatures face hunger. Nothing highlights how circles of compassion are integral to sustaining our ecosystem more than the universal need for food—from the smallest phytoplankton to the largest whales. Trees need nutrients from soil and light from the sun. Livestock can't survive without fresh water, grasses, and grains. You and I need fruits, vegetables, and grains to survive. A study by scientists at Dalhousie University in Nova Scotia, first published in the July 29, 2010 issue of *Nature*, reported that the global population of phytoplankton, at the base of the global food chain, has fallen about 40% since 1950. They take in carbon dioxide and produce much of the world's oxygen. Along with providing as much oxygen as all terrestrial plants and trees, phytoplankton feed many animals in our oceans, including whales, small fish, shrimp, zooplankton, and jellyfish who, in turn, provide food for other marine animals.

Research suggests that rising sea temperatures are responsible for the steady decline in phytoplankton populations. The US National Oceanic and Atmospheric Administration (NOAA) reports that the oceans are warming. Jay Lawrimore, chief of climate analysis at NOAA's National Climatic Data Center, told *Scientific American*, "The global temperature has increased more than 1 degree Fahrenheit [0.55 degrees C] since 1900 and the rate of warming since the late 1970s has been about three times greater than the century-scale trend."

Hunger and poverty in Asia and Africa have contributed to the extinction and near extinction of many larger animals. When I was in Nigeria, I often saw wild animals for sale on the roadside as "bushmeat." Transnational corporations and free-trade policies have encouraged timber harvesting and mining in many wilderness areas, but these wealthy companies often fail to provide adequate compensation to their workers or to local communities, causing people to poach increasing numbers of wild animals, including endangered species. Mining and logging have also destroyed native habitats. One solution suggested by experts with the Bushmeat Crisis Task Force to slow the killing of endangered wildlife is to introduce cattle and other livestock, but this contributes to deforestation, reducing the natural habitats needed to support native animals. Primatologist Dr. Jane Goodall has spent decades working with apes in Africa. She says, "The bushmeat crisis is the most significant and immediate threat to wildlife populations in Africa today."

The Jane Goodall Institute of Canada reports that over five million tons of bushmeat are shipped from the Congo Basin every year. Nearly 300 chimpanzees were slaughtered for bushmeat in The Republic of Congo alone in 2003. The total value of the bushmeat trade around the world is estimated to be approximately $1 billion annually.

At the same time that wildlife in the bush is being devastated in West Africa, the fisheries off its coast are also in danger. The United Nations Food and Agriculture Organization reports that all West African fisheries are now over exploited. Coastal fisheries there have declined 50% since the 1980s, mostly due to over fishing by fleets based in the European Union, using ships individually able to net tens of thousands of pounds of fish each day.

Industrial fishing is also driving marine species to extinction. The crisis is not limited to Africa. The British Broadcasting Corporation reports that "Around 85% of global fish stocks are over-exploited, depleted, fully exploited or in recovery from exploitation." Over 400 million people, many living in extreme poverty, depend on fish to survive. Scientists believe fish stocks in tropical seas could be reduced by another 40% by 2050, when many millions more people may be depending on fish for food.

Frances Moore Lappe's *Diet for a Small Planet* indicates that one way to reduce hunger and protect the environment is to introduce the public to a vegan diet. Lappe points out, "An acre of cereals produces five times more protein than an acre devoted to beef production," and that "it takes 16 pounds of grain to make a pound of meat." With every passing year, the need to encourage the public to change its eating habits has become more urgent.

Switching to a vegan diet is an effective way to reduce hunger, because it is possible to feed many more people on less land and with less water on a plant-based diet than on a meat-based diet. Cornell University scientists report that the U. S. could feed 800 million people with grain that is now fed to livestock. The grain that is currently fed to animals for global meat production could feed over two billion people. The World Watch Institute states that it takes 49 gallons of water to produce a pound of apples, 33 gallons to produce a pound of carrots, 24 gallons to produce a pound of potatoes, 23 gallons for a pound of tomatoes and 2,500 gallons of water to produce a pound of beef.

The U.S. Department of Agriculture says that one acre of farmland can produce 356 pounds of pro-

> ## "Sell a country! Why not sell the air, the clouds, and the great sea as well as the earth?"
>
> —Tecumseh, Address to General Wm. Henry Harrison, 1810

Preparation of evening meal in Bankgkok. Photo courtesy Food Not Bombs.

resources and ecosystem quality, and the average Italian diet had the greatest projected impact." Beef was the single food with the greatest projected impact on the environment; other foods estimated to have high impact included cheese, milk, and seafood.

Livestock farming generates an estimated 18% of the planet's greenhouse gas emissions, while all the cars, planes, trains, and boats on earth account for a combined 13%. The clear cutting of forests for grazing lands adds to the degradation of our atmosphere, while the high concentrations of methane from factory-farm meat production contribute significantly to climate change, as methane per molecule has approximately 20 times the impact of carbon dioxide. As well, factory meat farming dumps massive amounts of toxic waste into our waterways, and the chemicals used for corporate agriculture wash into our rivers and oceans, killing fish and destabilizing ecosystems. Researcher and author Eric Schlosser reports, in *Fast Food Nation*, that only two cattle mega-feedlots "outside Greeley [Colorado] produce more excrement than the cities of Denver, Boston, Atlanta, and St. Louis—combined." A vegan diet would be better for the environment, consume fewer resources, and would be healthier for us individually.

A vegan diet reflects our desire to create a nonviolent future, and reflects the principles central to living in and organizing an egalitarian, nonhierarchical society. In addition to eating a healthier diet, we encourage everyone to take direct action by uniting with others in their communities to cultivate, recover, and distribute food. Working on such projects helps to build trust, and trust is necessary to the transition to a nonhierarchical society in which everyone's needs will be met. It may take time, but the philosophy of anarchism can provide a foundation for a transition away from the disaster of capitalism and state control, and the hunger and environmental disaster they produce.

tein from soybeans, 265 pounds from rice, 211 from corn, or 192 from legumes. They report that when the same acre is used for animal production, these numbers drop drastically: only 82 pounds of protein from milk, 78 from eggs, and only 20 pounds of protein from beef.

Because of the large numbers of variables involved, the specific numbers cited in estimates of the amount of water and other resources used, and in estimates of the amounts of food produced per unit of land, vary considerably. But this is *not* a reason to ignore those estimates.

All agree that it's far more efficient to produce vegetables, fruits, and grains rather than meat.

The choices we make as a society about food production can help solve the climate change crisis. This ongoing disaster can be slowed if everyone eats a more plant-based diet, as The Intergovernmental Panel on Climate Change recommends. The Dietary Guidelines Advisory Committee, a federally appointed panel of nutritionists created in 1983 that helps set federal dietary guidelines, is recommending that Americans eat less meat because it's better for the environment, sparking outrage from industry groups representing the nation's purveyors of beef, pork, and poultry. The 571-page report published in 2015 says that "The organically grown vegan diet also had the lowest estimated impact on

101

"In sum, the workers fight over bread, they snatch mouthfuls from each other, one is the enemy of the others, because each searches solely for his own well-being without bothering about the well-being of the rest; and this antagonism between individuals of the same class, this deaf struggle for miserable crumbs, makes our slavery permanent, perpetuates our misery, causes our misfortunes—because we don't understand that the interest of our neighbor is our own interest, because we sacrifice ourselves for a poorly understood individual interest, searching in vain for well-being which can only be the result of our involvement in the matters which affect all humanity."

—Ricardo Flores Magón, Speech in El Monte, California, 1917

Conscious Eating

Why are we offering plant-based vegan recipes? We want you to enjoy the flavor and health benefits of a vegan diet, a diet that reflects your desire to live a conscientious life, reduce animal suffering, help slow climate change, protect our fresh water and oceans, and support your health and that of your family.

What is a vegan? Anyone who respects all life and seeks to end the exploitation and suffering of animals. Vegans eat a plant-based diet, with nothing coming from animals—no fish, poultry, meat, milk, eggs, or honey. A vegan also tries to avoid using leather, wool, silk and other animal products for clothing or any other purpose. Many vegans seek to enjoy whole organic meals cultivated and harvested by farm workers who are treated with respect and paid a living wage. Many vegans also support efforts to protect the rights of all animals by volunteering at sanctuaries and shelters, by engaging in campaigns to stop genetically engineered crops, and in their support of groups such as PETA, Food Not Bombs, Farm Animal Rights Movement, and their local vegan growers, restaurants, and grocery stores.

A vegan or plant-based diet can be balanced, and can improve your health because it contains fewer chemicals and less cholesterol and saturated fat than a meat-based diet. Vegan diets can be rich in protein, iron, vitamins, antioxidants, and fiber, and they can decrease the chances of suffering from medical problems such as heart disease, stroke, diabetes, and many cancers. If you remove added salt, oil, sugar, and processed foods from your plant-based diet, it can help you overcome many chronic illnesses. Many people find they have more energy and look younger through eating a plant-based diet, which is great for people of all ages, races, cultures, and genders. Even if you don't completely switch to veganism, the closer your diet comes to it the more benefits you'll reap.

A vegan lifestyle is a compassionate lifestyle. Industrial agribusiness has taken animal suffering to

unimaginable levels with millions of birds living tortured lives in tiny dark cages, cows forced by the millions into filthy feed lots or, even worse, killed brutally soon after birth. Millions of sheep, pigs, goats and other animals are treated as commodities, suffering miserable lives shortened in unsanitary feedlots and slaughterhouses. Along with the suffering of livestock, thousands of animals are murdered for fur and leather or used in experiments. Factory farm conditions are not only horrific for animals, but are largely responsible for foodborne illnesses, the decreasing effectiveness of antibiotics, and heart disease, strokes and other conditions that lead to the suffering of many people who eat these products.

A vegan lifestyle is also an effective way to protect the environment. Industrial meat farming produces large amounts of climate change gases. A University of Chicago study found that a typical meat-based diet in the United States generates the equivalent of nearly 1.5 tons more carbon dioxide per person per year than a vegan diet. The livestock industry is responsible for more than 18% of all global greenhouse gas emissions; it produces 90 million tons of carbon gas emissions through its use of fossil fuels each year, and also contributes heavily to methane production—a greenhouse gas far more potent than carbon dioxide. According to a Penn State study, meat production generates 27% of the methane emitted in the U.S.

Frances Moore Lappé's book *Diet for a Small Planet* notes that a plant-based diet requires around one-third of the land and water needed to produce a typical meat-based diet. Lappé also points out that vegetables, grains, and fruits—in a properly balanced diet—can provide more protein per acre than meat. Each sixteen pounds of perfectly edible human food in the form of grain fed to cattle produces only one pound of beef. An acre of cereals produces five times more protein then an acre devoted to beef production.

Animal agriculture is a chief contributor to wa-

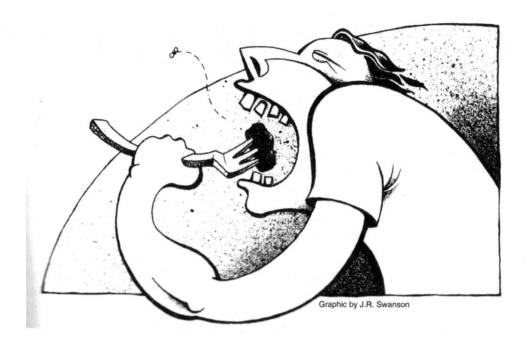

Graphic by J.R. Swanson

FORK, n. An instrument used chiefly for the purpose of putting dead animals into the mouth . . .

—from *The Devil's Dictionary*, by Ambrose Bierce

ter pollution. America's farm animals produce ten times the waste produced by the human population. Many species of wildlife are becoming extinct because of industrial farming and consequent habitat loss, and we are losing our rain forests to corporations like McDonalds and Burger King who require ever increasing land to grow feed and graze cattle. Eating more of a plant based diet is essential in our effort to protect our environment.

Why else switch to veganism? A vegan diet is delicious. Many cultures have wonderful vegan dishes and also experience fewer health problems than cultures relying on meat- and dairy-based diets. When Food Not Bombs first started to share vegan meals, much of our food was derived from Indian or other Asian cuisine featuring curries, dahl, tofu, tempeh, and rice dishes. However, we found that enjoyable vegan cuisine can be found in every corner of the world, an example being Mediterranean meals of pastas, salads, hummus, baba ghanoush, or a Mexi-can meal with rice, beans, salsa, and tortillas. Switch to veganism and you'll never run out of delicious and healthy choices.

104

RECIPES
FOR SMALL GROUPS

All recipes for small groups are for five or six people unless otherwise noted. Most of the dishes that involve sauteing or frying can be dry skilleted if you're avoiding oils. So, treat the cooking oil in these recipes as optional.

We recommend cast iron, stainless steel, pyrex, and ceramic-coated cookware. These are either inert or will add a tiny amount of a useful dietary mineral (iron) to your food. We recommend against aluminum and, especially, nonstick cookware. Aluminum cookware leaches minute amounts of aluminum into food during cooking, and, when heated, nonstick cookware emits carcinogenic and neurotoxic compounds. The nonstick coating will also oftentimes flake off into food if nonstick pots or pans are scratched.

If you're grilling, we recommend using a charcoal chimney (cost $10–$15) instead of petrochemical "lighter" fluid. Charcoal chimneys pay for themselves quickly, are environmentally friendly, and don't give your grilled food a nasty chemical taste.

Breakfast

Hash Browns

Russet potatoes (1 medium potato per serving)
granulated garlic (or powdered garlic)
black pepper
light cooking oil (not olive oil)

Bake or boil as many potatoes as needed the previous evening. Allow to cool for at least an hour. Place in refrigerator.

Lightly grease a large skillet (for small groups) or griddle (for large groups). Heat skillet on medium heat. Grate chilled potatoes onto heated surface. Flatten into patties about a quarter-inch thick, about the size of a 6" flapjack. Dust heavily with granulated garlic and black pepper. Cook approximately 4 minutes. Turn over with spatula when bottom is brown and allow to cook for another 2 minutes. Serve with habanero, cayenne, or tabasco sauce.

If using a griddle, grate potatoes into large bowl, then ladle out into individual portions on the griddle and flatten them. Prepare as above. Turn and take off in order ladled out.

Note: Russets work best with this recipe. Other types of potatoes tend to be too gummy.

Home Fries

6 to 8 potatoes, in strips or cubes
1 tablespoon sea salt

In a large pot, bring water to a boil. Carefully add potatoes so there is no splashing and bring to a second boil. Add salt. Continue boiling until potatoes just start to turn soft, after about 10 to 15 minutes. Drain and cool by running cold water over them in a colander.

4 cloves garlic, diced
2 or 3 onions, chopped
2 tablespoons nutritional yeast
4 tablespoons tamari or soy sauce
2 tablespoons cumin
cooking oil (just enough to coat bottom of pan)

Over high heat, sauté about 3 tablespoon of diced garlic for 30 seconds Add about 2 cups of onions and sauté until clear, about 3 to 5 minutes, stirring often. Then add enough potatoes to fill the skillet and fry until they start to brown. Keep stirring, and scrape the bottom of the skillet occasionally. Sprinkle in some of the yeast, cumin and tamari or soy sauce while stirring. (Hint: mix tamari or soy sauce with equal parts water for more even distribution when sprinkling.) Mix well and empty skillet into a large metal serving bowl. Serve homefries hot with dry roasted sunflower and sesame seeds and/or ketchup.

Granola

Makes about 3 pound of granola

Preheat oven to 300 degrees

1 pound rolled oats
1 pound barley flakes
1/4 cup almonds
1/4 cup shredded coconut
1/4 cup sunflower seeds
1/8 cup sesame seeds
1/4 cup cooking oil (optional)
1/4 cup maple syrup, molasses or dark agave
    nectar, bananas, raisins or apple cider
1 tablespoon vanilla
1 cup raisins or apple pieces
3/4 teaspoon salt (optional)
Alternatives — wheat flakes or rye flakes

Mix dry ingredients together in a large bowl. In a saucepan, heat oil, if using it, maple syrup and vanilla only until warm enough to soak into the dry ingredients. Pour this mixture over the dry ingredients and mix thoroughly, then spread into several flat baking trays. The layer of granola should be no more than one-inch thick. Toast in oven for 15 to 20 minutes, stirring every few minutes. Granola is done when golden brown. Mix in raisins at this point. When cool, serve granola with soy milk or fruit juice and sliced fresh fruit.

Oatmeal

2 tablespoons vanilla
1/4 cup maple syrup, molasses or dark agave
    nectar, bananas, raisins or apple cider
4 cups rolled oats

Optional Ingredients

2 teaspoons sea salt
1/2 cup raisins or chopped apples
1/4 cup shredded coconut
1 tablespoon nutmeg

Bring a half-gallon of water to a boil in a large pot. Add remaining ingredients, return to a boil, then turn to low heat. Stir often. Cook for 2 to 5 minutes. Remove from heat. You can serve with vegan margarine and sweetener or substitute bananas or apple juice to sweeten the oatmeal.

Scrambled Tofu

2 or 3 cloves of garlic, pressed
1/2 onion, chopped
3 pounds tofu (any variety, soft to extra firm)
3 teaspoons turmeric
6 teaspoons garlic powder or 10 cloves diced fresh
    garlic
6 teaspoons tamari or soy sauce
1/4 cup nutritional yeast
1/4 cup sesame seeds
cooking oil

Heat a large skillet. Sauté garlic for 30 seconds, then add onions and sauté until clear. Squeeze tofu like a sponge if using soft or medium tofu, until all excess water is removed, (skip this step if using firm or extra firm) then crumble into skillet and sauté until tofu starts to brown. Add turmeric, garlic powder, soy sauce and/or nutritional yeast. Mix well and remove from heat. Serve hot with dry roasted sunflower and sesame seeds and/or ketchup.

To dry roast sunflower and sesame seeds, heat a dry, clean skillet and add enough sunflower seeds to cover bottom. Stir constantly once they start to brown. They will smoke some but keep stirring until both sides of most seeds are brown. Then add sesame seeds. Keep stirring. The sesame seeds will start to pop and some will pop right out of the skillet. Roast the sesame seeds for 1 to 2 minutes more, until the popping starts to decrease. Remove seeds from skillet immediately and let cool in a metal or ceramic bowl. Tamari or soy sauce can be added to the seeds at the very end, if desired.

Lunch & Dinner

Artichoke Treat

5 globe artichokes
1 cup lemon juice
2 tablespoons Bragg's Liquid Amino or tamari
1/2 cup nutritional yeast
1/2 cup Dijon mustard

Cut artichokes in half from top to stem and place in pot with water. Steam artichokes for 45 minutes.

Sauce

Add Bragg's Liquid Amino (or tamari sauce), nutritional yeast, mustard and juice of lemon into food processor, blender and mix until smooth. Place in bowl and dip artichokes leaves and heart in sauce or to be fancy remove leaves and fibrous center of artichoke, place flat side down and dribble sauce over top.

Bad Ass Baba Ghanoush

1 large eggplant
1/4 cup tahini
1/4 cup lemon juice
2 teaspoons cumin
1 tablespoon chopped fresh parsley
1/4 cup black olives

Optional Ingredients

1 teaspoon salt
1 tablespoon extra virgin olive oil

Prepare a medium-hot fire in a grill or plan to use the flame on a gas stove. At the same time preheat an oven to 375°. While oven is heating up stick the eggplant with a fork on each side making holes in the outer skin. Put the eggplant on a grill or above stove flame at about 4 to 5 inches from the fire turning it frequently, until the skin blackens and blisters and the flesh just begins to become soft. This can take about 10 to 15 minutes.

After grilling, place the eggplant on a baking sheet and bake for 15 to 20 minutes until it is very soft.

Take eggplant from the oven, let cool slightly, and remove the skin from the flesh and compost. Smash the eggplant to a paste and add the tahini, the garlic, the lemon juice and the cumin and mix well. You can season with salt, tasting to see if you need to add tahini and/or lemon juice.

Place the mixture in a serving bowl and spread with the back of a spoon to form a place to pour the olive oil. Decoratively sprinkle the parsley and olives over the top.

Breaded Eggplants

2 black beauty eggplants
4 cups bread crumbs (whole wheat flour in a pinch)
2 tablespoons garlic powder
2 tablespoons onion powder
1 teaspoon salt (optional)
olive oil

Peel eggplants. (The skin is beautiful, but very bitter.) Cut into slices 1/2" to 3/4" thick. Coat with salt and let sit for an hour. Rinse. Turn over and repeat the process. (This further reduces the bitterness, which is the primary problem when cooking with eggplant.)

Mix flour and spices, spread on large plate or flat pyrex dish. Coat eggplant in olive oil on both sides and place slices on flour mixture and then turn over so slices are breaded on both sides.

Heat oil to a depth of about 1/4" in skillet on medium heat. When oil is hot, fry eggplant slices, approximately 2 to 3 minutes per side.

Breaded Eggplant Casserole

Breading is same as above, but bake instead as follows. First, make a tomato sauce:

5 large tomatoes, sliced
6 cloves garlic, diced or slivered
1 teaspoon salt (if using fresh tomatoes—omit if using tomato sauce)
2 tablespoons dry basil
1 tablespoon dry oregano

Optional / Alternative Ingredients

1 pound nondairy mozzarella equivalent, shredded
1 28-oz. can tomato sauce (instead of tomatoes)

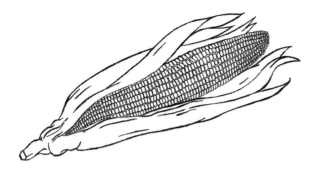

Put all ingredients in sauce pan. Simmer on low heat for 15 minutes or so. Turn off heat and set aside. Preheat oven to 350 degrees.

Place one layer of breaded eggplant slices on the bottom of a lightly greased pyrex baking dish. Cover with the tomato mixture and nondairy cheese. Put in a second layer—and a third if you have enough eggplant slices—and repeat the process, topping with the nondairy cheese. Bake for approximately 30 minutes.

This recipe will work without the tomato mixture/sauce or cheese, but it's better with them.

Burritos

3 pounds refried Beans (warm)
1-1/2 pounds cooked rice (warm)
pico de gallo or other salsa
6 large flour tortillas at least 12" in diameter

Optional Ingredient

1 pound guacamole

Warm tortilla over open flame for a few seconds. If using burner on stove, turn tortilla quickly so entire tortilla warms. Pile ingredients on toward one edge and roll over edge of tortilla so it forms a tube. Fold ends of tortilla inward and finish rolling.

Carrot Raisin Salad

6 cups carrots, grated
1 cup raisins
1 cup nondairy mayonnaise
1 or 2 lemons, juice of

Grate carrots, then mix all ingredients in a large mixing bowl. Serve cold.

You can make you own vegan mayonnaise by blending 1 cup of tofu, lemon juice, vinegar and 2 teaspoons of garlic powder.

Cold Bean Salad

The variations on this are almost endless. Have fun experimenting with them.

1 pound fresh green beans (or fresh wax beans)
    cut into one-to-two-inch lengths.
1 pound cooked black beans or red beans
1 pound cooked garbanzos
1/4 cup olive oil
1/2 cup vinegar (any type)
1/2 teaspoon salt
1/2 teaspoon black pepper

Optional Ingredients

1 small onion or 3 or 4 green onions, diced
1 fresh jalapeño or serrano chile, diced
1 or 2 Roma or other type dry tomatoes, chopped
1 small Bell Pepper, chopped
fresh basil, diced or minced
fresh cilantro, dice or minced

Mix all beans and vegetables together. Mix oil and vinegar along with basil or cilantro (not both) if using and pour over bean mixture. Mix all together again and serve.

Coleslaw (for 10)

6 cups carrots, grated
4 cups nondairy mayonnaise
1 tablespoon sea salt
2 heads green cabbage, shredded
1 tablespoon lemon juice
2 pinches of black pepper

Optional Ingredient

1 tablespoon sea salt

Shred cabbage and grate carrots, then mix all ingredients in a very large mixing bowl and serve immediately. Serve cold.

You can make you own vegan mayonnaise by blending 1 cup of tofu, lemon juice, vinegar and two teaspoons of garlic powder.

Curried Cauliflower

2 or 3 cloves of garlic, diced
2 onions, chopped
2 heads cauliflower, chopped
4 tablespoons curry powder
2 tablespoons cumin
5 tablespoons tamari
1 teaspoon white pepper
olive oil

Sauté the diced garlic for 30 seconds over high heat. Add about a cup or so of onions and sauté until clear, or about 3 to 5 minutes. Stir often. Add enough cauliflower to fill the skillet and fry until it starts to brown. Keep stirring and scrape the bottom of the skillet occasionally. While stirring, sprinkle in some of the curry, cumin, pepper and tamari. (Hint: mix tamari with equal parts water for more even distribution when sprinkling.) Mix well and empty the skillet into a large metal serving bowl. Place in a 150 degree oven to keep warm, and repeat the process until all the cauliflower is cooked. Serve hot over brown rice.

Curried Peas and Potatoes (for 5 to 10)

5 to 10 potatoes, washed and cubed
4 tablespoon olive oil
4 cloves of garlic, diced
1 or 2 onions, diced
1 cup nutritional yeast
1 cup curry powder
1 pound frozen peas
1 cup vegan margarine
1 tablespoon salt (optional)

In a large pot (4 quart or larger), bring water to a boil. If using salt, add it to water. Carefully add potatoes so there is no splashing and bring to a second boil. Boil until potatoes turn soft or about 15 to 25 minutes. Drain.

Sauté diced garlic for 30 seconds over high heat. Add onions and sauté until clear, or about 3 to 5 minutes. Add yeast and curry. If using salt, add it to water. Stir often. Add enough potatoes (already prepared) to fill the skillet. Mix well. Add a little water, if desired. When the spices are thoroughly mixed with the potatoes, add peas and margarine, if you wish. After the margarine has melted and is mixed in, empty skillet into a large metal serving bowl. Place

in a 150 degree oven to keep warm and repeat the process until all the spices, potatoes and peas are mixed together. Serve hot.

Grilled Asparagus (for 2 or 3)

1 pound (asparagus
1 tablespoon granulated garlic or garlic powder
2 ounces pine nuts or crumbled almonds or
   cashews
1/4 cup olive oil

Coat asparagus lightly with olive oil with brush, place in large pyrex baking dish. Dust with granulated garlic and crumbled nuts. Put dish in oven broiler pan, cook on medium heat (350 to 400) for approximately 5 minutes. Check frequently. Remove asparagus when soft.

Hot Rice

2 cups brown rice
4-1/2 cups water
1 tablespoon garlic powder or granulated garlic
3 or 4 small cayenne, thai, japanese chiles, or
   chiles de arbol, diced or minced; dried
   chiles work as well as fresh ones in this recipe

Put rice and water in a pot. Add garlic powder and chiles. Cook on low heat for approximately 50 minutes. Serve with almost any kind of spicy food.

Hummus

2 pound cooked garbanzos (chick peas)
1 tablespoon sea salt
2 cups tahini
5 lemons, juice of
1 head of garlic, diced

Optional ingredients

1/4 cup diced fresh parsley
1 small onion, diced
5 tablespoons toasted sesame oil

Soak garbanzos overnight. (They will double in volume so fill the container full of water after filling only half full of dry garbanzos.) Drain the water and place garbanzos in a large pot with 4 quarts of water and the salt, and bring to a rapid boil over high heat. Reduce heat and simmer for at least 1 hour (or until garbanzos are easily mashed between fingers—let cool before testing). In a very large mixing bowl, combine all ingredients and mash chick peas until smooth with a potato masher. (Alternatively, place all ingredients into a food processor or blender and blend until smooth.) Be sure to add water as necessary to create a creamy consistency. Let cool and serve as a sandwich in pita bread with sprouts and/or lettuce and cucumbers, or as a dip for cut vegetables and wedges of pita bread. If used as a dip, sprinkle paprika over top. If using oil, drip it on top.

Kebabs

Bell pepper(s)
Onion(s)
Potato(es)
Zucchini(s) or other soft squash
Mushroom(s)
Pineapple(s)

Cut veggies and pineapples into fairly large chunks, and spear with wooden skewers, alternating different types of veggies and the pineapple. Leave on grill, turning frequently, until done. Should take no more than two or three minutes of grilling.

For more even cooking—potato chunks, for instance, take longer to cook than mushrooms—put only one type of veggie per skewer, remove from skewers once done, mix all types in a large bowl, and serve.

Kebab Marinade

Dijon or other brown mustard, or ground mustard
    seeds
soy or tamari sauce
lemon, lime, or grapefruit juice

Optional Ingredients

Hot finely ground dried chiles or cayenne powder (very little)

Use quite a bit more citrus juice than mustard and soy sauce. It's cheaper that way, and you don't need a lot of soy sauce or mustard to impart flavor. Let kebabs steep in the marinade prior to cooking, or just coat them with it immediately before putting them on the grill.

Lasagna

1 or 2 cloves of garlic, diced
1 onions, chopped
3 or 4 fresh tomatoes, sliced (or 1-16 oz can sliced
    tomatoes)
1 tablespoon sea salt
1 tablespoon oregano
1 tablespoon basil
1 tablespoon thyme
2 or 3 bay leaves
1 tablespoon black pepper
olive oil (enough to coat bottom of pan)

Sauté diced garlic for 30 seconds in a heavy 4 quart saucepan. Add onions and spices, and sauté until onions are clear. Add tomatoes, bay leaves, and pepper. Add salt if you wish. Cover and simmer on medium-low heat for 30 minutes, stirring occasionally. Add salt or water, if you wish.

Filling

4 tablespoons olive oil
1 to 3 cloves of garlic, diced
1 or 2 onions, chopped
2 pounds tofu, drained (freeze for great texture)
10 oz frozen spinach (1 package)
    or 6 cups fresh spinach
1 tablespoon thyme
1 tablespoon basil
1 tablespoon oregano
1/8 cup tamari

Sauté diced garlic for 30 seconds over high heat. Add onions and sauté until clear, or about 3 to 5 minutes, stirring often. Add enough tofu to fill the skillet and fry until it starts to brown. Keep stirring and scrape the bottom of the skillet occasionally. While stirring, sprinkle in some of the thyme, oregano, basil and tamari; then add thawed, drained spinach. Mix well and cook until the excess water evaporates. Empty skillet into a large metal mixing bowl. Repeat the process until all the tofu is cooked. Mix all the tofu and spinach thoroughly and set aside.

Noodles

1 tablespoon salt
2 pounds lasagna noodles

In a large pot filled to within a couple of inches of the top, bring water to a boil, and cook the noodles about 10 minutes following the directions on the box. If using salt, add it to the water. Noodles ought to be *al dente* (still firm when bitten); do not overcook. Drain and rinse with cold water and set aside.

Soy or Nut Cheese

2 pounds soy or nut cheese (mozzarella style), grated (add more soy cheese if you like.)

Place a thin layer of tomato sauce in the bottom of each baking pan and place one layer of noodles over the sauce, completely covering the bottom. Place a layer of tofu-spinach mixture over the noodles and then sprinkle about 2 cups of nondairy cheese evenly over it. Cover completely with noodles. Place a generous layer of sauce over these noodles and repeat, starting with the mixture and ending with sauce. Sprinkle remaining soy cheese over top and bake at 350 degrees for 1 hour or until soy cheese starts to brown. Remove from oven and let stand for about 15 minutes before serving. The cheeseless sauce from the Macaroni and Cheeseless recipe can be used as a substitute for the soy cheese. You can also find nut based vegan cheeses.

Macaroni and Cheeseless

3 cups nutritional yeast
2 cups unbleached white flour
1 tablespoon garlic powder
1 tablespoon salt
3 tablespoons wet mustard

Optional Ingredient

1/4 cup vegan margarine

Boil macaroni until soft. Drain.

In a large mixing bowl, combine nutritional yeast, flour, garlic powder and salt, if desired. Mix well. Add boiling water, 1 quart at a time, using a whisk to stir. Add mustard and mix well. Add margarine if using.

Place the prepared macaroni in each of the baking pans. Cover with cheeseless sauce, making sure to coat each piece of macaroni. Sprinkle toasted sesame seeds or bread crumbs over top, and bake in 350 degree oven for 30 minutes or until hot and bubbling. Serve hot. (This dish freezes well.)

Mexican Pizza / Quesadilla (for 1)

1 large (burrito size) flour tortilla
6 to 8 oz nondairy cheese (cheddar, colby, jack, or mozzarella equivalent)
2 or 3 green onions, chopped
1 bell pepper
1 or 2 Roma or other dry tomato, chopped
1 Anaheim chile (de-seeded and de-veined, cut into strips)

Optional Ingredients

1/4 can black olives, crumbled
2 oz mushrooms, sliced

Place tortilla in bottom of skillet. Spread all vegetables on tortilla. Cover with nondairy cheese. Cover skillet with lid. Cook on medium heat until cheese melts, approximately 3 minutes. Serve with salsa, guacamole, and rice and beans as sides.

For a simple snack, make a quesadilla instead: omit the veggies, use any type of tortilla, cover with cheese, and cook as above. Serve with salsa.

Nopalitos

Nopalitos are the despined, skinned interiors of prickly pear cactus pads. You can sometimes buy them fresh in Mexican grocery stores, though they're more common in 28-oz cans. Either type will work fine. We recommend against despining and skinning the pads yourself, because it's time consuming and a pain, both figuratively and all too often literally.

There's a wide range of nopalito recipes. Here are two simple ones.

Nopalito Salad

2 pounds or 1 28-oz can of nopalitos
3 or 4 medium tomatoes, chopped
2 large carrots, in strips or grated
2 large jalapeño chiles or 1 large serrano chile, diced or cut into small circular cross sections
1/4 bunch cilantro
2 or 3 limes

Boil or steam nopalitos until tender (10 to 15 minutes). Set aside and chill in bowl. Once chilled, dice tomatoes, grate carrots, mince chile(s) and cilantro into bowl. Cut limes in half and squeeze over salad. Mix and serve.

Nopalitos with Black Beans

2 pounds or 1 28-oz can of nopalitos
3 medium tomatoes
2 large onions
2 large jalapeño chiles or 1 large serrano chile
1/2 bunch cilantro
2 pounds cooked black beans
3 or 4 large cloves of garlic
1/2 cup cooking oil

Coat bottom of skillet with oil and heat. Once oil hot, put in nopalitos and stir frequently. Slice onions, tomatoes and chiles, coarsely mince garlic and cilantro. Once nopalitos are almost soft, add onions and garlic, stir occasionally until they start turning clear, then add chiles; once onions are clear, add beans and cilantro, and mix. Cook over low heat until beans are same temperature as other ingredients. Serve as an entree with rice and warm flour or corn tortillas for complete protein.

Ratatouille

3 medium onions, sliced
1 large or 2 medium eggplants
5 or 6 medium tomatoes, chopped
5 or 6 large cloves garlic, finely chopped
3 medium zucchinis (10" long or so), cut into
    circular slices about 1/4" thick
1/2 cup finely chopped fresh basil
1/2 cup olive oil

Optional Ingredients

2 or 3 bay leaves
1 tablespoon thyme
1/4 cup chopped parsley
1/2 pound nondairy cheese

Skin eggplant, cut into slices about 1/2" thick, salt and let sit. Rinse off salt, turn eggplant slices over, salt again, let sit, and rinse. Cut into pieces about 1" on a side. Cut onion into slices, cut zucchini into slices about 1/4" thick. Cut tomatoes into medium-size pieces. Finely chop garlic and basil.

Cover bottom of large skillet with olive oil to a depth of about 1/8" and heat. When medium hot add eggplant pieces, stir and turn frequently. When they start to turn soft, add onions (and more oil if necessary), and stir. When onions start to turn clear, add zucchini slices, stir. When zucchini starts to turn soft, add garlic and stir. After another minute add tomatoes, basil (and other herbs, if using) and stir. Let cook another minute, turn off and serve. After letting sit for a couple of minutes.

If using nondairy cheese and a cast iron skillet, turn on oven to broil. Grate nondairy cheese over entire mixture while still cooking in pan. Turn off burner, stick in broiler, and broil until cheese turns brown. Turn off broiler, remove, and serve after letting sit for a few minutes. If skillet won't fit in broiler, leave on stove top, turn heat down to low, and turn off heat after cheese melts.

Refried Beans

2 pounds dry beans (black or pinto)
1 teaspoon salt
1 tablespoon cumin
1 tablespoon garlic powder

Optional Ingredients

2 tablespoons natural peanut butter
3 or 4 cayenne, Japanese, or Thai chiles, diced if
    fresh, crumbled if dry
1 tablespoon coriander (in place of cumin)

Soak beans overnight in about three times the volume of water to volume of beans—more water is okay—in a large pot. Drain beans in morning, pour in more water and drain again. Add water until it's about 1" above level of soaked beans. Add other ingredients except salt. Bring to boil, then immediately reduce heat to medium, cooking for about one hour. Add water if necessary to keep beans covered. Test beans, and add salt when they're not quite done. Cook until soft.

At this point, you can simply serve as whole beans. If you want refrieds, wait until beans aren't scalding hot and mash them with a potato masher.

Shepherd's Pie

Mashed Potatoes

3 pounds Yukon Gold potatoes
1 onion, diced
2 cloves garlic, minced
1 tablespoon dill
1 tablespoon black pepper

Steam potatoes or bake for 20 to 30 minutes at 350 degrees. Saute diced onion in frying pan with 2 ounces of water. Mash potatoes and mix in spices.

Filling

2 cups frozen corn kernels

Place corn in small pot or saucepan. Add water and steam for five minutes. Set aside.

1 onion, diced
2 cloves garlic, minced
1 tablespoon dried thyme
1 tablespoon coriander
1 tablespoon black pepper
1/2 cup bell pepper
1/2 cup zucchini
1/2 cup diced carrots

Crust

4 cups rolled oats
4 cups nutritional yeast
2 tablespoons Bragg's Liquid Amino or soy sauce
2 cloves garlic
1/2 cup cashews

Place cashews in food processor and blend into powder. Add rolled oats and blend into a flour. Add nutritional yeast and blend that into a flour. Add Bragg's Liquid Amino and blend until smooth. Spread over top of filling. Mash the potatoes across the bottom of the casserole dish. Cover potato mixture with a layer of cooked corn. Cover corn with vegetable filling then cover the filling with the oatmeal crust and place into oven for 20 to 30 minutes at 350 degrees.

Soy Chorizo Scramble

1 pound soy chorizo
3 medium onions, sliced
1 bulb garlic (approx. 10 to 12 cloves), sliced
1 large bunch chard (other greens will work, but chard is best), chopped
1/4 cup cooking oil (enough to coat bottom)

Optional Ingredient

1 cayenne, Japanese, or Thai chile, minced (other chiles not recommended)

Saute onions and garlic in skillet. When onions and garlic are mostly clear, add minced chile. Once onions are clear, add soy chorizo. Cook on medium heat for 2 minutes, stirring frequently. Add chard, continue to cook on medium heat stirring frequently for another 2 minutes or until chard is done (it gets limp and turns dark green).

Spicy Spaghetti Sauce (15 to 20 servings)

12 8-oz cans tomato sauce
3 large onions, sliced
12 cloves garlic, sliced or diced,
3 to 6 large Anaheim chiles (Hatch chiles will work; Anaheims are better for this recipe; do not use poblanos, jalapeños, or serranos),
2 large carrots, grated
1-1/2 cups TVP (textured vegetable protein)
1 16-oz can black olives
1 or 2 large bell peppers, cut into strips 2" to 3" long

1/4 cup dried basil
1/4 cup dried oregano
1 teaspoon salt
5 or 6 bay leaves
2 tablespoons powdered or granulated garlic
1/2 cup Mexican hot sauce (smooth variety such as Valentina or Tapatio)
vegetable oil (enough to coat bottom of skillet)

Optional Ingredients

1 eggplant, peeled and cubed
4 or 5 cayenne, Japanese, or Thai chiles, minced (avoid jalapeños, serranos, poblanos, or other chiles with a strong taste)

Cut up veggies. Drain olives and break them up into chunks with your hands. Heat oil in a very large skillet and, if using eggplant, saute it for 2 or 3 minutes on medium heat until it changes color, then add garlic and onions. Add more oil if necessary.

Stir frequently until onions turn clear. Add other veggies and stir again. When veggies are soft, add tomato sauce. Stir. Add herbs, spices, and bay leaves, pushing the leaves beneath the surface. Add TVP, and stir in. Let simmer for an hour, stirring frequently. If the sauce becomes too thick, add water and stir.

The number of chiles you use will depend on how hot they are—even the same types often vary considerably—and how hot you want to make the sauce. Initially, err on the side of mildness by putting in fewer chiles than you think necessary when cutting up the veggies, and then taste the sauted mix before adding the tomato sauce. If it needs to be hotter, add more chiles, stir them in, and saute for another couple of minutes before adding tomato sauce and spices.

Tofu Fajitas

1 pound extra firm tofu, cut into pieces approximately 1/2" X 1/2" X 2"
2 medium onions, sliced
10 cloves garlic, sliced
2 to 4 large Anaheim or Hatch chiles (depending on hotness of chiles), sliced into 2" to 3" strips, deveined and deseeded
2 large bell peppers, sliced into 2" to 3" strips
1/4 cup ground basil
1/4 cup Mexican hot sauce (smooth variety—e.g., Valentina or Tapatio)
1 cup cooking oil (not olive oil—something light)

Optional Ingredients

1 or 2 large carrots, cut into strips 2" to 3" long
2 tablespoons soy sauce

Fry tofu strips in skillet, turning frequently, until golden brown on all sides. Drain on a plate with paper towels on the bottom. Set aside.

While tofu is cooking, cut onions, garlic, bell pepper, into strips. Cut chiles in half and remove veins and seeds. Cut into strips. Set aside. Heat second skillet until oil is hot.

If using carrots, saute them first on low heat. After 3 minutes, add other vegetables. Stir frequently until onions are almost clear. Add basil and Mexican hot sauce. Stir thoroughly. Let simmer for another minute, add the tofu strips, cook all for another 1 or 2 minutes, stirring frequently, turn off the heat and you're done.

Serve with warmed corn or flour tortillas, refrieds, rice, guacamole, and salsa.

Tofu Sandwich Spread

1/4 cup miso
1/4 cup water
1 cup tahini
2 pounds crumbled tofu, soft probably the best
2 lemons, juice of

Optional Ingredients

2 teaspoons cumin or coriander
2 or 3 cloves crushed garlic
1 small onion, diced
2 stalks diced celery
1/8 cup seaweed

In one bowl, mix the miso and water into a smooth paste, then add tahini to the mix (add additional water to make a smooth, creamy paste). Drain tofu of excess water and crumble by hand into the very large bowl. Squeeze the lemon juice over the tofu. Add miso/tahini mixture and mix well. Add optional ingredients, if desired, and spread on your favorite bread with lettuce, sprouts and tomato slices.

Crush seaweed into the tofu spread to give it a tuna like taste. You can use alaria, dulse, kelp, nori, or any edible seaweed you happen to find. Harvesting seaweed yourself can also be rewarding, but be careful not to do it in polluted areas.

Tossed Salad

1 head lettuce, torn
2 large carrots, chopped
3 sticks of celery, chopped
3 or 4 large tomatoes, chopped
1 head red cabbage, shredded
1 green bell pepper, chopped
1 cucumber, sliced

Optional Ingredients

1/4 cup sunflower seeds
1/2 cup alfalfa, sunflower, or other sprouts
1 pound tempeh or tofu
1 cup cranberries

Saute tempeh in olive oil until crispy brown. Set aside.

Wash all vegetables and chop into bite-size pieces. Use additional ingredients which might be on hand, such as broccoli, cauliflower, onions, zucchini, beets, mushrooms, spinach, sprouts, apples, raisins, sunflower seeds, cooked whole beans (such as garbanzos, kidney beans and green peas) and so on. Use a smaller salad bowl for serving and only dress the salad in that bowl. Keep the rest on ice or refrigerated. Salad will keep overnight if undressed.

Tostadas

12 corn tortillas (6" diameter)
1-1/2 to 2 pounds refried beans (warm)
1 to 2 pints guacamole
1/4 head lettuce, shredded
3 large tomatoes, diced
cooking oil, enough to cover bottom of small skillet
   to depth of 1/2"

Shred lettuce, dice tomatoes, and set aside. Preheat beans and set aside. Heat oil in a skillet. When oil is quite hot, but not smoking (turn down heat if oil starts to smoke), put in a corn tortilla with tongs. It should immediately start snapping, crackling, and popping as the moisture in it boils. After about 10 or 15 seconds turn it over with the tongs. After another 10 or 15 seconds, remove it and set it to drain on a plate or cookie sheet covered with paper towels.

After all tortillas are fried, pile on the refried beans and smooth with a spoon. Do the same with the guacamole. Top with shredded lettuce, diced tomatoes, and salsa.

Guacamole Tostadas

Same as above, but omit the refrieds, increase the amount of guacamole, and use it in place of the refrieds.

Tremendous Tabouli

1 cup water
1 cup fine cracked wheat
1 cup minced fresh parsley
1/2 cup minced fresh mint leaves
1/2 finely chopped yellow onion
3 tomatoes diced
2 cucumbers seeded and diced
2 teaspoons olive oil
3 teaspoons lemon juice
1 teaspoon salt

In a large mixing bowl, pour the water over the wheat, cover and let stand for about 20 to 30 minutes until wheat is tender and water is absorbed. Mix in the chopped herbs and vegetables. Mix the oil, lemon juice, and salt in a separate bowl and add to wheat mixture. Serve chilled if possible.

Trident Subs

2 or 3 cloves of garlic, diced
1 or 2 onions, chopped
5 tablespoons olive oil
2 teaspoons thyme
3/4 teaspoon cayenne
1 teaspoon salt
1 teaspoon black pepper
1 or 2 16-oz cans tomatoes, or 2 to 4 fresh
   tomatoes, chopped
1 or 2 squash (zucchini, summer, etc.—must have
   soft skins)
3 to 5 root vegetables (carrots, potatoes, etc.)
1 or 2 bunches any dark green leafy vegetable
   (collards, kale, spinach, etc.)
1/2 cabbage or eggplant
Sandwich rolls

Sauté the chopped garlic and onions at medium-high heat in a large pot until the onions become clear. Add spices, then all the chopped vegetables and either fresh or canned tomatoes. (If you do not have any tomatoes, add a little water to start the vegetables cooking.) Stir often to prevent sticking. Once the liquid in the bottom starts to boil, lower heat to medium low. Cook until the vegetables are soft and the sauce is thick like stew, usually about 1 hour, but simmering longer enhances the taste. Adjust seasonings, especially salt, pepper and cayenne. Serve on a sandwich roll, or over bread or brown rice on a plate. This trident sub is spicy hot!

Sauces and Dressings

Lemon-Tahini Dressing

1/2 cup tahini
2 lemons, juice of
1/2 cup nutritional yeast
1 tablespoon toasted sesame oil
2 or 3 cloves of garlic
1/2 cup water

Optional Ingredients

apple juice or cider

Place ingredients in a blender and blend until smooth. Add more water, lemon or apple juice as necessary to make a thick, creamy dressing.

Oil and Vinegar Dressing

1/2 cup olive oil
1/4 cup balsamic vinegar
1 lemon, juice of
4 teaspoons fresh garlic, diced
2 teaspoons thyme
2 teaspoons basil
2 teaspoons oregano
2 teaspoons salt (optional)
2 teaspoons black pepper
2 teaspoons ginger powder

Put ingredients in jar and shake well. Shake again before every serving. Variations include removing the oil, using only lemon juice and no vinegar; using tamari instead of salt; adding nutritional yeast; adding apple or orange juice, and so on. (Have fun making your dressing tasty!)

Pico de gallo

This is a common and easy type of Mexican salsa.

2 medium red or yellow onions, diced
5 or 6 Roma or other type of relatively small, dry tomatoes (don't use beefsteaks or other juicy tomatoes), diced
2 or 3 jalapeños, diced or cut into circular slices
1 bunch cilantro, diced
2 limes, cut in half

Cut limes in half. Dice all other ingredients, mix, squeeze limes over the mixture.

This version of pico de gallo will be very hot. For a milder salsa, only use one chile or devein and deseed the jalapeños before dicing. If deveining and deseeding, wash your hands thoroughly with soap at least twice after handling the jalapeño interiors. Better, use latex gloves while deveining and deseeding, and then discard the gloves. It can be physically painful to the fingers/hands to devein and deseed chiles if you don't use gloves, and, trust us on this one, in that case you *really* don't want to rub your eyes or relieve yourself after doing so.

Simple Salsa

10 large chiles (any type, though Anaheims and Hatch chiles work well)
1 cup white vinegar
1/2 teaspoon salt
2 tablespoons oregano

Cut or pull stems off chiles and place in blender. Add vinegar to about one-third of the height of the chiles. Add water to bring to height equal to that of the chiles. Add salt and oregano or cilantro. Blend to desired consistency and place in jar(s). Always shake jars before serving, as ingredients will tend to separate.

Alternate Ingredients

lemon or lime juice in place of the vinegar
1/4 bunch cilantro in place of the oregano

Optional Ingredient

2 tomatoes (blend with other ingredients)

Soups

Miso Soup

1/4 cup olive oil
2 or 3 cloves of fresh garlic, diced
1 tablespoon thyme
1 tablespoon basil
10 cups water
2 cups miso

Optional Ingredients

1 teaspoon cayenne
1/8 cup arame (sea vegetable)
1/4 cup cabbage, shredded
1/2 cup tofu, cubed
1/4 cup chopped scallions

Sauté diced garlic and spices for 30 seconds. Add a small amount of water and add any combination of the ingredients except the miso. Bring to a boil. Remove from heat. You could heat the water in a kettle and pour it into each cup, mix in the miso and add the sautéed ingredients, then stir and enjoy. You can also pour the hot water into the pot of ingredients and stir in the miso. (Note: Do not pour boiling water over the miso; this kills the beneficial microorganisms.)

Potato Soup

5 tablespoons olive oil
2 or 3 cloves of garlic, diced
1 or 2 onions, chopped
1 tablespoon thyme
1 tablespoon basil
1 tablespoon oregano
1-1/2 gallons water
2 pounds potatoes, cubed
1 tablespoon salt
1 tablespoon white pepper
1 pound carrots, chopped

Sauté garlic for 30 seconds in a soup pot then add onions and spices. Sauté until onions start to brown on their edges. Add water, potatoes, carrots and pepper. If using salt, add to water. Bring to a boil, then reduce heat to low and cover. Simmer for 30 minutes or until potatoes are soft. Ladle about half of the soup into a blender and blend until smooth. (Be careful to hold the lid very tightly onto the blender; the soup is very hot and will burn you if it splashes out.) Put the blended soup back in the pot, stir and serve.

(Note: add 1/2 cup of dill and make this Potato Dill Soup.)

Vegetable Soup

5 tablespoons olive oil
2 or 3 cloves of garlic, diced
1 or 2 onions, chopped
1 tablespoon thyme
1 tablespoon basil
1 tablespoon oregano
1 tablespoon tarragon
1-1/2 gallons water
1 tablespoon salt
2 teaspoons black pepper
1 or 2 bay leaves
1 pound potatoes, cubed
2 tomatoes, chopped
1 pound zucchini, chopped
2 or 3 stalks of celery, chopped
1 pound carrots

Optional Ingredients

1 or 2 cups cooked macaroni
1 or 2 cups cooked garbanzos
1 or 2 cups peas
1 or 2 cups cooked brown rice

Sauté garlic for 30 seconds in a soup pot, then add onions and spices. Sauté until onions start to brown on their edges. Add water, pepper, and bay leaves. If using salt, add to water. Bring to a boil, and add chopped vegetables and other ingredients. Bring to a second boil, then reduce heat to low and cover. Simmer for 45 minutes or until vegetables are cooked to desired softness. Serve hot. This soup can simmer for as long as you like if you keep adding water. Serve hot.

117

Yellow Pea Soup

5 tablespoons olive oil
2 or 3 cloves of garlic, diced
1 onion, chopped
1 teaspoon thyme
1 teaspoon basil
1 teaspoon oregano
1-1/2 gallons water
2 cups dry yellow peas
1/2 cup barley
1 tablespoon salt
1 tablespoon black pepper
4 or 5 potatoes, cubed
1 or 2 cups carrots, chopped
2 to 4 stalks of celery, chopped

Sauté garlic for 30 seconds in a soup pot, then add onions and spices. Sauté until onions start to brown on their edges. Add peas and spices, stir until heated, then add water, barley and bring to boil. If using salt, add it to water. Add chopped vegetables and bring to a second boil, then reduce heat to low and cover. Stir occasionally and simmer for 45 minutes or until peas are cooked to desired softness. Serve hot.

Snacks

Garnet Yam Fries

2 or 3 large garnet yams (or other sweet potatoes
    or yams)
1/4 cup olive oil

Optional Ingredients

salt
cayenne powder
cajun or creole seasoning

Preheat oven to 400 degrees. Cut yams into french fry-size strips, 1/4" to 3/8" on a side, and 4" to 6" in length. Place in bowl, and coat very lightly with oil by brushing it on or pouring a small amount over fries and turning by hand. Place fries in single layer on a lightly greased cookie sheet, dust lightly with any (but not all!) of the optional ingredients if desired, place in oven, and let bake for approximately

15 to 20 minutes. For juicier fries, cover the fries on cookie sheet with aluminum foil. For dry fries, do not cover. For really dry fries, don't coat them lightly with oil, and just bake them.

Guacamole

3 large avocados
1/2 teaspoon garlic salt
1 to 2 ounces lime juice (lemon juice will work)

Mash avocados, add garlic salt and lime juice, and mash in.

Optional Ingredients

1 or 2 green onions, diced.
1 Roma tomato, diced

Tofu Dill Dip

1 pound tofu, drained
5 tablespoons olive oil
5 tablespoons vinegar
2 lemons, juice of
2 to 5 cloves of garlic
1 onion
5 tablespoons dill
1 tablespoon salt
1 tablespoon white pepper

Optional Ingredients

apple juice or cider

Squeeze tofu like a sponge to remove excess water, then crumble it into a blender or bowl to use with a whisk. Add 1 quarter each of the remaining ingredients. Blend until smooth, adding water or apple juice as necessary to achieve a thick, creamy consistency. Repeat 3 more times. Chill and serve with cut vegetables or chips.

Tortilla Chips

1 package of 36 corn tortillas (6" diameter)
cooking oil (light—canola, sunflower, etc.)
salt

Pour oil to depth of about an inch in skillet. Turn burner to medium heat. Cut stack of tortillas into quarters. When oil is hot put tortilla pieces in oil, making sure all pieces are covered. Cook for approximately 30 seconds, turning while cooking. Remove chips with sieve when they're rigid, but before they start turning brown. Let drain on dish or cookie sheet covered with paper towels. Salt to taste.

Trail Mix

Proportions don't matter much with trail mix. No matter what proportions you use, the result should taste good. It also doesn't matter much if you omit one or two of the ingredients.

dried fruit (apples, cranberries, bananas, pineapple, mango, etc.)
unsalted nuts (almost any kind)
date pieces
raisins
unsalted sunflower seeds

Desserts

Apple-Pear Crisp

Filling

5 apples or 5 pears
1 lemon, juice of
3 tablespoons vanilla
1 tablespoon cinnamon
1 tablespoon powdered ginger
1 teaspoon nutmeg
1 teaspoon allspice

Optional Ingredients

1 cup maple syrup, agave nectar, or brown sugar

Core and slice apples and pears (peeling is not necessary if organic). In a mixing bowl, mix sliced fruit with remaining ingredients until every piece of fruit is covered. Place into greased baking pans in an even layer.

Topping

2 cups rolled oats
2 cups whole wheat flour

1 tablespoon cinnamon
1 tablespoon nutmeg
1 tablespoon allspice
2 teaspoons ground cloves
1/4 cup vegan margarine

Optional Ingredients

1/4 cup maple syrup, molasses, brown sugar, or
    agave nectar
5 tablespoons vanilla
1 teaspoon salt

In a large bowl, mix the oats, flour, and spices. Break margarine into small pieces and work into the dry mixture with your hands. Mix syrup and vanilla together, then add to the topping and mix very well. Crumble the topping over the fruit in the baking pans and bake in oven at 350 degrees for at least 1 hour, until the topping is golden brown, the fruit is soft, and there is liquid on the bottom. Serve hot with nondairy ice cream or sherbet.

Baked Apples

6 apples (one per person)
1 cup brown or turbinado sugar
1 tablespoon ground cinnamon

Optional Ingredients

1/2 cup lemon juice
1 teaspoon nutmeg
1/2 to 1 cup walnut pieces

Preheat oven to 350 degrees. Lightly grease covered baking dish. Cut apples in half and place cut side up in baking dish. Mix brown sugar with cinnamon and nutmeg. Sprinkle lemon juice on apples, then crumble on brown sugar mix and, if using, walnut pieces. Cover baking dish, bake for half an hour and serve.

Cranberry Stuffed Bell Peppers

6 large red, orange, or yellow bell peppers (not
    green ones)
1-1/2 to 2 pounds cranberries (fresh or frozen)

Core bell peppers, stuff with cranberries (if using frozen cranberries, allow to thaw first), put on grill, turning frequently, until bell peppers are soft. Remove from grill and wait one or two minutes before serving.

To make even sweeter, add a teaspoon of brown sugar or dark agave syrup to each of the cored and stuffed bell peppers prior to grilling. If you use brown sugar, it'd be easier to mix in one teaspoon per serving (per bell pepper) with the cranberries prior to stuffing.

Bread

Uprising Bread for The Change We Knead!
(four loaves)

2 tablespoons dry yeast
5 cups hot water
1/2 cup oil
1/2 cup warm water
2 tablespoons salt
1/2 cup organic sugar or apple juice
12 cups organic whole wheat, organic unbleached white flour or organic rice flour (or 7 cups whole wheat flour & 5 cups white flour or any combination of flours adding up to 12 cups)
1 tray ice cubes (if using conventional oven)

Sprinkle yeast into 1/2 cup warm water. It should not be even close to boiling when adding the yeast or the bread will not rise. Let stand 10–15 minutes. Add 1 tablespoon of sugar or juice to the warm water and yeast. Slowly combine the remaining 4-1/2 cups hot water with 7 cups flour in a large bowl. Add salt, oil, sugar, and prepared yeast to mixture and blend thoroughly. Continue mixing until well blended. Continue to add flour and water until it is a ball of dough.

Knead the dough for 10 minutes or until it has a consistency like cookie dough. You may add flour as you go. A stickier dough will result in moister bread. Oil hands and divide dough into four parts and place in greased pans. Cover loaves with damp cloth or pot lid and let rise until they've gained at least a third in bulk. This should take one to two hours.

Toward the end of this time, preheat your oven to 375 degrees. Place pans on top shelf and a ceramic or pyrex dish containing the ice cubes on the bottom shelf. Bake for approximately 35 to 50 minutes.

If using a solar oven, place lids on the pans or insert an empty loaf pan on top of each loaf of dough.

Place in solar oven by 11 a.m. Cook 4 to 6 hours, periodically turning over towards the sun. As the aroma of baked bread drifts from the oven you know it won't be long before it is time to unlock the oven to remove your four loaves. Remember the bread pans will be hot enough to burn your fingers so use pot holders to lift the pans out of your oven.

Drinks

Sun Tea

1/3 to 1/2 ounce loose tea or 8 to 12 tea bags per gallon

Fill a gallon jar with fresh water and put in the tea bags or loose tea—obviously, the more you put in the stronger the tea will be. Put the jar out in the sun and let it sit for a few hours. Serve it hot, or take it out of the sun, let it cool, then refrigerate it and serve it cold. The most refreshing teas are mint, hibiscus, darjeeling, oolong, and green.

Tofu Smoothy

5 cups fruit (any type; a mixture is better than a single type)
½ pound soft tofu
1 cup water

Optional/Alternative Ingredients

1/2 cup nondairy vanilla protein powder (good in addition to tofu, but can be used in place of it)
1/4 teaspoon vanilla (if not using vanilla protein powder)

Cut the fruit into chunks. Add the fruit to water and soft tofu in a blender or food processor. Blend until smooth. Add more water if necessary to bring to right consistency.

COOKING
FOR LARGE GROUPS

Cooking for large numbers of people can be very intimidating. It is very different to cook a dinner for six at home than to cook for several hundred people; but don't be overwhelmed. It can be done, and with the right equipment and a few skills it can be easier and more fun than you might think.

It isn't necessary to make huge pots of two or three items, although that is one way to provide hundreds of people with a meal. Your group can make a variety of foods, dishing out five or six items to each person. It can be surprising how many hundreds of people you can feed when you prepare different dishes.

Equipment

The first task is getting together a few people who are willing to help with food preparation, transportation, and serving. These are not jobs to be done alone. The second task is acquiring the proper equipment. Most people don't have five or ten gallon pots or extra-large mixing bowls in their kitchens. However, most churches do, as do many community centers, food service programs, and restaurants. Sometimes, one or more of these organizations will allow you to borrow their equipment; at other times, you might have to buy it. Used restaurant equipment stores, going-out-of-business auctions, and rummage or yard sales are excellent places to obtain the necessary cooking tools.

You can start by getting a few very large pots, large bowls or plastic buckets, large spoons, and a cutting board and knife for each cook. You should be able to find most of this at yard sales or thrift stores, but you might have to buy some of it retail. In general, the more time you have to gather equipment, the less you'll have to buy from restaurant supply or other stores.

In general, the equipment you'll need will include:

- 2 or 3 very large pots
- 2 or 3 large cast iron skillets (or woks)
- Several large bowls
- Large kitchen spoons and ladles
- Several large knives
- Several cutting boards
- Several various sized plastic containers with lids
- 1 bread box with lid and attached pair of tongs
- 1 large coffee urn with spout
- 1 or 2 large ice chests or coolers
- 1 or 2 propane 2-burner or 3-burner stoves
- 3 large plastic bins
- Sponges or cloths
- 1 or more portable tables
- 1 or more banner(s)
- Personal eating utensils (plates, bowls, cups, spoons, forks, and napkins)

For one-off large events, it might make sense to use disposable utensils, though there are obvious environmental drawbacks to this. However, using paper products made from post-consumer waste paper, avoiding styrofoam, and collecting used plasticware for recycling mitigates these problems.

If you'll be doing ongoing events, it makes much more sense, both economically and environmentally, to buy large numbers of durable plastic plates, bowls, and metal flatware from flea markets and yard sales at very low prices, cheap enough that if you lose a few at each event it won't matter much. Even though these items will need to be washed during or after each meal in a sanitary way, it is a great way to inspire a move away from a disposable society.

Portable tables are another story. You can get six-foot portable tables at most building supply stores. They even have ones that fold into a three-foot

121

square. To save money, ask if they have one they have already been using for display and ask if they would be willing to mark it down. A forty-dollar table can become a twenty dollar table just by asking. Another way to make a sturdy portable table is to use a plain, hollow core interior door (without the doorknob) and a pair of sawhorses made from metal joiners and lumber. The material for the saw horses can be bought at a hardware store or lumberyard for less than fifteen dollars, and hollow core doors are easy to find at used building supply stores; often you can find most of this material for free on craigslist. A hollow core door is very light, and the joiners allow the sawhorse legs to be easily assembled and disassembled, allowing easy set-up, takedown, and transportation. Some groups have used plastic milk or drink crates and have stacked them to table height. However, even if you found the crates discarded in an alley, the police can still arrest you for possession of "stolen" property if there are dairy company names or other identifying marks on the crates, so we recommend against using them.

Tips on Cooking for Large Numbers

Cooking for 100 is not much different from cooking for 10, except that most of the quantities are 10 times greater. However, for a few things this is not true. Spices and salt in particular should not just be multiplied when increasing the size of a recipe. Proportionally, much less is needed in most dishes—let your taste buds be your guide.

In group cooking, it can be useful to have a "bottom liner" who adds the spices so that the dishes are not over spiced. Every once in a while, a group will find that four or five volunteers are all adding pepper, salt or another popular spice, and before long, the meal is inedible. The same is true for the amount of preparation time each dish requires: the larger the volume, the more efficient you'll be, so overall prep time will be relatively small. When a particular ingredient is in several dishes on the menu, prep enough of this ingredient for all the dishes at the same time. This can often be done for events that last several days, depending on your available storage space and labor.

If you need to feed a lot of people in a hurry at an event lasting for hours or days, start with soup. While it is heating, start chopping and adding vegetables, and add spices. Once the vegetables start to soften, remove half the soup and serve it. With the remaining half, add more water and vegetables, check it for spice balance, add a little more if necessary, and keep cooking. This can go on indefinitely creating a never-ending pot of soup.

This same concept can be used when the stove is too small for several large soup pots. Follow the normal recipe for vegetable soup, and when the vegetables have been added and the broth just begins to boil, drain off most of the broth and save it in another container. Add more vegetables and a small amount of water to the first pot and continue cooking. This pot should now contain enough vegetables and spices for two or more pots of soup, but little broth. When the vegetables are cooked, mix them and the broth you've set aside in several containers and transport to the serving site. This can make two or more pots worth of soup using only one cooking pot and only a little more time. If you have tofu, wheat gluten or tempeh, you can sauté that in another pan and keep adding that to the soup as the day goes along.

Field Kitchens

Preparing to feed hundreds of people at strikes, blockades, occupations, or during relief operations is a challenge, but not impossible. Several key issues must be resolved.

Water

The first priority is a source of fresh water. You may be able to access water from a hose tap on a nearby building. Pliers, vice grips, or a tap key can come in handy in this case. You may need to access water from a nearby restaurant, grocery, hotel, or other commercial establishment. This may require some diplomacy and gentle persuasion.

In emergencies, you may need to open a fire hydrant or even tap into an irrigation system. At times you may need to haul water from one of these sources because none of them are located near the place that is best for your field kitchen.

No matter where you obtain water, you will need containers to collect, transport, and store it. You can buy, borrow, or find plastic containers such as insulated plastic ice chests, five-gallon water jugs, or buckets. You may be able to borrow or rent a water truck. This can be a huge asset at large and ongoing events.

OCCUPATION KITCHEN

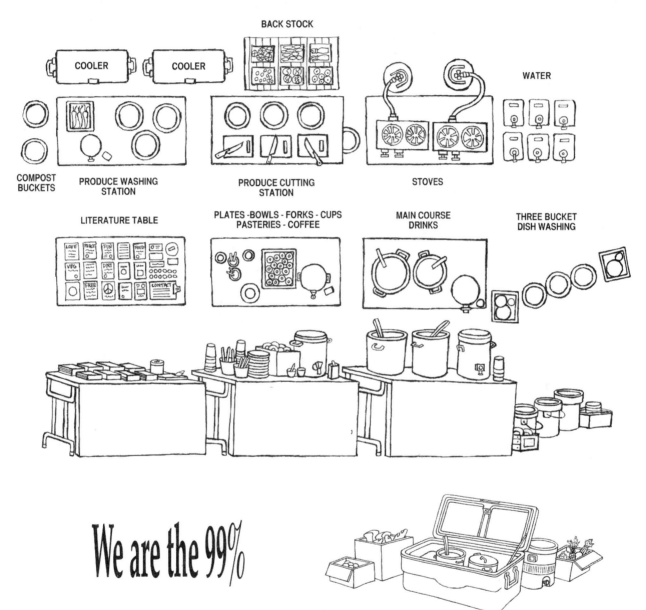

Fire

It's fairly cheap to acquire propane stoves and five-gallon propane tanks. You can get the tanks from hardware stores, groceries, or gas stations. You may also have local propane distribution companies or be able to find refills at RV campgrounds.

In emergencies, if you can't buy propane you can use wood, coal, or solar ovens. If logs and sticks are not available you may need to collect paper, cardboard, and scrap wood from pallets to make your fire. If using coal or wood, it is wise to wipe dish soap on the outside of your cooking pots to make it easier to clean off the soot from the fire.

Kitchen layout

There are several factors in kitchen layout. The first consideration is the location. It's usually very helpful to set up your field kitchen near the place where you plan to share food. Find a location where you are close to the action, which should reduce logistical problems. If you are providing meals at a rally, concert, or occupation you can seek a location on the edge of the event as close to your source of water as possible while still in view of those participating in the event. One advantage of this is that you can often recruit additional help for your kitchen, since people can see that they can help out and at the same time feel connected to the action. This also provides a chance for you and the other volunteer cooks to have dialog with those who came to participate in the event.

Interference from the authorities or other factors may make it necessary to set up your kitchen at some distance from the action. But try to be as close to it as you can, set up your serving area near the event, and organize volunteers to make regular deliveries to this remote serving location. If this is the case, those delivering the food should probably return to the kitchen with dirty dishes, forks, spoons, empty pots, and trash.

Once you determine the location of your field kitchen, you'll need to consider the layout. You may want to set up a row of tables or prep stations that relate to the type of food you expect to prepare. One table or area could be dedicated to garlic, onions, or leeks. Another for hard vegetables such as potatoes, turnips, carrots, and other root vegetables. A third area or table could be dedicated to softer vegetables, and yet a fourth area could be set aside for the preparation of fruit, or you could have a table dedicated to making bread and other baked goods. This is determined by what type of food you're serving. After setting out the tables or prep areas you can set out cutting boards and knives at each place where you expect a volunteer. You can also provide a bowl or bucket for the cut produce at every station. You can also provide compost buckets at strategic locations so those preparing the produce can discard food waste.

Serving Area

Consider the logistics of your serving area. Determine the direction that people will take along your serving line. Is there a direction people will be arriving from, or do you want people to move in a particular direction?

Here are a few things that can help with the flow and logistics of your serving area. First, it's necessary to place the plates, bowls, and utensils at the beginning of the line. It's also often good to share your tossed salad first, followed by rice, beans or pasta, followed by whatever you'll serve on top of your grains, beans, or pasta. You can share soup in bowls or cups after you fill the guests' plates so they spend as little time as possible in line with a liquid that could spill. If you have pastries, bread, and fruit salads, it's good to place them toward the end of the line, so people will have their plates filled with more nutritious food before they get to the comfort foods. It's also helpful to have your salad dressing, salt, and other condiments located away from the serving line. If you have your condiments with the stack of plates, bowls, and utensils, or with the foods they're intended to season, people will slow down the line as they add condiments.

Drinks Area

It's often a good idea to have a table or area dedicated to drinks. You'll need to provide cups even if you've asked those attending to bring their own, as not everyone will remember to do so.

Wash Station

You could provide disposable paper plates and utensils, but this is wasteful and can limit you to providing as many meals as you have paper products for. You have no limit to the number of people you can feed if you use reusable plates, bowls, cups, and utensils, because you can continue washing them as they are used by setting up a three-basin wash station. Start with a compost bucket immediately prior to the wash station. Its first basin or bucket contains soapy water; the second contains water with a disinfectant such as chlorine, vinegar, or other sterilizing agent; and the third basin contains rinse water. Provide a draining station for the washed dishes; don't put them out again while they're still wet.

You should provide a way for cooks and those coming to eat to wash their hands. This could be set up at the same area or table as the station for washing dishes. Hand soap and towels for drying hands are also good.

124

Field Kitchen Equipment

- Two or three 2- or 3-burner propane stoves
- Two to four 165-quart coolers or ice chests
- Four 5-gallon propane tanks
- Ten to twenty 6 foot by 3 foot folding tables
- One or two pop-up tents
- Twenty 5-gallon buckets, some with lids
- Ten mixing bowls
- One 26-inch wok
- Five to ten pots from 30 to 60 quarts with lids
- Two 2-quart sauce pans

Kitchen Box

The kitchen box holds the equipment you will need to prepare food. This can include:

- 10 to 20 cutting boards
- 10 to 20 kitchen knives
- 5 to 10 large spoons
- 1 long paddle for big pots
- Latex or plastic gloves
- One or two graters
- One or two colanders
- One or two tongs
- Two to four spatulas

Serving Box

The serving box contains the items you'll need to share your meals.

- Four to six tongs
- Five to ten serving spoons
- Two to four ladles
- Four bread knives
- Two to four spatulas
- Serving bowls
- Four to six hotel-type trays
- Condiments, salt, pepper, salad dressing, salsa, mustard, catsup, nutritional yeast, soy sauce or liquid amino sauce
- Flatware for 50 to 100
- Fifty to 100 plates
- Fifty to 100 bowls
- Fifty to 100 cups
- Sponges

> "All authoritarian organizations are organized as pyramids: the state, the private or public corporation, the army, the police, the church, the university, the hospital; they are all pyramidal structures with a small group of decision-makers at the top and a broad base of people whose decisions are *made for them* at the bottom. Anarchism does not demand the changing of the labels on the layers, it doesn't want different people on top, it wants us to clamber out from underneath."
>
> —Colin Ward, *Anarchy in Action*

Food Handling and Storage

There are health and safety concerns related to food handling and storage. Keep the length of time that you handle or store food as short as possible. If you do not handle any animal products and if the length of time between food pickup and delivery is a matter of hours rather than days, there is almost no danger. Keep the food in a cool, dry place out of the sun, and wash your hands before handling it. Always wash vegetables before cooking them. If you are out in the field, this can be accomplished by having a five gallon bucket of water into which you dip and scrub produce. Obviously, anybody who has a cold or the flu should not prepare or serve food until they are well.

After events, there is sometimes leftover food. Try to donate this to a local soup kitchen, shelter, or group home rather than trying to find ways to store and refrigerate it. In general, the longer food is stored the less nutritious and more susceptible to spoilage it becomes. It also requires additional energy to keep food refrigerated or frozen. Meanwhile, the food industry continues to produce more surplus every day. If you have no one to donate your prepared food to, divide it up among the volunteers and take it home.

A number of anarchist groups have placed refrigerators in places with public access to provide a

125

> "The principle at issue is that a man may be said to have a right to what he produces by his own labour, but not to what he gets from the labour of others; he has a right to what he needs and uses, but not to what he does not need and cannot use. As soon as a man has more than enough, it either goes to waste or it stops another man having enough.
>
> This means that rich men have no right to their property, for they are rich not because they work a lot but because a lot of people work for them; and poor men have a right to rich men's property, for they are poor not because they work little, but because they work for others. Indeed, poor people almost always work longer hours at duller jobs in worse conditions than rich people. No one ever became rich or remained rich through his own labour, only by exploiting the labour of others."
>
> —Nicolas Walter, *About Anarchism*

temperature by the time you serve them. If storing, use refrigerators or coolers. Volunteers who smoke should wait to do so until they are finished cooking or serving the meal, and should remember to wash their hands before returning to cook or share food. Washing your hands with soap and warm water after going to the toilet is absolutely essential; it's dangerously irresponsible not to do so.

Simple low-tech practices, such as washing our produce and our hands and preparing only vegan meals shortly before serving, protect the community we are feeding.

way for people to help themselves between meals. In some locations the low temperatures during winter make it possible to store food on enclosed porches or in basements using the spaces as natural refrigerators. In warm climates, shade is important for items you intend to keep from becoming warm, even if just while you are sharing a meal.

Follow these simple steps to make sure your meals are always safe. First, make sure all food is vegan or vegetarian and serve it as quickly as possible, before harmful bacteria have a chance to grow. Bacteria multiply most rapidly between 40° and 140°, a range known as the food temperature danger zone; after only two or three hours in this zone, bacteria may start to become a safety issue, particularly if the meal includes meat or dairy. Your meals should leave the stove above 140° and still be at that

RECIPES

FOR LARGE GROUPS

Breakfast

Oatmeal for 100

Need: 24 quart cooking pot
Prep time: 1 minute
Cooking Time: 10 to12 minutes

3 gallons water
1 cup vanilla
1 cup maple syrup, molasses, dark
    agave nectar, bananas, raisins or apple cider
2 tablespoon salt
12 pounds rolled oats

Optional Ingredients

10 cups raisins or chopped apples
8 cups shredded coconut
4 tablespoons nutmeg

Bring water to a boil in a large pot. Add oats. When again boiling, add remaining ingredients, return to a boil, then turn to low heat. Stir often. Cook for 2 to 5 minutes. Remove from heat. You can serve with margarine and sweetener or substitute bananas or apple juice to sweeten the oatmeal.

Granola for 100
(makes about 40 pounds of granola)

Need: large mixing bowl; medium saucepan;
    several flat baking trays
Preheat oven to 300 degrees
Prep Time: 30 minutes
Bake time: 45 to 60 minutes

10 pounds rolled oats
10 pounds barley flakes (or wheat or rye flakes)
5 pounds almonds
5 pounds shredded coconut
2 pounds sunflower seeds
1 pound sesame seeds
3 pints cooking oil (sunflower, safflower)
5 cups maple syrup, molasses or
dark agave nectar, bananas, raisins or apple cider
1/2 cup vanilla
5 pounds raisins or chopped apples
1 tablespoon salt (optional)

Mix dry ingredients together in a large bowl. In a saucepan, heat oil, maple syrup and vanilla only until warm enough to soak into the dry ingredients. Pour this mixture over the dry ingredients and mix throughly, then spread onto several flat baking trays. The layer of granola should be no more than 1-inch thick. Toast in a 300 degrees oven for 15 to 20 minutes, stirring every few minutes. Granola is done when golden brown. Mix in raisins at this point. When cool, serve granola with soy milk or fruit juice and sliced fresh fruit.

Scrambled Tofu for 24

Equipment: very large skillet
Prep time: 15 minutes
Cooking time: 30 to 40 minutes

2 or 3 bulbs garlic, pressed
5 onions, chopped
10 pounds tofu
3 tablespoons turmeric
1/4 cup garlic powder
1/4 cup tamari or soy sauce

2 cups nutritional yeast
1 cup sesame seeds
olive oil

Heat a very large skillet. Sauté garlic for 30 seconds, then add onions and sauté until clear. Squeeze tofu like a sponge until all excess water is removed, then crumble into skillet and sauté until tofu starts to brown. Add turmeric, garlic powder, Tamari or soy sauce and nutritional yeast. Mix well and remove from heat. Serve hot with dry roasted sunflower and sesame seeds and/or ketchup. To dry roast sunflower and sesame seeds, heat a dry, clean skillet and add enough sunflower seeds to cover bottom. Stir constantly once they start to brown. They may smoke some but keep stirring until both sides of most seeds are brown. Then add sesame seeds. Keep stirring. The sesame seeds will start to pop, and some will pop right out of the skillet. Roast the sesame seeds for 1 to 2 minutes more, until the popping starts to decrease. Remove seeds from skillet immediately and let cool in a metal or ceramic bowl. Tamari or soy sauce can be added to the seeds at the very end, if desired.

Homefries for 100

Equipment: 40 quart pot and 1 very large skillet
Preheat oven: 150 degrees
Prep time: 2 hours (parboiled potatoes)
Cooking time: 1 hour 15 minutes

6 gallons water
100 potatoes, washed and cubed or cut in strips
1/4 cup salt

In a very large pot (40 quart or larger), bring water to a boil. Carefully add potatoes so there is no splashing and bring to a second boil. Continue boiling until potatoes just start to turn soft, after about 10 to 15 minutes. Drain and cool, or immediately sauté. Cool potatoes by running cold water over them in a colander or just fill the pot with cold water after draining it.

1 pint olive oil
4 bulbs garlic, diced
15 onions, chopped
4 cups nutritional yeast
2 cups tamari or soy sauce
1 cup cumin

Over high heat, sauté about 3 tablespoon of diced garlic for 30 seconds. Add about 2 cups of onions and sauté until clear, which takes about 3 to 5 minutes; stir often. Then add enough potatoes to fill the skillet and fry until they start to brown. Keep stirring and scrape the bottom of the skillet occasionally. Sprinkle in some of the yeast, cumin, and tamari or soy sauce while stirring. (Hint: mix tamari or soy sauce with equal parts water for more even distribution when sprinkling.) Mix well and empty skillet into a large metal serving bowl. Place in a 150 degree oven to keep warm. Repeat the process until all the potatoes are cooked or everyone is fed. Serve homefries hot with dry roasted sunflower and sesame seeds and/or ketchup.

Lunch and Dinner

Tofu Sandwich Spread for 100

Equipment: medium mixing bowl, very large mixing bowl
Prep time: 2 hours

3 cups miso
3 cups water
8 cups tahini
25 pounds crumbled tofu (firm is best; other types will work)
25 lemons, juice of

Optional Ingredients

2 tablespoons cumin or coriander
1/2 cup garlic powder
8 cups diced onion
8 cups diced celery
3 cups Alaria, Dulse, Kelp, Nori, or other seaweed

In the medium bowl, mix the miso and water into a smooth paste, then add tahini to the mix (add additional water to make a smooth, creamy paste). Drain tofu of excess water and crumble by hand into the very large bowl. Squeeze the lemon juice over the tofu. Add miso/tahini mixture, and mix well. Add optional ingredients, if desired, and spread on your favorite bread with lettuce, sprouts, and tomato slices.

Vegan Tuna-like Tofu Spread

Crush seaweed into the tofu spread to give it a tuna-like taste. You can use alaria, dulse, kelp, nori, or any other edible seaweed.

(Harvesting seaweed yourself can be rewarding, but it's important to stay clear of areas where the seaweed could be contaminated with oil, radiation, or other toxins.)

Rice and Beans in one pot for 100

Equipment: 40 quart pot with a tight fitting lid
Prep time: 30 minutes
Cooking time: 50 minutes

8 gallons water
1/4 cup salt
4 cups cumin or coriander
1/4 cup black pepper
10 pounds pinto beans (soak the night before)
15 pounds long-grain brown rice (dry)
10 onions, chopped

Bring water to a boil in a 40 quart pot with a tight fitting lid. Add beans and boil for 45 minutes, then add rice and spices. Bring to a rapid boil again, stir once, being sure to stir the beans up from the bottom. Then cover, reduce to very low heat and let simmer for another 45 minutes. Do not stir or open cover until it is done so the rice is fluffy. Remove from heat and serve hot, plain or with cooked vegetables or tomato sauce.

Tomato Sauce with Vegetables for 100

Equipment: 24 quart pot with a lid
Prep time: 1 hour
Cooking time: 1 hour or more

1 cup olive oil
1 bulb garlic, diced
10 onions, chopped
10 pounds canned tomatoes
10 pounds assorted vegetables, chopped finely
2 tablespoons basil
2 tablespoons thyme
10 bay leaves
2 tablespoons sea salt
2 tablespoons black pepper

Heat a heavy, 24 quart pot and add oil. Add garlic and sauté for 30 seconds. Add onions and spices and sauté until onions are clear. Add tomatoes, bay leaves, salt and pepper. Chop any vegetables you have on hand, especially broccoli, green peppers, beets, carrots, mushrooms, eggplant and so on, and add to the sauce. Cover and simmer on medium-low heat for at least 1 hour, stirring occasionally. Add salt, if you desire. Serve over rice, pasta, bread, or use as a base for vegan chili.

Trident Subs for 100

Equipment: 20 quart or larger pot
Prep time: 30 minutes
Cooking time: 1 hour or longer

2 bulbs garlic, diced
8 to 12 onions, chopped
1/2 cup olive oil
1 tablespoon thyme
2 teaspoons cayenne powder
2 tablespoons sea salt
2 tablespoons black pepper
3 or 4 16-oz cans tomatoes, or 15 to 20 fresh tomatoes, chopped
4 to 6 squash (zucchini, summer, etc., with soft skins)
12 to 15 of any root vegetable (carrots, potatoes, etc.)
2 bunches any dark green leafy vegetable (collards, kale, spinach, etc.)
2 or 3 cabbages or 5 or 6 eggplants
100 sandwich rolls

Sauté the chopped garlic and onions in a dry pan or in oil over medium high heat in a 20 quart or larger pot until the onions become clear. Add spices, then all the chopped vegetables and either fresh or canned tomatoes. (If you do not have any tomatoes, add a little water to start the vegetables cooking.) Stir often to prevent sticking. Once the liquid in the bottom starts to boil, lower heat to medium low. Cook until the vegetables are soft and the sauce is thick like stew, usually about 1 hour, but simmering longer enhances the taste. Adjust seasonings, especially salt, pepper, and cayenne. Serve on a sandwich roll, bread, or brown rice. We call this a trident sub because it is spicy "hot"!

Hummus for 100

Equipment: 40 quart pot, very large mixing bowl
Cooking time: 2 hours
Prep time: 2 hours

20 pounds cooked garbanzos (chickpeas)
3 tablespoons sea salt
20 cups tahini
50 lemons, juice of
2 bulbs garlic, diced
6 gallons water

Optional Ingredients

10 cups diced fresh parsley
4 cups diced onions
1 cup toasted sesame oil

Soak garbanzos overnight. (They will double in volume, so fill the container with water to twice their level.) Drain the water and place garbanzos in a 40 quart pot with 6 gallons of fresh water. Salt, and bring to a rapid boil over high heat. Reduce heat and simmer for at least 1 hour (or until garbanzos are easily mashed between fingers—remove from pot and let cool before doing this). In a very large bowl, combine all ingredients, and then mash garbanzos until smooth. Combine. (Alternatively, place all ingredients into a food processor or blender, and blend until smooth.) Be sure to add water as necessary to create a creamy consistency. Let cool and serve as a sandwich in pita bread with sprouts and/ or lettuce and cucumbers, or as a dip for cut vegetables and wedges of pita bread. If used as a dip, sprinkle paprika over top. If using oil, drip it on top.

Macaroni and Cheeseless for 90

Equipment: 40 quart pot, very large mixing bowl,
   3 12" x 18"baking pans
Preheat oven: 350 degrees
Prep time: 1 hour 30 minutes
Baking time: 30 minutes

Elbow Macaroni

8 gallons water
5 tablespoons sea salt
20 pounds elbow macaroni

Bring the water to a rapid boil in a 40 quart pot. Add macaroni and return to a boil. If you use salt, you can add it to the boiling water. Cook for about 10 minutes. Macaroni ought to be *al dente* or firm, but not hard; do not overcook. Drain and rinse with cold water until all macaroni is rinsed and cold, then set aside.

Cheeseless

36 cups nutritional yeast
12 cups unbleached white flour
1/2 cup garlic powder
1/2 cup sea salt
4-1/2 gallons boiling water
6 pounds vegan margarine
1 cup wet mustard

In a large mixing bowl, combine nutritional yeast, flour, garlic powder, and salt. Mix well. Add boiling water, 1 quart at a time, using a whisk to stir. Add mustard and margarine and mix well.

Place the prepared macaroni in the baking pans. Cover with cheeseless sauce, making sure to coat each piece of macaroni. Sprinkle toasted sesame seeds or bread crumbs over the top, and bake at 350 degrees for 30 minutes or until the mac and cheeseless is hot and bubbling. Serve hot.

(This dish freezes well.)

Cauliflower Curry for 100

Equipment: large skillet, large metal serving bowl
Pre-heated oven: 150 degrees
Prep time: 1 hour 15 minutes
Cooking time: 1 hour 20 minutes

1 cup olive oil
3 bulbs garlic, diced
20 onions, chopped
24 heads cauliflower (1 case), chopped
4 cups curry powder
1 cup cumin
1 cup tamari
4 tablespoons white pepper

Sauté the diced garlic for 30 seconds at high heat. Add the 20 chopped onions and sauté until clear, which should take about 3 to 5 minutes. Stir often. Add enough cauliflower to fill the skillet, and fry until it starts to brown. Keep stirring, and scrape the bottom of the skillet occasionally. While stirring, sprinkle in some of the curry, cumin, pepper, and tamari. (Hint: mix tamari with equal parts water for more even distribution when sprinkling.) Mix well and empty the skillet into a large metal serving bowl. Place in a 150-degree oven to keep warm and repeat the process until all the cauliflower is cooked. Serve hot over brown rice.

Brown Rice for 100

Equipment: 20 quart pot with a tight fitting lid
Prep time: 30 minutes
Cooking time: 50 minutes

3 gallons water
3 tablespoons sea salt (optional)
15 pounds long grain brown rice

Bring water to a boil in a 20 quart pot with a tight-fitting lid. Add rice and bring to a rapid second boil. If using salt, add it to the water. Stir once, cover and reduce heat to very low. Let simmer for exactly 40 minutes. Do not uncover or stir until done so it will be fluffy. You can add 1 quart of water if cooking at high altitudes, and turn the heat off after 30 minutes.

Potato-Pea Curry for 100

Equipment: 40 quart pot, large skillet, large metal
    serving bowl
Preheat oven: 150 degrees
Prep time: 2 hours
Parboiling potatoes: 1 hour 15 minutes
Cooking time: 1 hour 15 minutes

Parboiled Potatoes

6 gallons boiling water
1/4 cup sea salt (optional)
100 potatoes, washed and cubed

In a very large pot (40 quart or larger), bring water to a boil (approximately 1 hour). If using salt, add it to water. Carefully add potatoes so there is no splashing and bring to a second boil. Boil until potatoes turn soft or about 15 to 25 minutes. Drain.

Curry for 100

2 cups olive oil
4 bulbs garlic, diced
15 onions, diced
6 cups nutritional yeast
6 cups curry powder
4 tablespoons sea salt
25 pounds fresh or frozen peas
6 pounds vegan margarine

Sauté 4 bulbs of diced garlic for 30 seconds over high heat. Add onions and sauté until clear or about 3 to 5 minutes. Add yeast and curry. If using salt, add it too. Stir often. Add enough potatoes (already prepared) to fill the skillet. Mix well. (You can add a little water, if needed.) When the spices are throughly mixed with the potatoes, add two packages of frozen peas and 1 stick of margarine. After the margarine has melted and is mixed in, empty skillet into a large metal serving bowl. Place in a 150-degree oven to keep warm and repeat the process until all the spices, potatoes, and peas are mixed together. Serve hot.

Tofu-Spinach Lasagna for 100

1 cup olive oil
2 bulbs garlic, diced
10 onions, chopped
10 16-oz cans of tomatoes
2 tablespoons sea salt
3 tablespoons oregano
2 tablespoons basil
2 tablespoons thyme
10 bay leaves
2 tablespoons black pepper

Sauté garlic in a heavy 24 quart saucepan for 30 seconds. Add onions and spices, and sauté until onions are clear. Add tomatoes, bay leaves, pepper. and salt. Cover and simmer on medium-low heat for 30 minutes, stirring occasionally. Add water, if needed.

Filling

1 cup olive oil
1 bulb garlic, diced
10 onions, chopped
20 pounds tofu, drained

20 10-oz boxes of frozen spinach or about 12
      pounds fresh spinach
3 tablespoons thyme
2 tablespoons basil
3 tablespoons oregano
2 cups tamari

Sauté diced garlic for 30 seconds over high heat in a skillet. Add about 2 cups of onions and sauté until clear, or about 3 to 5 minutes, stirring often. Add enough tofu to fill the skillet and fry until it starts to brown. Keep stirring and scrape the bottom of the skillet occasionally. While stirring, sprinkle in some of the thyme, oregano, basil and tamari; then add thawed, drained spinach. Mix well and cook until the excess water evaporates. Empty skillet into a large metal mixing bowl. Repeat the process until all the tofu is cooked. Mix all the tofu and spinach thoroughly and set aside.

Noodles

4 gallons water
2 tablespoons sea salt (optional)
5 pounds lasagna noodles

Bring the water to a boil in a 20 quart pot, and cook the noodles about 10 minutes, following the directions on the boxes. If using salt, add it to the water. Noodles ought to be *al dente* (still firm when bitten); do not overcook. Drain and rinse with cold water and set aside.

Soy cheese

20 pounds soy cheese (mozzarella style), grated (add more soy cheese if you like)

Place a thin layer of tomato sauce in the bottom of each baking pan and place one layer of noodles over the sauce, completely covering the bottom. Place a layer of tofu-spinach mixture over the noodles and then sprinkle about 2 cups of soy cheese evenly over it. Cover completely with noodles. Place a generous layer of sauce over these noodles and repeat, starting with the mixture and ending with sauce. Sprinkle remaining soy cheese over top and bake at 350 degrees for 1 hour or until soy cheese starts to brown. Remove from oven and let stand for about 15 minutes before serving. The cheeseless sauce from the Macaroni and Cheeseless recipe can be used as a substitute for the soy cheese.

Salads

Tossed Salad for 100

Equipment: very large mixing bowl, smaller serving
      bowl
Prep time: 2 to 3 hours

8 heads lettuce, torn
10 pounds carrots, chopped or shredded
3 bunches celery, chopped
20 tomatoes, chopped
2 heads red cabbage, shredded
20 bell peppers, chopped
10 cucumbers, sliced

Optional Ingredients

3 cups sunflower seeds
8 cups alfalfa, sunflower or other sprouts
5 cups tempeh cubed sautéed in olive oil until
      crispy brown (tofu if you don't have tempe)
3 cups cranberries

Wash all vegetables and chop into bite-size pieces. (For ease of tossing and transporting, use 30 gallon plastic food storage bags, but be sure to double them to be on the safe side.) Use additional ingredients which might be on hand such as broccoli, cauliflower, onions, zucchini, beets, mushrooms, spinach, sprouts, apples, raisins, sunflower seeds, cooked whole beans (such as garbanzos, kidney beans, and green peas), and so on. Use a smaller salad bowl for serving and only dress the salad in that bowl. Keep the rest on ice or refrigerated. Salad will keep overnight if undressed.

Carrot Raisin Salad for 100

Equipment: large mixing bowl
Prep time: 1 to 2 hours

25 pounds carrots
6 pounds raisins
10 cups nondairy mayonnaise
20 lemons, juice of

Grate carrots, then mix all ingredients in a large mixing bowl. Serve cold.

You can make you own nondairy mayonnaise by blending 10 pounds of tofu with lemon juice, vinegar, and two teaspoons of garlic powder. You can add a touch of olive oil, if you wish.

Coleslaw for 100

Equipment: large mixing bowl
Prep time: 1 hour

5–10 pounds carrots, grated
15 cups nondairy mayonnaise
1 tablespoon sea salt (optional)
10 heads green cabbage, shredded
2–4 lemons, juice of
1 tablespoon black pepper

Shred cabbage and grate carrots, then mix all ingredients in a very large mixing bowl and serve immediately. Serve cold.

Salad Dressings

Oil and Vinegar Dressing for 100

Equipment: 2 quart jars with lids
Prep time: 1 hour

8 cups olive oil
2 cups balsamic vinegar
10 lemons, juice of
4 tablespoons fresh garlic, diced
2 tablespoons thyme
2 tablespoons basil
2 tablespoons oregano
2 tablespoonssea salt (optional)
2 tablespoons black pepper
2 tablespoonsginger powder

Put half of all ingredients in each jar and shake well. Shake again before every serving. Variations include leaving out the oil, using only lemon juice and no vinegar; using tamari instead of salt; adding nutritional yeast; adding apple or orange juice, and so on. (Go ahead, be creative!)

Tahini-Lemon Dressing for 100

Equipment: blender or whisk
Prep time: 1 hour

10 cups tahini
10 lemons, juice of
2 cups nutritional yeast
4 tablespoons toasted sesame oil (optional)
10–15 cloves of garlic
4 cups water

Optional Ingredients

apple juice or cider

Place half of all ingredients in a blender and blend until smooth. Add more water, or lemon or apple juice as necessary, to make a thick, creamy dressing. Repeat.

Tofu Dill Dip for 100

Equipment: blender or whisk
Prep time: 1 hour 15 minutes

10 pounds tofu, drained
5 cups olive oil
2 cups vinegar
20 lemons, juice of
20 cloves garlic
10 onions
1 cup dill
2 tablespoons sea salt
2 teaspoons white pepper

Optional Ingredients

apple juice or cider

Squeeze tofu like a sponge to remove excess water, then crumble 2-1/2 pounds of it into a blender. Add 1 quarter each of the remaining ingredients. Blend until smooth, adding water or apple juice, as necessary to achieve a thick, creamy consistency. Repeat three more times. Chill and serve with cut vegetables or chips.

Soups

Miso Soup for 100

Equipment: 30 quart to 50 quart soup pot
Prep time: 40 minutes
Cooking time: 1 hour

1 cup olive oil
2 bulbs fresh garlic, diced
2 tablespoons thyme
2 tablespoons basil
4 gallons water
2 pounds miso

Optional Ingredients

1 tablespoon cayenne powder
2 cups arame (sea vegetable)
1 head cabbage, shredded
6 pounds tofu, cubed
4 cups chopped scallions

Sauté diced garlic and spices for 30 seconds in a soup pot. Add water and any combination of optional ingredients. Bring to a boil. Remove from heat. Pour 1 to 2 quarts of broth into a large mixing bowl, mix with miso paste (miso varies in strength so use about 2 to 3 tubs or pounds). When all the miso is smoothly mixed into the broth, pour into pot of vegetables, stir and serve. (Note: Do not boil the miso; this kills its beneficial microorganisms.)

Yellow-Pea Soup for 100

Equipment: 20 quart soup pot
Prep time: 1 hour
Cooking time: 1 hour or more

1/2 cup olive oil
2 bulbs garlic, diced
5 onions, chopped
2 tablespoons thyme
2 tablespoons basil
2 tablespoons oregano
3 gallons water
12 pounds yellow peas
2 pounds barley
3 tablespoons sea salt (optional)
1 tablespoon black pepper
10 potatoes, cubed
2 pounds carrots, chopped
2 heads celery, chopped

Sauté garlic for 30 seconds in a soup pot, then add onions and spices. Sauté until onions start to brown on their edges. Add peas and spices, stir until heated, then add water and barley and bring to a boil. If using salt, add it to water. Add chopped vegetables and bring to a second boil, then reduce heat to low and cover. Stir occasionally and simmer for 45 minutes or until peas are cooked to desired softness. Serve hot. (Note: The soup can simmer for as long as you like, if you continue adding water. It can also be made with any type of bean or combination of breans in place of the yellow peas.) For the grain, barley works best but rice, whole oats, wheat berries, or another whole grain will also work if you do not have barley.

Vegetable Soup for 100

Equipment: 30 quart soup pot
Prep time: 1 hour 30 minutes
Cooking time: 1 hour or more

1/2 cup olive oil
2 bulbs garlic, diced
12 onions, chopped
2 tablespoons thyme
2 tablespoons basil
2 tablespoons oregano
2 tablespoons tarragon
3 gallons water
1/4 cup sea salt (optional)
1 tablespoon black pepper
10 bay leaves
6 pounds potatoes, cubed
20 tomatoes, chopped
2 pounds zucchini, chopped
2 heads celery, chopped
2 pounds carrots, chopped

Optional Ingredients
:
4 cups cooked macaroni
4 cups cooked garbanzos
2 pounds peas
Almost any other vegetable

Sauté garlic for 30 seconds, then add onions and spices in a soup pot. Sauté until onions start to brown on their edges. Add water, pepper, and bay leaves. If using salt, add to water. Bring to a boil, and add chopped vegetables and other ingredients. Bring to a second boil, then reduce heat to low and cover. Simmer for 45 minutes or until vegetables are

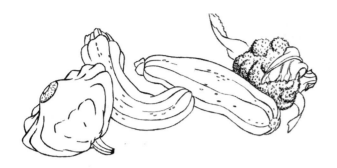

cooked to desired softness. Serve hot. This soup can simmer for as long as you like if you keep adding water. Serve hot.

Potato Soup for 100

Equipment: 30 quart soup pot
Prep time: 1 hour
Cooking time: 1 hour or more

1/2 cup olive oil
2 bulbs garlic, diced
12 onions, chopped
2 tablespoons thyme
2 tablespoons basil
2 tablespoons oregano
3 gallons water
10 pounds potatoes, cubed
3 tablespoons sea salt
2 tablespoons white pepper
4 pounds carrots, chopped

Sauté garlic for 30 seconds in a soup pot, then add onions and spices. Sauté until onions start to brown on their edges. Add water, potatoes, carrots, and pepper. If using salt, add to water. Bring to a boil, then reduce heat to low and cover. Simmer for 30 minutes or until potatoes are soft. Ladle some of the soup into a blender and blend until smooth. (Be careful to hold the lid tightly onto the blender; the soup will be very hot and will burn you if it splashes out.) Blend about half of the soup, leaving some chunks of potato, and pour back into pot with the unblended soup. (Note: Adding 1/2 or 1 cup of dill will make this into Potato Dill soup.)

Desserts

Fruit Salad for 100

Equipment: large mixing bowl, small serving bowl, plastic storage buckets with lids.
Prep time: 1 hour

100 pieces assorted fruit (apples, oranges, pears, peaches, bananas, pineapples, berries, raisins, and so on)
20 lemons, juice of

Cut fruit into bite-size pieces. In a large mixing bowl, mix fruit together with lemon juice, coating all pieces. (The lemon juice helps retard the browning which occurs when fruit is exposed to the air.) Store fruit in plastic "tofu" buckets with tight fitting lids and refrigerate, if possible. Serve in small portions using a small serving bowl. This salad also tastes great with granola, shredded coconut, or nondairy ice cream or sherbet.

Apple-Pear Crisp for 100

Equipment: 3 12" x 18" baking pans.
Preheat oven: 350 degrees
Prep time: 1 hour 30 minutes.
Cooking time: 1 hour

Filling

50 apples
50 pears
10 lemons, juice of
5 cups maple syrup, agave nectar (Optional)
1/4 cup vanilla
1/2 cup cinnamon
2 tablespoons powdered ginger
1 tablespoon nutmeg
1 tablespoon allspice

Core and slice apples and pears (peeling is not necessary if organic). In a mixing bowl, mix sliced fruit with remaining ingredients until every piece of fruit is covered. Place into baking pans in an even layer.

Topping

15–20 cups rolled oats
15–20 cups whole wheat flour
1/2 cup cinnamon
2 tablespoons nutmeg
2 tablespoons allspice
1 tablespoons ground cloves
1 tablespoons sea salt (optional)
4 pounds vegan margarine
5 cups maple syrup or agave nectar (optional)
1/2 cup vanilla

In a large mixing bowl, mix the oats, flour, and spices. Break margarine into small pieces and work into the dry mixture with your hands. Mix syrup and vanilla together, then add to the topping and mix very well. Crumble the topping over the fruit in the baking pans and bake in oven at 350 degrees for at least 1 hour, until the topping is golden brown, the fruit is soft, and there is liquid on the bottom. Serve hot with nondairy ice cream or sherbet.

Drinks

Sun Tea

1/3 to 1/2 oz loose tea or 8 to 12 teabags per gallon

Sun tea provides a refreshing touch to a day at the literature table, tabling at concerts, or the enjoyment of regular meals. Nothing brings renewed enthusiasm to the picket line during a strike or blockade more than refreshing sun tea.

Collect empty gallon glass jars from restaurants; if you can't get free ones, you can sometimes buy them at discount or dollar stores.

Fill a gallon jar with fresh water and put in the teabags or loose tea—obviously, the more you put in the stronger the tea will be. Put ithe jar out in the sun and let it sit for a few hours. Serve the tea hot, or take it out of the sun, let it cool, then refrigerate it and serve it cold. The most refreshing teas are mint, hibiscus, darjeeling, oolong, and green.

Bread

Uprising Bread for The Change We Knead!
(four loaves)

2 tablespoons dry yeast
5 cups hot water
1/2 cup oil
1/2 cup warm water
2 tablespoons salt
1/2 cup organic sugar or apple juice
12 cups organic whole wheat, organic unbleached white flour or organic rice flour (or 7 cups whole wheat flour & 5 cups white flour or any combination of flours adding up to 12 cups)
1 tray Ice cubes (if using conventional oven)

Sprinkle yeast into 1/2 cup warm water. It should not be boiling or close to boiling when adding the yeast or the bread will not rise. Let stand 10 to 15 minutes. Add 1 tablespoon of sugar or juice to the warm water and yeast. Slowly combine the remaining 4-1/2 cups hot water with 7 cups flour in a large bowl. Add salt, oil, sugar, and prepared yeast to the mixture and blend thoroughly. Continue mixing until well blended. Continue to add flour and water until it is a ball of dough.

Knead the dough for 10 minutes or until there is a consistency like cookie dough. You may add flour as you go. A stickier dough will result in moister bread. Oil hands and divide dough into four parts and place in greased pans. Cover loaves with damp cloth or pot lid and let rise until they've gained at least a third in bulk. This should take one to two hours.

If using a conventional stove, toward the end of this time preheat your oven to 375 degrees. Place pans on top shelf and a ceramic or pyrex dish containing the ice cubes on the bottom shelf. Bake for approximately 35 to 50 minutes.

If using a solar oven, place lids on the pans or insert an empty loaf pan on top of each loaf of dough. Place in solar oven by 11 a.m. Cook 4 to 6 hours turning stove towards the sun. As the aroma of baked bread drifts from the oven you'll know it won't be long before it is time to unlock the oven to remove your four loaves. Remember the bread pans will be hot enough to burn your fingers so use pot holders to lift the pans out of your oven.

SPICES AND HERBS

Herbs and spices help make any meal a work of art. Herbs are generally the green leafy parts of plants, and spices come from roots, nuts, bark, or seeds.

Food has six universally recognized basic tastes: sweet, sour, picante (hot), bitter, salty, and savory or umami (and, arguably, astringent). The key to preparing great tasting meals is primarily in creating a balance of these six tastes. Attention to the aroma, texture, taste, color, and presentation of a meal is essential to making the food you prepare enjoyable. You can add spices at any time when preparing your dish, as their flavor generally increases as the food is cooking. Herbs on the other hand should be added towards the time when you will stop heating, as their flavor can diminish when cooked too long.

If a dish you prepare isn't as good as you'd like, it's often because there's too much of one taste and too little of a complementary taste. For example, with hot and sour dishes, you might tend too much toward the hot or sour. With the preceding recipes, experiment with the spice and herb balance, using our suggestions as a starting point.

Allspice (*Pimenta dioica*) The dried, dark brown berries from an evergreen tree. Clove-like flavor, but smoother, mellower with undertones of cinnamon, and nutmeg.

Arrowroot (*Marantha arundinacea*) Arrowroot is a white powder extracted from the root of a West Indian plant, *Marantha arundinacea*, used by a native people, the Arawaks, who used it to draw out toxins from people wounded by poison arrows. It looks and feels like cornstarch. It is used as a thickening agent for sauces, fruit pie fillings, glazes, and puddings. Arrowroot has no flavor. Arrowroot mixtures thicken at a lower temperature than mixtures made with flour or cornstarch. Mix arrowroot with cool liquids before adding hot liquids, then cook until mixture thickens. Remove immediately to prevent mixture from thinning. Two teaspoons of arrowroot can be substituted for 1 tablespoon of cornstarch. One teaspoon of arrowroot can be substituted for 1 tablespoon of flour.

Anise (*Pimpinella anisum*) Sold in seed form, anise smells like black licorice, though it is actually a member of the parsley family. Anise is native to the eastern Mediterranean region and throughout Southwest Asia.

Basil, sweet (*Ocimum basilicum*) The bright green leaves of a mint family herb, basil has a special affinity for tomato and tomato-flavored dishes. Basil can be used fresh or dried. Fresh basil and dried basil provide different flavors, and may not always be freely substituted for each other.

Bay Leaf (*Laurus nobilis*) The large, olive-green leaves of the sweet-bay or laurel tree. Bay leaf is often used in tomato sauces and can also be used in soups.

Black Pepper (*Piper nigrum*) The dried, mature berries of a tropical vine. The whole dried berry (peppercorn) is used for black pepper. Commonly used as a seasoning in down-home American cooking, and as a garnish on baked potatoes and salads.

Caraway (*Carum carvi*) The hard, brown, scimitar-shaped seeds of an herb of the parsley family. Caraway is native to western Asia, Europe and Northern Africa, and is sometimes used a topping for bagels and other baked goods.

Cardamom (*Elettaria cardamomum, Amomum costatum or Amomum subulatum*) Most often used in powdered form, cardamom consists of a papery pod with dark brown seeds from a ginger family plant. Green cardamom is one of the most expensive spices

by weight, but has a strong flavor so little is needed. Cardamom is best stored in its seed pods to protect the flavor. It's native to India, Pakistan, Nepal, and Bhutan, and is commonly used in Indian food.

Cayenne Pepper (*Capsicum annuum*) This very hot chile is named for the city of Cayenne in French Guiana. It's normally sold in powdered form, but green or red (ripe) whole chiles can be used in Thai, Japanese, or other Asian dishes in place of Japanese or Thai chiles. Powdered cayenne is quite hot, so use it cautiously. Whole cayenne chiles are not strongly flavored and are roughly as hot as serrano chiles. Use them where you want heat but don't want chile flavor to overwhelm your other spices.

Chili powder (*Capsicum spp.*—classic blend) Such spices as allspice, cloves, coriander, and ginger may be included along with mild powdered chiles. Not useful for much of anything other than making chili sin carne, or if you're an omnivore, chili con carne.

Cilantro/Coriander (*Coriandrum sativum*) Also known as Chinese Parsley and Mexican Parsley, cilantro has a distinctive flavor and is an excellent addition to fresh salsa. Cilantro also works well in marinades and a large variety of other dishes. It usually comes fresh in bunches.

Cinnamon (*Cassia vera*) and (*Cinnamomum lverum*) Cinnamon is made from the inner bark of a number of small evergreen trees. *Cinnamomum verum* is tan colored, with a mild, sweet flavor. *Cassia vera* is reddish brown, with a stronger flavor. Cinnamon is customarily used in powdered form in sweet baked goods.

Cloves (*Syzygium aromaticum*) The dried, unopened flower buds of an evergreen tree. Intriguing, nail-like shape makes cloves an exotic garnish. Ground cloves are very strongly flavored and are quite bitter tasting. For nonvegans, cloves are an excellent addition to hot buttered rum.

Coriander consists of dried cilantro seeds. The two flavors are very different, and while fresh cilantro is commonly used in Mexican cooking, coriander is customarily used in Indian dishes, with the dried seeds being ground before use. Coriander has a mild, delicately fragrant aroma with lemony/sage undertones. It can be mixed with cumin to make a very special flavor.

Cumin (*Cuminum cyminum*) The small, elongated, yellowish-brown seeds of a plant of the parsley family. Cumin provides the aromatic flavor note in chili powder and is essential in curries.

Curry powder. This mixture consists of ground cumin, ground coriander and fenugreek seeds, turmeric, black and red chiles and other ingredients including cinnamon, ginger, cardamom, nutmeg, allspice, garlic, dill and celery seeds, and sometimes salt. Imported curry powders often contain such other ingredients as flour, peanuts, asafetida, and kari leaves. Mix with coconut milk to make curry.

Dill herb or weed (*Anethum graveolens*—herb) The green, feathery leaves of the dill plant, dill is strongly flavored and is much used in sauces, salads, dressings, and potato dishes.

Fennel (*Foeniculum vulgare*) The small, yellowish-brown, watermelon-shaped seeds from a bulbous plant, fennel is related to the celery and parsley families, and has a strong anise-like flavor. It's often used in Italian cooking and provides the distinctive note in Italian sausages, both sweet and hot.

Fenugreek (*Trigonella foenum-graecum*) Fenugreek consists of the very small, reddish-brown seeds of a member of the pea family. It has a pleasantly bitter flavor with a curry-like aroma. It's essential in curries.

Garam Masala. An Indian spice blend with a warm, earthy flavor. Ingredients vary but may include black pepper, cardamom, cinnamon, cloves, coriander, cumin, fennel, ginger, and nutmeg. ("Garam" means "hot" in Hindi.)

Garlic (*Allium sativum*) Garlic consists of the bulbs of an annual plant. It's a cousin to the onion and a member of the lily family. It's a strong flavored, somewhat hot herb. Dehydrated garlic is milled to particle sizes ranging from powdered, to granulated, to minced. It's essential to Italian cooking and is widely used in Mexican cooking. Homegrown garlic tends to be much hotter and stronger than store-bought garlic; be aware of this and use correspondingly less if cooking with homegrown garlic.

Ginger (*Zingiber officinale*) Ginger consists of the dried roots (rhizomes) of a member of the zingiber family. Smooth, straw-colored ginger roots have been peeled or bleached. Fresh ginger has a very sharp, somewhat hot flavor, and is commonly used in stir fries, where it's minced prior to adding it to the mix. Powdered ginger is a common ingredient in curries and can also be used with stir fries.

Horseradish (*Armoracia rusticana*) First cultivated in Eastern Europe, horseradish root has been used for its sharp, hot taste for thousands of years. The roots are tasteless until grated, smashed, or diced. Horseradish is commonly used as a garnish.

Italian seasoning. A blend of typical Italian herbs, such as thyme, oregano, basil, savory, marjoram, rosemary, fennel, and sage. The herbs are normally in crushed leaf form and salt is not usually added.

Jalapeño chiles (*Capsicum annum*) In the U.S., the most common type of chile. Medium hot with a pronounced, distinctive flavor. Very common in salsa and pico de gallo. Because of their strong flavor, jalapeños should not be used in place of Thai or Japanese chiles in Asian food.

Lemongrass (*Cymbopogon citratus*) Available in fresh, dried, and powdered forms, lemon grass comes from a long, coarse grass-like plant and is used extensively in Thai and Indonesian cooking. It adds a lemon-like yet distinctive flavor. In a pinch, lemon zest can be substituted for lemon grass.

Mace (*Myristica fragrans*) The lacy, scarlet-colored aril (covering—orange when dried) which surrounds the seed of the nutmeg fruit. Its flavor is a mix of cinnamon and pepper, similar to nutmeg but much more subtle.

Marjoram (*Origanum majorana*) The grayish-green leaves of a member of the mint family. It's closely related to oregano, but has a milder and more complex flavor.

Mint (*Mentha spp.*) There are 25 species and hundreds of varieties of mint. Most common are the dark green leaves of the peppermint and spearmint plants, which are used as noncaffeinated tea.

Mustard (*Sinapis alba*) Mustard consists of the tiny yellow or brownish seeds of a cabbage family member. Ground mustard seeds are commonly used in prepared mustard. The yellow and white seeds have a sharp bite, but no aromatic pungency. The brown seeds are aromatically pungent as well as biting.

Nutmeg (*Myristica fragrans*) The brown seed of the fruit of an evergreen tree. Nutmeg is used in a wide variety of Asian dishes, including some curries.

Oregano (*Origanum vulgare*) Consists of the bright green leaves of a member of the mint family. It's essential to Italian cooking, often used in tomato-based sauces, and is sometimes used in Mexican salsa.

Paprika (*Capsicum annuum*) Powdered paprika is derived from the pods of certain sweet, mild chile plants. Paprika has a pleasant red color and is used frequently as a garnish.

Parsley (*Petroselinum crispum*) The bright green leaves of the parsley plant. There are several different varieties of parsley: American, Italian, and Chinese or Mexican (see Cilantro). Italian parsley has broader leaves and a stronger flavor than its American counterpart, which is very mild and commonly used as a garnish.

Rosemary (*Rosmarinus officinalis*) The green, needle-like leaves of a mint family shrub. A bitter, aromatic herb often used in Italian cooking.

Saffron (*Crocus sativus*) The dried flower stigmas of a member of the crocus family. By the pound, the most expensive spice, but a pinch goes a long way. Saffron has a sweet taste and imparts an attractive golden color to dishes.

Sage (*Salvia officinalis*) The long, slender leaves (silver-gray when dried) of a member of the mint family, sage is customarily used in ground or powdered form. It's mild flavored and a bit peppery, and is used in stuffings and also in Italian and Middle Eastern cooking.

Savory (*Satureja hortensis*) Derived from an annual plant, savory is customarily used in powder form and is sometimes used as a substitute for sage. It's commonly used in meat sauces and in some Eastern European cooking.

Sesame (*Sesamum indicum*) The small, oval, pearly white seeds of an annual plant native to Africa and India. Sesame is mostly used in the United States in, or as a topping for, baked goods. It's used, either as seeds or as a paste, in a wide variety of world cuisines.

Star Anise (*Illicium verum*) The large, brown, star-shaped fruit of an evergreen tree. Each point contains a seed; the whole fruit is used. It has an anise-like flavor, and is used in Chinese and Indian food.

Tarragon (*Artemisia dracunculus*) The slender, dark green leaves of a member of the aster family. Distinctive for its hint of anise flavor. Widely used in French cooking.

Thyme (*Thymus vulgaris*) The grayish green leaves of a member of the mint family. One of the strongest herbs. Used in stuffings, clam chowder, and innumerable herb blends.

Turmeric (*Curcuma longa*) The orange-colored roots (rhizomes) of a member of the ginger family. Turmeric provides color for prepared mustards, curry powder, sauces, pickles, and relishes, and is widely used in Indian and other Asian cooking.

Vanilla (*Vanilla planifolia*) Vanilla Beans are the long, greenish-yellow seed pods of a tropical orchid plant, and vanilla extract is produced by soaking the pods in alcohol. Vanilla is widely used in baking. It's wise to avoid artificial vanilla extract.

Wasabi (*Wasabia japonica*) Wasabi is an essential Japanese garnish. It is difficult to cultivate, so colored horseradish is often used as a substitute—almost universally so in Japanese restaurants in the U.S.

White Pepper (*Piper nigrum*) The light, tan-colored seeds of the pepper berry from which the dark outer husk has been removed. White pepper has the heat but not the bouquet of black pepper. It can be freely substituted for black pepper and is often used in light colored soups and sauces.

140

GARDENING

There are many good reasons to garden: personal, political, social, economic, and ecological. Working in a cooperative garden is a good way to make new friends, deepen friendships with those you already have, and build a political community. It also helps to make people less dependent on the corporations that control the global food chain.

Ecologically, it reduces the amount of fossil fuels used in the production of fruits and vegetables. Factory farming is energy intensive. One widely cited study from the 1980s estimated that vegetables used in Chicago were shipped on average over 1,500 miles. While there are economies of scale in factory farming, local production of high-yield fruits and vegetables does reduce, even if marginally, the amount of fossil fuels used in food transport.

However, only 11% of fuels used to power agribusiness are used in transport. The rest are used in production, in part in the production and distribution of chemical fertilizers, herbicides, and pesticides. Frederick M. Fishel, of the University of Florida, reports that in 2007 U.S. agribusiness used approximately 680 million pounds of herbicides and pesticides costing approximately $7.9 billion on to-a-large-extent GMO monocultural crops.

In contrast, organic gardening uses no chemical fertilizers, herbicides, or pesticides, and (if you plant heirloom varieties) helps to preserve biodiversity. Organic gardening also contributes to eating healthier, more ecologically friendly food than that in the average American diet. As an example of the benefits of eating a healthier diet, the Johns Hopkins School of Public Health reports that "if Americans followed a solely plant-based diet one day per week, they could cut more GHG [greenhouse gas] emissions than by following an entirely local diet."

Gardening is good for you, your family and friends, your community, and the planet. In itself, gardening will not bring about "the revolution," but it's a useful and enjoyable thing to do, and it brings us a few steps closer to the society we want.

Gardening Basics

Since this book will be read in many different areas, we'll restrict ourselves to general notes.

First, be prepared for at least partial failure, especially if you're new to gardening. If you are, start small—cultivate no more than about 100 square feet. You'll be amazed at how much produce you can raise in such a small space.

In places with good soil, such as the U.S. East, Midwest, and Plains States, you can just turn the soil over to a depth of eight or nine inches (roughly the length of the blade of the average garden shovel) and plant without adding soil amendments. In subsequent years, though, you will want to add some compost and manure when you turn the soil over.

In places with poor soil, mostly desert and semi-desert areas, such as the U.S. Southwest, preparing soil is more complicated. First, dig down to a depth of eight or nine inches, and once you've dug up your entire plot shovel out the soil, putting it to one side. Dig down another eight or nine inches. Once you've done that, put at least three inches (8 cm) of compost or steer manure on the soil in the hole and thoroughly mix. (Using horse manure is not a good idea; it's nitrogen poor and contains a lot of salts.) Shovel the first layer of soil back in, put at least three inches of compost and/or steer manure on top of it, and mix thoroughly. In arid regions, put a lip of at least three inches around the edges of the entire plot in order to conserve water.

In most places, you'll want your plot to be shaded during at least part of the day, especially the afternoon. If no partially shaded spots are available, suspend shade cloth six or seven feet above your plot. Use the 50%-blocking rather than the 80% blocking type; using the 80% type can cause problems with flowering and setting.

Because shade cloth is expensive (though very durable), it's advisable in your first year or two—while you're figuring out if you want to continue gardening—to use old sheets instead. They'll deteriorate rapidly, but they cost next to nothing, and they get the job done.

Now it's time to plant. When to do that will vary with your altitude and with how far north or south of the equator you are.

In your first year of growing a summer garden, you'll probably want to buy starts unless you already know gardeners who will give you some. Rather than buying starts at big-box store garden departments (expensive and very limited variety), plant nurseries are generally a better bet, but there are even better places to get starts. In many places there are organic gardening associations, and they almost always have events where members sell starts during the spring planting season. Farmers markets can be another good source.

Once you've grown your first crop, you can harvest seeds and then raise your own starts in subsequent years. Plant the seeds in starter containers about six to eight weeks prior to the beginning of spring planting season. The easiest types of vegetables and herbs from which to harvest seeds are eggplants, bell peppers, chiles, beans, squash, okra, melons, peas, lettuce, broccoli, chard, cilantro, and tomatoes.

Harvest seeds only from the largest mature vegetables. In most cases, this simply means removing the seeds, spreading them out on a tray, and letting them dry. Tomatoes are a different matter. Using only the largest, most mature tomatoes, drain the seeds and the liquid they're in into a bowl, add a little water, and let sit at room temperature for two to four days until a scum forms on top. Skim off the scum, drain the liquid, and then let the seeds dry for several days. This will drastically increase the germination rate when you plant the seeds.

In preparing starts, it's a good idea to recycle small plastic containers (yogurt containers, sawed off soda bottles, sawed off pint milk bottles, etc.) and poke several holes in the bottoms with a knife to facilitate drainage. It works well to use cheap commercial potting soil mixed with compost and manure in about a 4:2:1 ratio. Put in several seeds per container, and a few weeks after they've come up you can thin the seedlings, replanting the thinned ones in other containers. If you live in an area with occasional freezes prior to the planting period, it's a good idea to put your starts on trays so that you can take them inside on nights that it freezes.

With winter gardens (in relatively warm climates, such as Tucson's) it's generally not necessary to prepare starts for most winter crops; it's okay to just stick seeds directly into the ground. However, it's a good idea to prepare starts for cruciform vegetables such as broccoli, cauliflower, and cabbage about six weeks before you plan to plant them.

In dry areas, you'll want to use mulch to hold in soil moisture. Straw is common, good, inexpensive mulch. Put down a layer about three inches thick all around your plants. Water it immediately once you've put it down, so it doesn't blow away in the wind. (Figure one bale per every 150 square feet.) Before you buy a bale or two of straw at your local feed store, ask what kind it is. Because it contains seeds which will sprout in your garden, and which you'll need to weed out, wheat straw is the best choice. Barley straw is acceptable, though a bit more of a pain to deal with, and under no circumstances buy sorghum straw, which will produce a weeding nightmare for years to come.

A note on preparation: Even before you start your garden, you'll want to start composting. It's a simple process. You don't need to buy an expensive container to do it, just find an out-of-the way spot in your yard, and start throwing your kitchen waste there, as well as vegetation waste from your yard (weeds which haven't yet seeded, fallen leaves, etc.), shredded paper, and occasionally soil when necessary to cover kitchen waste (if you don't have yard waste or shredded paper available). Unless you live in an area with a lot of rain, water the compost pile regularly.

Good practices with compost include keeping a covered bucket in your kitchen for kitchen waste, emptying it onto the compost pile whenever it's near full, and occasionally poking holes roughly six inches apart all the way down through your compost pile with a piece of rebar or steel pipe. This will help with aeration and the growth of aerobic bacteria which turn waste into compost. Turn the entire pile over with a pitchfork every couple of months. Finally, compost weeds *before* they go to seed. Unless you're prepared to do an ungodly amount of unnecessary weeding, do *not* compost seeding weeds; throw them in the trash.

This all sounds like a lot of work, and it is, but gardening is restful, ecologically friendly, and there's nothing like eating your own produce and sharing it with your family, friends, and neighbors.

BIBLIOGRAPHY

Anarchism

Antliff, Allan. *Only a Beginning: An Anarchist Anthology*. Vancouver, BC: Arsenal Pulp Press, 2004.

Avrich, Paul. *Anarchist Portraits*. Princeton, NJ: Princton University Press, 1988.

Bakunin, Mikhail. *God and the State*. New York: Dover, 1970.

Bakunin, Mikhail. *Marxism, Freedom and the State*. London: Freedom Press, 1984.

Bakunin, Mikhail (Sam Dolgoff, ed.). *Bakunin on Anarchy*. New York: Knopf, 1972.

Berkman, Alexander. *What Is Anarchism?* Oakland: AK Press, 2003.

Bookchin, Murray. *Post-Scarcity Anarchism*. Oakland: AK Press, 2004.

Bookchin, Murray. *Remaking Society*. Cambridge, MA: South End Press, 1990.

Chomsky, Noam. *On Anarchism*. New York: New Press, 2013.

Dark Star Collective (eds.) *Quiet Rumours: An Anarcha-Feminist Reader, New Edition*. Oakland: AK Press, 2012.

Ehrlich, Howard and a.h.s. boy (eds.). *The Best of Social Anarchism*. Tucson, AZ: See Sharp Press, 2013.

Ehrlich, Howard (ed.). *Reinventing Anarchy Again*. Oakland: AK Press, 2001.

Fabbri, Luigi. *Bourgeois Influences on Anarchism*. Edmonton, Alberta: Thoughtcrime Ink, 2010.

Fernández, Frank. *Cuban Anarchism: The History of a Movement*. Tucson, AZ: See Sharp Press, 2001.

Flores Magón, Ricardo (Mitchell Verter and Chaz Bufe, eds.). *Dreams of Freedom: A Ricardo Flores Magón Reader*. Oakland: AK Press, 2005.

Goldman, Emma. *Anarchism and Other Essays*. New York: Dover, 1969.

Goldman, Emma. *Living My Life* (volumes 1 & 2). New York: Dover, 1970.

Guerin, Daniel. *Anarchism: From Theory to Practice*. New York: Monthly Review Press, 1996.

Kropotkin, Peter. *Anarchism and Anarchist Communism*. London: Freedom Press, 1987.

Kropotkin, Peter. *The Conquest of Bread*. New York: Dover, 2011.

Kropotkin, Peter. *Fields, Factories and Workshops Tomorrow*. New York: Harper Torchbooks, 1974.

Kropotkin, Peter. *Mutual Aid*. Boston, Porter-Sargent, n.d.

Kroptkin, Peter. *Kropotkin's Revolutionary Pamphlets*. New York: Dover, 1970.

Malatesta, Errico. *Anarchy*. London: Freedom Press, 1984.

Malatesta, Errico (Vernon Richards, ed..). *Life and Ideas: The Anarchist Writings of Errico Malatesta*. Oakland: PM Press, 2015.

Marshall, Peter. *Demanding the Impossible: A History of Anarchism*. Oakland: PM Press, 2010.

Mbah, Sam and Igariwey, I.E. *African Anarchism: The History of a Movement*. Tucson, AZ: See Sharp Press, 1997.

Meltzer, Albert. *Anarchism: Arguments For & Against*. Edinburgh: AK Press, 1996.

Rocker, Rudolf. *Anarchism and Anarcho-Syndicalism*. London: Freedom Press, 1988.

Rocker, Rudolf. *Anarcho-Syndicalism: Theory and Practice*. Oakland: AK Press, 2004.

Rooum, Donald. *What Is Anarchism?* London: Freedom Press, 1992.

Ward, Colin. *About Anarchism*. London: Freedom Press, 2002.

Ward, Colin. *Anarchism: A Very Brief Introduction*. Oxford: Oxford University Press, 2004.

Ward, Colin. *Anarchy in Action*. London: Freedom Press, 1992.

Woodcock, George. *Anarchism*. Toronto: University of Toronto Press, 2004.

Anarchist Science Fiction

Banks, Iain M. *The Player of Games*. New York: Orbit, 1988.

Banks, Iain M. *Matter*. New York: Orbit, 2008.

Banks, Iain M. *Surface Detail*. New York: Orbit, 2010.

Carlsson, Chris. *After the Deluge*. San Francisco: Full Enjoyment Books, 2004.

Danvers, Dennis. *The Fourth World*. New York: Avon, 2000.

Harrison, Harry. *The Stainless Steel Rat Gets Drafted*. New York: Bantam, 1987.

Hogan, James P. *Voyage from Yesteryear*. New York: Doubleday, 1982.

LeGuin, Ursula. *The Dispossessed*.N ew York: Harper, 1974.

Macleod, Ken. *The Stone Canal*. New York: Tor, 1996.

Macleod, Ken. *The Cassini Division*. New York: Tor, 1998.

Oakley, Nicholas P. *The Watcher*. Tucson: See Sharp Press, 2014.

Rucker, Rudy. *Software*. New York: Eos, 1987.

Rucker, Rudy. *Wetware*. New York: Eos, 1988.

Rucker, Rudy. *Freeware*. New York: Eos, 1997.

Stross, Charles. *Neptune's Brood*. New York: Ace, 2014.

Teflon, Zeke. *Free Radicals: A Novel of Utopia and Dystopia*. Tucson: See Sharp Press, 2012.

Wilson, Robert Anton and Shea, Bob. *The Illuminatus Trilogy*. New York, Dell, 1975.

Art & Anarchism

Antiff, Allan. *Anarchist Modernism: Art, Politics, and the First American Avant-Garde*. Chicago: University of Chicago Press, 2007.

Antiff, Allan. *Anarchy and Art: From the Paris Commune to the Fall of the Berlin Wall*. Vancouver, BC: Arsenal Pulp Press, 2007.

Harper, Clifford. *The Education of Desire: The Anarchist Graphics of Clifford Harper*. London: Anarres, 1984.

Harper, Clifford. *Anarchy: A Graphic Guide*. London: Camden Press, 1987.

Kinney, Jay. *Anarchy Comics: The Complete Collection*. Oakland: PM Press, 2012.

Rooum, Donald. *Wildcat: Anarchist Comics by Donald Rooum*. London: Freedom Press, 1985.

Rooum, Donald. *Wildcat: Twenty Year Millenium, A selection celebrating 20 years of Wildcat appearances in Freedom newspaper*. London: Freedom Press, 1999.

Weire, David. *Anarchy and Culture: The Aesthetic Politics of Modernism*. Amherst, MA: University of Massachusettes Press, 1997.

Cookbooks

Calvo, Luz. *Decolonize Your Diet: Plant-Based Mexican-American Recipes for Health and Healing.*Vancouver, BC: Arsenal Pulp Press, 2013.

Chef AJ. *Unprocessed: How to achieve vibrant health and your ideal weight.* Los Angeles: CreatSpace, 2011.

Goldhammer, Alan. *The Health Promoting Cookbook.* Summertown, TN: Book Publishing Co., 1997.

Hagler, Louise and Bates, Dorothy. *The New Farm Vegetarian Cookbook.* Summertown, TN: Book Publishing Co., 1988

Kalper, Michael A. *The Cookbook for People Who Love Animals.* Kapa'au, HI: Gentle World, 1981.

Katzen, Mollie. *The Enchanted Broccoli Forest.* Berkeley, CA: Ten Speed Press, 1995

Katzen, Mollie. *Moosewood Cookbook.* Berkeley, CA: Ten Speed Press,, 2000

Kloss, Jethro. *Back to Eden.* Santa Barbara: Woodbridge Press, 1972.

Moskowitz, Isa Chandra. *Vegan with a Vengeance*: *Over 150 Delicious, Cheap, Animal-Free Recipes That Rock.* Cambridge, MA: Da Capo Press, 2005

Robertson, Laurel. *Laurel's Kitchen: A Handbook for Vegetarian Cookery and Nutrition.* Berkeley, CA: Nilgiri Press, 1971.

Shurtleff, William. *The Book of Miso.* New York: Ballantine, 1976.

Thomas, Ann. *The Vegetarian Epicure.* New York: Vintage, 1972

Direct Action

Beck, Julian. *The Life of the Theatre.* San Francisco: City Lights Books, 1972.

Billboard Liberation Front. *The Art & Science of Billboard Improvement.* Tucson: See Sharp Press, 2000.

Boyle, Francis. *Defending Civil Resistance Under International Law.* Dobbs Ferry, NY: Transnational Publishers, 1987.

Crimethinc. *Recipes for Disaster:An Anarchist Cookbook.* Salem, OR: Crimethinc, 2005

DAM Collective. *Earth First! Direct Action Manual.* Earth First!, 1997.

Flynn, Elisabeth G. and Smith, Walker C. *Direct Action and Sabotage!* Chicago: IWW, 1991.

Foreman, Dave (ed.). *Ecodefense: A Field Guide to Monkeywrenching.* Chico, CA: Abbzug Press, 1993.

Hedemann, Ed. (ed.). *War Resisters League Organizers Manual.* New York: War Resisters League, 1981.

Lane, James H. *Direct Action and Desegregation 1960–1962: Towards a Theory of the Rationalization of Protest.* Brooklyn, NY: Carlson Publishers, 1989.

Thoreau, Henry David. *Walden and Civil Disobedience.* New York: Signet, 2012.

Economics

Albert, Michael. *Looking Forward: Participatory Economics for the Twenty First Century.* Boston: South End, 1999.

Albert, Michael. *Of the People, By the People: The Case for a Participatory Economy.* Oakland: AK Press, 2001.

Albert, Michael. *Parecon: Life After Capitalism.* New York: Verso, 2004.

Albert, Michael. *Thinking Forward: Learning To Conceptualize Economic Vision.* Winnipeg: Arbeiter Ring, 1997.

Alperovitz, Gar. *America Beyond Capitalism: Reclaiming Our Wealth, Our Liberty, and Our Democracy, 2nd Edition.* Boston: Democracy Collaborative Press/Dollars and Sense, 2011.

Alperovitz, Gar. *What Then Must We Do?: Straight Talk about the Next American Revolution.* White River Jct., Vermont: Chelsea Green, 2013.

Hahnel, Robin. *Of the People, By the People: The Case for a Participatory Economy.* Oakland: AK Press, 2012.

Hahnel, Robin. *The ABCs of Political Economy: A Modern Approach.* London: Pluto Press, 2015.

Hahnel, Robin and Wright, Erik Olin. *Alternatives to Capitalism: Proposals for a Democratic Economy.* New Left Project, 2014.

Wolff, Richard. *Capitalism Hits the Fan: The Global Economic Meltdown and What to Do About It.* Northampton, MA: Interlink, 2013.

Wolff, Richard. *Democracy at Work: A Cure for Capitalism.* Chicago: Haymarket Books, 2012.

Wolff, Richard. *Occupy the Economy: Challenging Capitalism.* San Francisco: City Lights, 2012.

Zweig, Michael. *The Working Class Majority.* Ithaca, New York: ILR Press, 2011.

Environment

Bertell, Rosalie. *No Immediate Danger: Prognosis for a Radioactive Earth.* Summertown, TN: Book Publishing Co., 2000.

Bertell, Rosalie. *Planet Earth: The Latest Weapon of War.* London: Quartet Books, 2002.

Carson, Rachel. *Silent Spring.* New York: Mariner Books, 2002.

Hartmann, Thom. *The Last Hours of Ancient Sunlight: Revised and Updated: The Fate of the World and What We Can Do Before It's Too Late.* New York: Three Rivers Press, 2004.

Leopold, Aldo. *A Sand County Almanac: Outdoor Essays & Reflections.* New York: Ballantine Books, 1986.

McKibben, Bill. *End of Nature.* New York: Random House, 2006.

McKibben, Bill. *Earth: Making a Life on a Tough New Planet.* New York: Times Books, 2010.

Tokar, Brian. *Redesigning Life?: The Worldwide Challenge to Genetic Engineering.* London: Zed Books, 2001.

Tokar, Brian. *Gene Traders: Biotechnology, World Trade, and the Globalization of Hunger.* Burlington, VT: Toward Freedom, 2004.

Tokar, Brian and Eiglad, Erik. *Toward Climate Justice.* Porsegrunn, Norway: Communalism Press, 2010.

Food Politics

Aoki, Keith. *Seed Wars: Cases and Materials on Intellectual Property and Plant Genetic Resources.* Druham, NC: Carolina Academic Press, 2007.

Bello, Walden. *The Food Wars.* London, Verso, 2009.

Berry, Wendell. *The Unsettling of America: Culture and Agriculture.* San Francisco: Sierra Club, 1986.

Blood Root Collective. *The Political Palate.* Bridgeport, CT: Sanguinaria Publishing, 1980.

Boyd, Billy Ray. *For The Vegetarian in You.* San Francisco: Taterhill Press, 1987.

Collins, Joseph. *Food First.* New York: Ballantine, 1977.

Collins, Joseph. *World Hunger: Twelve Myths.* New York: Grove Press, 1986.

Cribb, Julian. *The Coming Famine: The Global Food Crisis and What We Can Do to Avoid It.* Berkeley, CA: University of California Press, 2010.

Gottlieb, Robert. *Food Justice: Food, Health, and the Environment.* Cambridge, MA: MIT Press, 2010.

McHenry, Keith. *Hungry for Peace: How You Can Help End Poverty and War with Food Not Bombs.* Tucson: See Sharp Press, 2012.

Katz, Sandor Ellix. *The Revolution Will Not Be Microwaved: Inside America's Underground Food Movements.* White River Jct., VT: Chelsea Green, 2006.

Lappé, Frances Moore. *Diet for a Small Planet.* New York: Random House, 1991.

Nestle, Marion. *Food Politics: How the Food Industry Influences Nutrition and Health.* Berkeley, CA: University of California Press, 2002.

Patel, Raj. *Stuffed and Starved: The Hidden Battle for the World Food System.* Brooklyn, NY: Melville House, 2008.

Pollan, Michael. *The Omnivore's Dilemma: A Natural History of Four Meals.* New York: Penguin Press, 2006.

Robbins, John. *Diet for a New America.* Novato, CA: H.J. Kramer, 1998.

Robbins, John. *The Food Revolution: How Your Diet Can Help Save Your Life and Our World*. Newbury Port, MA: Conari Press, 2001.

Schlosser, Eric. *Fast Food Nation*. New York: Houghton Mifflin, 2002.

Shiva, Vandana. *The Hijacking of the Global Food Supply*. Boston: South End Press, 2007.

Shiva, Vandana (ed.). *Manifestos on the Future of Food and Seed*. Boston: South End Press, 2007.

Shiva, Vandana. *Soil Not Oil*. Boston: South End Press, 2008

Sinclair, Upton. *The Jungle: The Uncensored Original Edition*. Tucson: See Sharp Press, 2003.

Tokar, Brian and Magdoff, Fred. *Agriculture & Food in Crisis: Conflict, Resistance and Renewal*. New York: Monthly Review Press, 2010.

Tuttle, Will. *The World Peace Diet: Eating For Spiritual Health And Social Harmony*. New York: Lantern Books, 2005.

Wolfe, David. *Superfoods: The Food and Medicine of the Future*. Berkeley, CA: North Atlantic Books, 2009.

Gardening

Bartholomew, Mel. *All New Square Foot Gardening, Second Edition: The Revolutionary Way to Grow More In Less Space*. Minneapolis: Cool Springs Press, 2013.

Brookbank, George. *The Desert Gardener's Calendar: Your Month-by-Month Guide*. Tucson: University of Arizona Press, 1999.

Brookbank, George. *Desert Gardening: The Complete Guide*. Boston: Da Capo Press, 1991.

Fell, Derek. *Vertical Gardening: Grow Up, Not Out, for More Vegetables and Flowers in Much Less Space*. Emmaus, PA: Rodale, 2011.

Flores, Heather. *Food Not Lawns: How to Turn Your Yard into a Garden and Your Neighborhood into a Community*. White River Jct., VT: Chelsea Green, 2010.

Fukuoka, Masanobu. *The One-Straw Revolution: An Introduction to Natural Farming*. New York: NYRB Clasics, 2008.

Logsdown, Gene. *Holy Shit: Managing Manure To Save Mankind*. White River Jct., VT: Chelsea Green, 2010.

Markham, Brett. *Mini Farming: Self-Sufficiency on 1/4 Acre*. New York: Skyhorse Publishing, 2010.

Madigan, Carleen. *The Backyard Homestead: Produce all the food you need on just a quarter acre!* North Adams, MA: Storey, 2009.

Nyhuis, Jane. *Desert Harvest: A Guide to Vegetable Gardening in Arid Lands*. Tucson: Growing Connections, 1982.

Owens, David. *Extreme Gardening: How to Grow Organic in the Hostile Deserts*. Phoenix: Poco Verde, 2000.

Smith, Edward. *The Vegetable Gardener's Bible*. North Adams, MA: Storey Publishing, 2009.

Wilson, Peter Lamborn and Weinberg, Bill (eds.). *Avant Gardening Ecological Struggles in the City & the World*. New York: Autonomedia, New York, 1999.

Labor

Boyer, Richard and Marais, Herbert. *Labor's Untold Story*. UE, 1979.

Brecher, Jeremy. *Strike!* (exp. ed.). Oakland: PM Press, 2014.

Brinton, Maurice. *For Workers' Power*. Oakland: AK Press, 2004.

Lynd, Staughton. *Doing History from the Bottom Up: On E.P. Thompson, Howard Zinn, and Rebuilding the Labor Movement from Below*. Chicago: Haymarket Books, 2014.

Ness, Immanuel. *New Forms of Worker Organization: The Syndicalist and Autonomist Restoration of Class-Struggle Unionism*. Oakland: PM Press, 2014.

Ness, Immanuel and Azzellino, Dario (eds.). *Ours to Master and to Own: Workers' Control from the Commune to the Present*. Chicago: Haymarket Books, 2011.

Pannekoek, Anton. *Workers' Councils*. Oakland: AK Press, 2002.

Thompson, Fred and Bekken, Jon. *The Industrial Workers of the World: Its First 100 Years*. Chicago: IWW, 2006.

Nonviolence

Cohen, Tom. *Three Who Dared*. New York: Avon, 1971.

Gandhi, Mohandas. *Gandhi An Autobiography: The Story of My Experiments With Truth*. Boston: Beacon Press, 1993.

Gandhi, Mohandas. *The Essential Gandhi: An Anthology of His Writings on His Life, Work, and Ideas*. New York: Vintage, 2002.

King, Martin Luther Jr. *Where Do We Go from Here: Chaos or Community?* Boston: Beacon Press, 1968.

King, Martin Luther Jr. *Letter from the Birmingham Jail*. New York: Harper Collins, 1994.

King, Martin Luther Jr. *The Autobiography of Martin Luther King, Jr.* New York: Grand Central Publishing, 2001.

Peace Pilgrim. *Peace Pilgrim: Her Life and Work in Her Own Words*. Santa Fe, NM: Ocean Tree Books, 1992.

Sharp, Gene. *Waging Nonviolent Struggle: 20th Century Practice and 21st Century Potential*. Manchester, NH: Extending Horizons Books, 2005.

Sharp, Gene. *The Politics of Nonviolent Action*. Boston: Porter Sargent, 1973.

Political / Social Theory & Change

Bey, Hakim. *TAZ: Temporary Autonomous Zones*. New York: Autonomedia, 1985.

Biehl, Janet. *Rethinking Ecofeminist Politics*. Boston: South End, 1991.

Biehl, Janet and Staudenmaier, Peter. *Ecofascism: Lessons from the German Experience*. Oakland: AK Press, 1995.

Bookchin, Murray. *Social Anarchism or Lifestyle Anarchism: An Unbridgeable Chasm*. Edinburgh: AK Press, 1995.

Bookchin, Murray. *Re-enchanting Humanity*. New York: Cassell, 1995.

Carlsson, Chris. *Nowtopia*. Oakland: AK Press, 2008.

Castle, Marie Alena. *Culture Wars: The Threat to Your Family and Your Freedom*. Tucson: See Sharp Press, 2013.

Chomsky Noam. *Necessary Illusions: Thought Control in Democratic Societies*. Boston: South End Press, 1989.

Chomsky, Noam. *Manufacturing Consent: The Political Economy of the Mass Media*. Boston: South End Press, 1988.

Debord, Guy. *Society of the Spectacle*. Detroit: Black & Red, 2000.

French, Marilyn. *Beyond Power: On Women, Men and Morals*. New York: Ballantine, 1986.

Fussell, Paul. *Class: A Guide Through the American Status System*. New York: Touchstone, 1992.

Gelderloos, Peter. *Consensus*. Tucson: See Sharp Press, 2006.

Goodman, Paul. *Utopian Essays and Practical Proposals*. New York: Vintage, 1962.

Greenleaf, Phyllis. *Our Changing Sex Roles*. Somerville, MA: New England Free Press, 1979.

Grogan, Emmett. *Ringolevio: A Life Played for Keeps*. Secaucus, NJ: Citadel, 1990.

Guerin, Daniel. *Fascism and Big Business* (2nd ed.). New York: Pathfinder, 2000.

Hedges. Chris. *American Fascists: The Christian Right and the War on America*. New York: Nation Books, 2008.

Hedges, Chris and Sacco, Joe. *Days of Destruction, Days of Revolt*. New York: Nation, Books, 2014.

Hedges. Chris. *Empire of Illusion: The End of Literacy and the Triumph of Spectacle*. New York: Nation Books, 2015.

Hedges. Chris. *Wages of Rebellion*. New York: Nation Books, 2015.

Klein, Naomi. *The Shock Doctrine: The Rise of Disaster Capitalism*. New York: Picador, 2009.

Klein, Naomi. *No Logo*. New York: Picador, 2009.

Knabb, Ken (ed.). *Situationist International Anthology*. Berkeley, CA: Bureau of Public Secrets, 2007.

Korten, David C. *The Great Turning: From Empire to Earth Community*. San Francisco: Berrett-Koehler, 2007.

Korten, David C. *When Corporations Rule the World*. San Francisco: Berrett-Koehler, 2001.

Kropotkin, Peter. *Memoirs of a Revolutionist*. New York: Doubleday, 1962.

Kunstler, James Howard. *The Long Emergency: Surviving the Converging Catastrophes of the Twenty-First Century*. New York: Atlantic Monthly Press, 2005.

Malcolm X. *The Autobiography of Malcolm X: As Told to Alex Haley*. New York: Ballantine, 1992.

Morris, Brian. *Social Change and Social Defense*. London: Freedom Press, 1993.

Ott, Jeff. *My World: Ramblings of an Aging Gutter Punk*. North Hills, CA: Hopeless Records, 2000.

Reich, Wilhelm. *The Mass Psychology of Fascism*. New York: Farrar, Straus & Giroux, 1980.

Ross, John. *¡Zapatistas! Making Another World Possible: Chronicles of Resistance 2000–2006*. New York: Nation Books, 2007.

Roy, Arundhati. *Public Power in the Age of Empire*. New York: Seven Stories, 2004.

Sampson, Ronald V. *The Psychology of Power*. New York: Vintage, 1965.

Scahill, Jeremy. *Dirty Wars: The World Is a Battlefield*. New York: Nation Books, 2014.

Shiva, Vandava. *Staying Alive*. Boston: South End Press, 2010.

Spring, Joel. *A Primer of Libertarian Education*. New York: Free Life Editions, 1975.

Sprouse, Martin (ed.). *Sabotage in the American Workplace*. San Francisco: Pressure Drop Press, 1992.

Starhawk. *The Spiral Dance*. New York: Harper and Row, 1979.

Taibbi, Matt. *The Great Derangement: A Terrifying True Story of War, Politics, and Religion*. New York: Spiegel & Grau, 2011.

Taibbi, Matt. *Griftopia: A Story of Bankers, Politicians, and the Most Audacious Power Grab in American History*. New York: Spiegel & Grau, 2009.

Taibbi, Matt. *The Divide: American Injustice in the Age of the Wealth Gap*. New York: Spiegel & Grau, 2014.

Uzcátegui, Rafael. *Venezuela: Revolution as Spectacle*. Tucson: See Sharp Press 2010.

Vaneigem, Raoul. *The Revolution of Everyday Life*. Oakland: PM Press, 2012.

Wilde, Oscar. *The Soul of Man Under Socialism*. Tucson: See Sharp Press, 2009.

Zinn, Howard. *A People's History of the United States*. New York: Harper, 2005.

Poverty and Homelessness

Davis, Mike. *Planet of Slums*. New York: Verso, 2007.

Day, Dorothy. *The Long Loneliness: The Autobiography of the Legendary Catholic Social Activist, Dorothy Day*. New York: HarperOne, 1996.

Ehrenreich, Barbara. *Nickel and Dimed: On (Not) Getting By in America*. New York: Holt, 2008.

Fanon, Franz. *The Wretched of the Earth*. New York: Grove, 2005.

Freire, Paolo. *Pedagogy of the Oppressed*. London: Continuum, 2000.

Piven, Frances Fox and Cloward, Richard. *Poor People's Movements: Why They Succeed, How They Fail*. New York: Vintage, 1979.

Piven, Frances Fox and Cloward, Richard. *Regulating the Poor: The Functions of Public Welfare*. New York: Vintage, 1993.

Roy, Arundhati. *Capitalism: A Ghost Story*. Chicago: Haymarket Books, 2014.

Steinberg, Michael. *Homes Not Jails!* San Francisco: Black Rain Press, 1998.

Wasserman, Jason and Clair, Jeffrey. *At Home on the Street: People, Poverty, and a Hidden Culture of Homelessness*. Boulder, CO: Lynne Rienner, 2009.

Russian Revolution

Avrich, Paul. *Kronstadt, 1921*. Princeton, NJ: Princeton University Press, 1991.

Berkman, Alexander. *The Bolshevik Myth*. London: Pluto Press, 1989.

Berkman, Alexander. *The Russian Tragedy*. London: Phoenix, 1986.

Brinton, Maurice. *The Bolsheviks and Workers' Control*. London: Solidarity, 1970. (now a part of *For Workers' Power*. Oakland: AK Press, 2004)

Goldman, Emma. *My Disillusionment in Russia*. New York: Dover, 2003.

Goldman, Emma. *My Further Disillusionment in Russia*. New York: Dover, 2003.

Maximoff, Gregory Petrovich. *The Guillotine at Work: The Leninist Counter-Revolution*. Sanday, Orkney: Cienfuegos Press, 1979.

Voline (E.K. Eichenbaum). *The Unknown Revolution*. Detroit: Black & Red, 1974.

Spanish Revolution

Bolloten, Burnett. *The Grand Camouflage*. New York: Prager, 1961.

Bolloten, Burnett. *The Spanish Civil War*. Chapel Hill, NC: University of North Carolina Press, 1979.

Bookchin, Murray. *The Spanish Anarchists: The Heroic Years (1868–1936)*. Oakland: AK Press, 2001.

Borkenau, Franz. *The Spanish Cockpit*. Ann Arbor, MI: University of Michigan Press, 1971.

Dolgoff, Sam (ed.). *The Anarchist Collectives*. New York: Free Life Editions, 1974.

Gómez Casas, Juan. *Anarchist Organization: The History of the FAI*. Montreal: Black Rose, 1986.

Leval, Gaston. *Collectives in the Spanish Revolution*. London: Freedom Press, 1975.

Mintz, Frank. *Anarchism and Workers Self-Management in Revolutionary Spain*. Oakland: AK Press, 2013.

Peirats, José. *Anarchists in the Spanish Revolution*. London: Freedom Press, 1987.

Porter, David (ed.). *Vision on Fire: Emma Goldman on the Spanish Revolution*. Oakland: AK Press, 2006.

INDEX